THE OVERLOOK MARTIAL ARTS DICTIONARY

THE OVERLOOK MARTIAL ARTS DICTIONARY

by
Emil Farkas
and
John Corcoran

THE OVERLOOK PRESS
New York

First published in 1983 by
The Overlook Press
Lewis Hollow Road
Woodstock, New York 12498

Library of Congress Cataloging in Publication Data
Farkas, Emil, 1946–
The overlook martial arts dictionary.

Bibliography: p.
1. Martial arts—Dictionary. I. Corcoran,
John, 1948– . II. Title.
GV1101.F37 796.8′15′03 81-47415

ISBN 0-87951-133-8 (cloth) AACR2
ISBN 0-87951-996-7 (paper)

First paperback printing 1985
Second paperback printing 1990

CONTENTS

Acknowledgments vi

The Role of the Dictionary vii

Guide to Using This Dictionary ix

Pronunciation Key xiii

Dictionary of Martial Arts 1

ACKNOWLEDGMENTS

To those who gave so willingly of their time and effort, the authors would like to extend wholehearted appreciation. To the following primary contributors: Jhoon Rhee of Washington, D. C., the "Father of American tae kwon do" and author of five books on the subject, whose help with the Korean terminology was indispensable; San Francisco's Richard Kim, America's foremost karate historian and author of *The Weaponless Warriors,* who tirelessly supplied countless literal translations and definitions for the Japanese nomenclature; San Francisco's Michael P. Staples, noted kung-fu photojournalist and author of four books about his specialty, who contributed all but a few of the Chinese terms herein; American kenpo pioneer Ed Parker of Los Angeles, who created and defined more than one hundred fighting theories used in this book.

The authors also acknowledge the assistance in a lesser capacity of several secondary contributors: Daniel M. Furuya of Los Angeles, a specialist in Japanese culture and history, whose additional work on the Japanese portion was integral to this book; Hee Il Cho of Los Angeles, a renowned tae kwon do master and author of *The Complete Martial Artist,* who supplied additional material for the Korean terminology; New York's Hidy Ochiai, consummate karate master, for his original direction regarding the Japanese portion of this book; Tacoma's Steve Armstrong, for his expert advice on certain Okinawan arts; and Terry Dunn, whose initial help with the Chinese nomenclature was interrupted by his departure to Hong Kong.

Numerous photographs accompanying this text are the property of *Inside Kung Fu* and *Kick Illustrated* magazines, whose publisher, Curtis Wong, kindly granted us reprint permission.

THE ROLE OF THE DICTIONARY

Ideally, a dictionary is an accurate record of a language as it is employed by those who speak and write it. But the martial arts language, in its present use alone, not to mention its exotic past, exists on such a vast scale that no single work is likely to do justice to it in its entirety. Of necessity, the authors were compelled to exercise a degree of selectivity to bring together those aspects of the language that will best serve the needs of those who consult this book.

We have assumed that this work will be chiefly used by those within the martial arts community. For that reason, we have intentionally included entries to appeal to a wide range of martial artists from beginner to black belt. Black belt instructors will find this work not only a most useful reference, but can benefit immeasurably by recommending its purchase to their students. It will save the instructor endless hours of answering the standard questions students pose.

At the same time, we have attempted to define the more popular terms in a general manner to make the book equally practical for the lay person. In this capacity, *The Overlook Martial Arts Dictionary* constitutes a reliable guide for journalists, researchers, and the general public.

It is impossible to include all variants because dialect research and English conversion is ongoing. Reliable information regarding many words of the martial arts language is not yet readily available. The foreign nature of these words and their transmission through time and distance establish a zone of disputed items about which there may be considerable difference of opinion, even among authorities of equal experience and eminence.

A researcher comparing the works of various authorities is likely to find a broad divergence of attitude and philosophy, ranging from a fairly wide permissiveness to a nervous reluctance to admit any deviation from the most rigid adherence to approved formal usage of a century or more ago. This conservative approach has been applied to the stylized movements of many of the traditional martial arts systems. It is understandable, then, that this attitude would also be seen in the language. That is not to say, however, that alternatives other than those appearing in this dictionary are unacceptable.

Of all the material contained in this book, the Japanese entries by far outnumber those of their counterparts in China and Korea. Korea, throughout history, has maintained some semblance of standard and order about its native forms of combat. China and Japan, on the other hand, developed a staggering number of armed and unarmed combatives, many of which, even today, remain a mystery.

In particular, China, the acknowledged pre-Christian birthplace of the Asian fighting arts, has suffered from a reluctance to reveal information pertinent to its hundreds of diverse styles. Many traditional kung-fu masters refrain from documenting their practices lest they betray closely guarded "secrets" entrusted to them through ancestral transmission. Most of these styles were passed down verbally and, primarily, physically. Very little in comparison to what exists has been made available in print. More and more, however, the communication barriers between Chinese masters and the outside world are crumbling and more information becomes available each year. It is because of this communications barrier that the dictionary contains much less data on the Chinese arts of combat.

GUIDE TO USING THIS DICTIONARY

1. Main entries appear in large, boldface type and are listed alphabetically by letter, regardless of whether composed of one or more words.

KARATE
KARATE-JUTSU

A main entry may consist of letters set solid, of letters joined by a hyphen, or of letters separated by one or more spaces:

KARATE
KARATE CHOP
KARATE-JUTSU

2. Pronounciations are enclosed in parentheses immediately following the main entry:

BUJUTSU (boo-jut'soo)

The pronunciation is given phonetically and is usually that most widely used whenever it has been possible to determine extent of usage.

Pronunciation is not given if the individual elements of a phrase are separately entered in proper alphabetical order.

3. The language of origin—Japanese, Korean, Chinese, and so on—appears in italics immediately following the pronunciation:

BUJUTSU (boo-jut'soo) *Jp.*

The derivation is not given for English-language entries since it will be evident to the user.

4. Abbreviations and symbols commonly used are:

Ch.	Chinese
(EP)	Ed Parker, who names and defines the entry
Ind.	Indian
Indo.	Indonesian
Jp.	Japanese
Kr.	Korean
Phil.	Filipino
Hind.	Hindustani
Poly.	Polynesian

5. Literal translations are used for most of the terms appearing in this work:

BUJUTSU (boo-jut'soo) *Jp.* "military art(s)"

Because of the difficulties of converting the characters and scripts of the Asian languages to English romanization, many entries embrace two and sometimes more literal translations. The authors have in these instances included those literal translations most commonly recognized and used in the martial arts.

6. In entries for words having several senses, the order in which the definitions appear is, whenever possible, that of frequency of use. Each such definition is preceded by a numeral:

ATE-WAZA (aw-tay-waw'za) *Jp.* "striking techniques" "smashing techniques" 1. In karate, the classification under which elbow and knee strikes are categorized. 2. In judo, another name for atemi-waza (vital-point techniques).

Closely related meanings may be defined under the same number.

7. Small capital letters are used to identify:

a) A cross-reference from a variant form to the entry where the term is defined:

BAKKAT-CHIGI: See BAKURO TAERIGI.

b) A cross-reference to a closely related entry containing supplementary information:

FOLLOW THROUGH To continue execution of a technique to its absolute completion. See also ZANSHIN.

c) A cross-reference to a synonymous meaning or an entry where a full definition will be found:

ADVANCED FOOT SWEEP: See DE-ASHI-HARAI.

8. In numerous cases, an entry is both singular and plural:

SENSEI can also be **SENSEIS** (pl.)
SIFU can also be **SIFUS** (pl.)
DOJO can also be **DOJOS** (pl.)

In these instances the singular is always preferred; therefore we have not indicated these irregular forms.

9. Certain forms of speech and writing are commonly accepted in the martial arts. However, discrepancies on the basis of geography and continental transmission have inevitably surfaced. There are also distinct

regional differences within the same continents. These variations will be most apparent to martial arts scholars.

At the outset of its worldwide migration, the language of the mother countries was, for the most part, accepted and used by those cultures adopting martial arts practices. But as some cultures acquired more and more independence and experience, as in America, new variations of the language emerged. When Anglicized, many of the original terms were inadvertently distorted. This led to a series of inaccuracies that, through mass diffusion, remains to this day a major problem plaguing the martial arts.

Still, it must be realized that despite all the differences throughout the world, the unity of martial arts language in the many countries in which it is practiced far outweighs the diversity. Overall, the martial arts community still recognizes the traditional vocabulary indigenous to each member's style or system. This is especially true of judo, where the terminology has been meticulously documented and standardized throughout the world.

The authors have included those words and phrases that are most standard to the genre and that are advocated by leading books and periodicals in the field.

10. Hyphens are used to separate the parts of a compound noun when it is so treated in this dictionary. The punctuation of compounds is too inconsistent to be generalized in a rule; uses by scholars themselves vary with respect to particular compounds.

The authors have in all cases attempted to use the preferred form of a compound—whether written solid, with a hyphen, or as a phrase of two or more words.

Some compounds appear with a space between the parts:

AIKI TAISO

Some are written solid:

AIUCHI

Most appear with a hyphen:

AIKI-JUTSU

The meaning of many combinations of words is sometimes easily apparent by combining the senses of their constituents.

11. Occasionally, a term will be pronounced but not defined. In most of these instances, the literal translation sufficiently conveys the entry's meaning and its context becomes self-evident.

KENSHI (kehn'shee) *Jp.* "fencer."

GUIDE TO USING THIS DICTIONARY

EXAMPLES

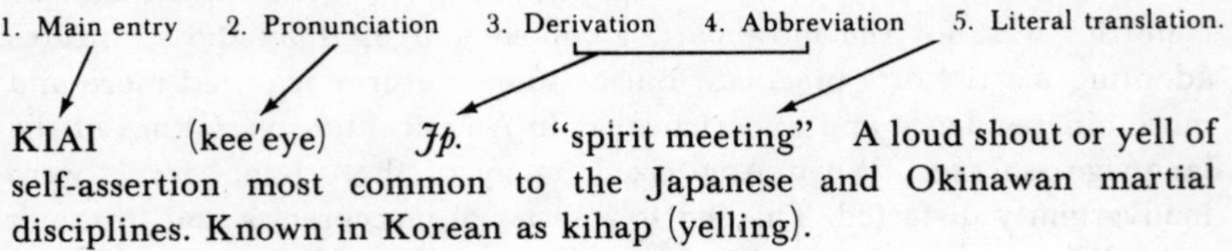

1. Main entry
2. Pronunciation
3. Derivation
4. Abbreviation
11. Short entry
5. Literal translation.
KIMA SOGI (kee'ma soh'ghee) *Kr.* "riding stance"
KIAI (kee'eye) *Jp.* "spirit meeting" A loud shout or yell of self-assertion most common to the Japanese and Okinawan martial disciplines. Known in Korean as kihap (yelling).

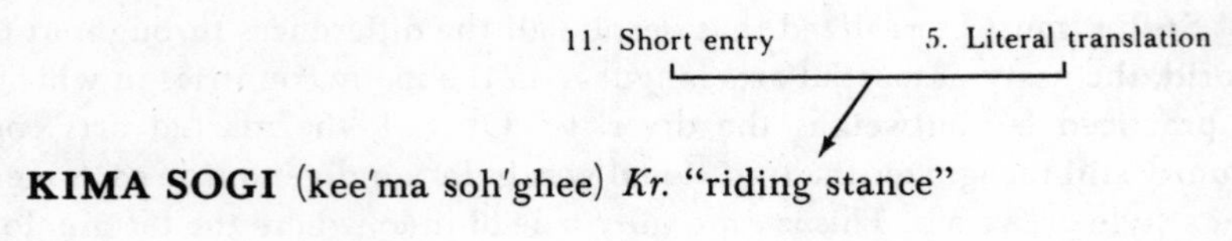

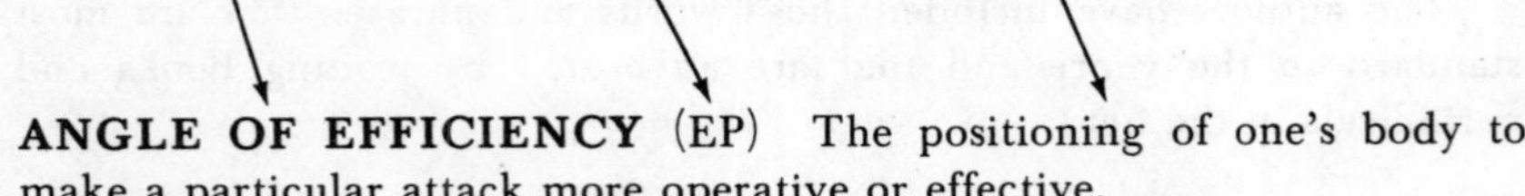

PRONUNCIATION KEY

Immediately following most main entries is a pronunciation enclosed in parentheses. Because so much martial arts terminology has been indiscriminately bastardized, the use of standard romanization tables is futile if not impossible. After several false starts, the authors decided finally to use the closest English phonetic equivalent to convey an appropriate pronunciation. This method proved to be the simplest and least complex for the purpose of this dictionary.

The stress mark (′) is placed after the syllable bearing the accent. Approximately 90 percent of the Japanese martial arts language is accented on the second to last syllable.

Phonetic Equivalent Symbol	*Example*
aw	d*aw*n, s*aw*
au	c*ou*ch, *ou*t
a	f*a*ther, c*a*r
ay	d*ay*, f*a*de
eh	b*e*d
ee	b*ea*t, bl*ee*d
i	b*i*t, f*i*t
eye	r*y*e, t*i*e
oh	b*o*ne, kn*ow*
oo	y*ou*th, s*ue*
u	b*oo*k, f*oo*t
uh	sab*er*, fav*or*
oy	b*oy*, c*oy*

The Chinese use an ideographic writing. The Chinese character for "crane," for instance, is an ideograph composed of some twenty-one different strokes of the brush or pen, none of which has any meaning whatsoever to those not familiar with Chinese writing.

Moreover, the Chinese language is tonal and any pronunciation without the proper intonation is incorrect. To compound the complexities, there are a great many dialects spoken in China and each dialect is as different from the other as, say, German is from French.

To be sure, there are several romanization systems used to translate the sound of Chinese words, including the Yale, Wade-Giles, Pin Yin, and the Meyer-Wempe systems. However, since the romanization systems are not part of the native Chinese tongue, a great deal of confusion can arise in translating precise pronunciations. It was the authors' decision therefore to omit most of the pronunciations for the Chinese terms appearing in this work. Only in rare cases is a phonetic equivalent provided.

ABANIKO (ab-ah-niko) *Phil.* "fan" In the Filipino art of arnis, a style of striking, with a short stick, that resembles the motion of a fan.

ACUPUNCTURE A traditional Chinese therapeutic science in which the placement of needles in specific locations, or "points" of the body, along passageways through which chi (vital energy) flows, called meridians, can restore physical health. It is often included as part of the healing arts studied by kung-fu students.

ADVANCED FOOT SWEEP: See DE-ASHI-HARAI.

ADVANCED LEVEL A stage of sophisticated study in the martial arts, usually commencing at brown belt level.

AGE-UKE (aw-gay-oo'kay) *Jp.* "rising block" A karate blocking technique in which the arm is raised in front of the body to nullify a strike directed to the face or head.

AGEUM-SON: See BANDAL SON.

AGE-ZUKI (aw-gay-zoo'kee) *Jp.* "rising punch" A karate punch delivered from a lower to a higher plane by way of a semicircle from the hip to the target.

AGGRESSIVE OFFENSE (EP) The activating of the first attacking move of which the opponent is not aware.

AGO-OSHI (aw-goh-oh'shee) *Jp.* "jaw squeeze" The fifth technique of ju-no-kata, the judo forms of gentleness and suppleness.

AGURA-WO-KAKU (aw-goo-raw woh kaw-koo) *Jp.* "informal sitting" The sitting position often used in the Japanese martial arts. One assumes it by sitting with the legs crossed, tailor fashion.

AHOP (a'hohp) *Kr.* "nine" The number nine.

AI (eye) *Jp.* "harmony" The aikido principle of harmony, which, when mastered, enables a practitioner to combine an opponent's force with his or her own.

AI-GAMAE (eye gaw-maw-eh) *Jp.* "matching stance" A normal standing used in aikido.

AIKI (eye'kee) *Jp.* "harmony meeting" or "spirit meeting" The aikido principle of integrating one's attitude with that of an opponent and thus becoming one with the opponent's movements in order to control him or her.

AIKIDO (eye-kee'doh) *Jp.* "way of harmony" or "way of the spirit meeting" An unarmed method of self-defense founded in Tokyo in 1942 by Morihei Uyeshiba, and based on the principle of harmony and nonresistance to one's opponent. Aikido is essentially noncombative and noncompetitive. Its primary purpose is to develop a healthy mind and body together with a wholesome spirit.

An aikidoist attempts to lead the attacker in a generally circular path, turning around the defender's center axis. The circular motion allows the practitioner to neutralize the aggressive action by gaining control of the attacker's momentum. Aikido execution requires considerable skill. The proper technique must be executed at the precise time with sufficient force to attain one's objective.

Aikido ranks are similar to those of most other Japanese martial arts. They are divided into two major categories: kyu grades and dan ranks. Kyu represent the student grades, rising from the lowest, normally sixth or fifth kyu, and they are usually denoted by various colored belts. Dan ranks, characterized by a black belt, progress from first dan to eighth dan, and in rare cases, above. In some sects only black belts wear a hakama (divided

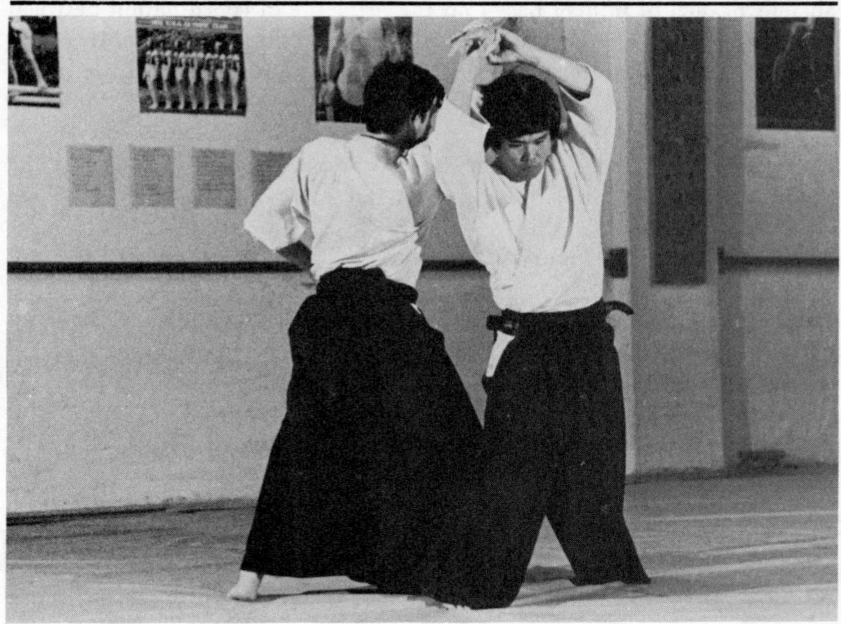

Aikido

skirt); in others it is optional; in some schools everyone wears the hakama and still others prefer women to wear it regardless of rank.

Aikido has certain definite links with Eastern philosophy, particularly Zen and Shinto, the national faith of Japan. Zen followers believe the center for meditation and the seat of mental power is the tanden, a point situated about one and one-half inches below the navel. This center is emphasized as the source of power in aikido and the point from which ki (spirit) originates.

More than thirty different sects of aikido exist today. The major sects are Uyeshiba's, which stems from Daito ryu aiki-jutsu; Gozo Shioda's Yoshin style, which is combat-oriented and closely approximates classical aiki-jutsu; Kenji Tomiki's system, containing practical elements of self-defense and practiced competitively; Minoru Hirai's korindo aikido, which is strictly self-defensive; and Yoichiro Inoue's style, called shinwa taido, a blend of self-defense and sport. Other eclectic systems of aikido are also extant. All of them, however, can be traced back to Uyeshiba's intrinsic teachings.

AIKI-JUTSU (eye-kee jut'soo) *Jp.* "technique of harmonious spirit" An ancient branch of jujutsu based on the principle of coordination between attack and defense. Aiki-jutsu was founded by Shinra Saburo Miyamoto during the Kamakura era (1185–1382) in Japan. It is the art from which aikido grew.

AIKI TAISO (eye-kee teye'soh) *Jp.* "harmonizing spirit exercises" The basic exercises of aikido.

AITE (eye'teh) *Jp.* "opponent" or "partner" An adversary in a contest.

AITE-NO-TSUKURI (eye-teh noh tsu-koo-ri) *Jp.* "condition or make-up of opponent" In judo, the preparing of an opponent in preliminary action in order to execute a throw.

AIUCHI (eye-oo'chee) *Jp.* "mutual striking down or simultaneous point" 1. A simultaneous score by both competitors in the sport aspects of the Japanese martial arts resulting in no point being awarded to either. 2. Mutual slaying in samurai combat.

ALTER (EP) To vary a weapon and/or target within a technique sequence.

ALTERNATE PUNCH: See RENZUKI.

AMATEUR KARATE The branch of competition in which participants compete in light-contact or noncontact sparring contests, as well as regulation form competition, without receiving financial rewards. Amateur karate in the United States has since 1972 come under the jurisdiction of the Amateur Athletic Union (although most amateur tournaments are not AAU sanctioned); its international governing body is the World Union of Karate-do Organizations (WUKO).

AMERICAN KARATE A hybrid form of traditional karate, which integrates techniques and philosophies from all styles to suit the needs of the American practitioner.

ANANKU (aw-nawn-ku) *Jp.* A kata practiced in the Matsubayashi-ryu style of shorin-ryu karate. While its history is obscure, it is believed to be named after a Chinese master who taught in Okinawa.

AN-CHIGI: See ANURO TAERIGI.

ANGLE OF CANCELLATION (EP) A controlled angle that places an opponent in a precarious position, thus minimizing or even nullifying the use of his or her weapons.

ANGLE OF DEFLECTION (EP) The increased angle caused by a block, parry, or the like, that widely diverts the weapon from its target.

ANGLE OF DELIVERY (EP) The positioning of one's natural weapons to make the execution of a movement accurate and effective.

ANGLE OF DESIRED POSITIONING (EP) Another phrase to describe the angle of efficiency.

ANGLE OF DISTURBANCE (EP) The angle that, when a move is executed, does not injure an opponent but instead upsets his or her balance.

ANGLE OF EFFICIENCY (EP) The positioning of one's body to make a particular attack more operative or effective.

ANGLE OF EXECUTION (EP) Any angle that, when an attack is executed, produces maximum results.

ANGLE OF GREATEST MOVEMENT (EP) An ideal positioning of the body, which enables one to move rapidly, easily, and without hesitation.

ANGLE OF OPPORTUNITY (EP) An encompassing phrase involving any and all of the angular classifications that, when taken advantage of, result in the success desired and/or intended.

ANGLES OF ATTACK (EP) The eight directions from which either opponent can attack.

ANKLE LOCKING In judo and jujutsu, the use of bone-locking techniques upon the ankles to gain a submission from an opponent.

ANKLE THROW A judo ashi-waza technique in which an opponent is thrown with the foot or leg.

AN MAKGI; AN MARKI (awn maw'ghee; awn mar'key) *Kr.* "inside block" A tae kwon do blocking technique.

ANNUN SOGI (awn-nun'soh-gee) *Kr.* "sitting stance" A tae kwon do stance assumed with the feet spread to the side about one and one-half shoulder widths and with the knees bent as if sitting.

AN PALJA SOGI (awn pal'jaw sew-ghee) *Kr.* "inner open stance" A tae kwon do preparatory stance assumed with the feet spread and the toes pointing slightly inward.

ANTEI (awn'tay) *Jp.* "balance," "stability," or "equilibrium."

ANURO CHAGI: See NOOLLO CHAGI.

ANURO MAKGI; ANURO MARKI (on'a-ro maw'ghee; on'a-ro mar'key) *Kr.* "inward block" A tae kwon do blocking technique.

ANURO TAERIGI (on'a-row tay'ree-ghee) *Kr.* "inward strike" A tae kwon do attacking technique, which moves from an outward direction inward toward the center of the body. Also known as an-chigi.

ANYO (An-joh) *Phil.* "form" Dancelike techniques practiced in the Filipino art of arnis.

APCHA BUSIGI: See AP-CHAGI.

AP-CHAGI (awp chaw'gee) *Kr.* "front kick" A tae kwon do kicking technique directed forward. When used in a snapping manner it is known as apcha busigi (front snap kick).

AP CHA OLLIGI (awp'chaw awl-lee'ghee) *Kr.* "front rising kick" A tae kwon do blocking technique using the foot.

APCHOOK (awp'chook) *Kr.* "ball of the foot."

AP CHOOMUK (awp choo'muk) *Kr.* "forefist" A striking surface used in tae kwon do punching.

APE-CHIGI: See AP TAERIGI.

APEX (EP) The uppermost point of any circular or linear movement whether delivered offensively or defensively.

APKUMCHI (awp-koom'chee) *Kr.* "ball of the foot."

APMAKGI; AP MARKI (awp maw'gee; awp mar'kee) *Kr.* "front block" A tae kwon do blocking technique in which the body directly faces the target.

APSEOGI; AP SOGI (both awp soh'gee) *Kr.* "front stance" A tae kwon do stance in which one foot is placed slightly in front of the other and supports 60 to 70 percent of the body weight.

AP TAERIGI (awp tay'ree-gee) *Kr.* "front strike" A tae kwon do hand technique applied when directly facing an opponent. Also known as apechigi.

ARAE-MAKKI: See NAJUNDE MAKGI.

ARBIR (r-bir) *Indo.* A halberd weapon of pentjak-silat approximately five feet in length that features a shallow groove in the plane of the blade running the length of the shaft.

ARC-HAND: See BANDAL SON.

ARIT (a-reet) *Indo.* A sickle with pronounced crescent-blade patterns and a short handle used in pentjak-silat.

ARM LOCK A restrictive hold in which one is rendered helpless by a twisting grip or a locking force on the arm joints. It is widely used in judo, jujutsu, and aikido.

ARNIS; ARNIS DE MANO (ar'nis da maw'no) *Phil.* "harness of hand" The best known and most systematic fighting art of the Philippines. Originally known as *kali,* arnis centers around three distinct phases: stick, blade, and empty-hand combat. As a fighting art, arnis has three forms of play: *espada y daga* (sword and dagger), in which a long wooden sword and a short wooden dagger are used; the *solo baston* (single stick), in which a single long stick made of wood or a rattan cane is employed; and the *sinawali,* a native term applied because the intricate movements of the two *muton* (sticks) resemble the crisscross weave of a *sawali,* a pattern used in walling and matting.

Arnis embraces three principal training methods: the *muestrasion* or *pandalag,* which teaches the artistic execution of the swinging movements and striking for offense and defense in repetitive drills; the *sangga at patama* or *sombra tabak* wherein striking, thrusting, and parrying in a prearranged manner are taught; and the *larga muton* or *labanang totohanan,* in which two trainees engage in free-style practice. The last is the ultimate phase of arnis.

There are certain key principles to be learned in arnis, which are

Arnis De Mano

divided into two categories, physical and psychological. Under the physical, the practitioner must emphasize speed of hands and feet for rapid delivery and also of the eyes for spotting an opponent's weak points. Toward this end, the student is conditioned to stare for long periods without blinking. Under the psychological principles, the student must learn to be calm and composed in order to fully concentrate on an opponent. Above all, the student must develop the will to fight and to win.

Arnis is most effective in close-range combat. Striking and parrying skills must therefore be developed with the utmost dexterity. The expert use of the leg to offset balance and throw an opponent must be perfected. Unlike other martial arts that make use of the entire body, early kali as well as modern arnis emphasize the use of the stick and hand-arm movements.

Many of the antiquated techniques and weapons have been modernized to prevent injury to students. These major changes were introduced by Remy Presas, the "founder of modern arnis."

Arnis is also known as escrima. See also KALI.

ART 1. Any specific skill or application. 2. In the Japanese martial arts, any jutsu (art) discipline that antedates its 20th-century counterpart, a do (way) discipline.

ASHI (aw'shee) *Jp.* "foot" or "leg."

ASHI-ATE (aw-shee aw'teh) *Jp.* "foot strikes" or "leg strikes" A set of karatelike techniques taught in advanced judo and based on methods of attack with the knee, ball of the foot, and the heel. These techniques are prohibited in judo competition.

ASHI-BARAI: See ASHI-HARAI.

ASHIBO-KAKE-UKE (aw-shee-boh kaw-keh oo-keh) *Jp.* "leg-hooking block" A karate blocking technique in which the leg is raised to the side and swung in a circle to deflect an opponent's side kick to the abdomen. When the ankle is similarly employed to block an opponent's front kick, the technique is called ashikubi-kake-uke (ankle-hooking block).

ASHI-GARAMI (aw-shee gaw-raw'mee) *Jp.* "leg entanglement" A judo dislocation technique in which the user entangles the opponent's foot with his or her own and applies leverage to inflict injury on the knee joint. It is the fifteenth technique of katame-no-kata (forms of grappling or holding).

ASHI-GATAMI (aw-shee gaw-taw'mee) *Jp.* "leg lock" A judo armlock applied with the leg.

ASHI-GATANA (aw-shee-gaw-taw'na) *Jp.* "footsword" A karate kick in which the toes are turned up and the outer edge of the foot is used as the striking point.

ASHI-GURUMA (aw-shee guh-roo'maw) *Jp.* "leg wheel" A judo leg throw in which the user extends his or her leg across the opponent's at knee level and throws the opponent in a large arc over his or her own leg.

ASHI-HARAI (aw-shee haw-raw-ee) *Jp.* "foot sweeping" A judo foot or leg technique that employs the sweeping action of the leg to apply one's body power in throwing an opponent. Known also as ashi-barai.

ASHI-HISHIGI (aw-shee hee-shee-gee) *Jp.* "leg lock" or "leg crunch" A judo dislocation technique in which pressure is applied to an opponent's lower calf to pin the opponent to the mat.

ASHIKUBI-KAKE-UKE: See ASHIBO-KAKE-UKE.

ASHIKUBI-WAZA (aw shee koo-bee waw'zuh) *Jp.* "ankle-locking techniques" Judo techniques performed by forcing down or twisting an opponent's foot sideways, thus causing dislocation of the ankle joint. In sport judo all such techniques are forbidden.

ASHI NO URA (aw'shee noh u'ra) *Jp.* "sole of the foot" A striking surface and occasional blocking point in karate, and in other Japanese martial arts.

ASHI SABAKI (aw-shee saw-baw-kee) *Jp.* "foot work" or "foot movement."

ASHI-WAZA (aw-shee waw'zuh) *Jp.* "foot techniques" or "leg techniques" A collective name for all judo techniques employing the foot or leg to throw an opponent.

ATAMA (aw-taw'maw) *Jp.* "head" or "top of the head."

ATE (aw'teh) *Jp.* "to strike" or "striking."

ATEMI (a-teh'mee) Jp. "body strikes" A method of attacking an opponent's pressure points, and one of the bases for the original empty-hand combat systems that came to be classified as jujutsu. The term is also used by contemporary martial artists to refer to any and all techniques of ate-waza (striking techniques).

ATEMI-WAZA (a-teh-mee-waw'zuh) *Jp.* "body striking techniques" or "techniques for attacking vital points" One of the three basic groups of techniques constituting judo. Known also as ate-waza, they are somewhat similar to the striking and kicking techniques of karate and are prohibited in judo competition.

ATE-WAZA (aw-teh waw'zuh) *Jp.* "striking techniques" or "smashing techniques" 1. In karate, the classification under which elbow and knee strikes are categorized. 2. In judo, another name for atemi-waza.

ATOSHIBARAKU (aw-toe-she-bah-rah-ku) *Jp.* "afterwards a few seconds" A term used in karate competition to signal that there are thirty seconds to the end of the match.

ATO-UCHI (aw-toh oo'chee) *Jp.* "delayed strike" In Japanese karate, the term representative of feinting.

ATTENTION STANCE Any of numerous preparatory positions in which a karate student awaits a command to begin executing techniques during a formal workout.

AU (aw'oo) *Jp.* "to meet" To encounter an opponent in any Japanese martial arts contest.

AUGMENT The act of using the support of the opposite hand and/or arm to strengthen a block or strike in Okinawan and Japanese karate.

AUGMENTED FOREARM BLOCK: See MOROTE-UKE.

AUN NO GYO *Kr.* A tae kwon do breathing exercise in which one crouches low while inhaling and rises on the toes with the arms extended upward while exhaling.

AWASE-WAZA (aw-wa-seh waw'zuh) *Jp.* "combining techniques or points" In judo competition, a victory obtained by scoring any two incomplete techniques worth a half-point each.

AWASE-ZUKI (aw-waw-seh tsoo-kee) *Jp.* "combined strike" or "double punch" A double karate punch in which both fists strike simultaneously, one to the face and the other to the solar plexus or abdomen. Known also as yama-zuki.

Awase-Zuki

AXE KICK A hybrid tae kwon do technique, similar to the spinning crescent kick, in which the kicking foot traverses above the opponent's head in a wide elliptical arc and lands downward on the opponent's neck or shoulder.

AYUMI-ASHI (aw-yoo-mee aw'shee) *Jp.* "stepping foot" A judo method of footwork in which the feet move alternately one ahead of the other, each sliding along the mat. It is one of two basic types of shintai (movement).

B

BACK-ARM SWEEPING BLOCK: See HAIWAN NAGASHI UKE.

BACKFIST: See URAKEN; DUNG JOOMUK.

BACKHAND; BACKHAND BLOCK: See HAISHU.

BACK KICK: See USHIRO-GERI.

BACK PIERCING KICK: See DWITCHA BUSIGI.

BACK SACRIFICE TECHNIQUES: See MA-SUTEMI-WAZA.

BACK SNAP KICK: See USHIRO-GERI; DWITCHA BUSIGI.

BACK SOLE: See DWIKUMCHI.

BACK STANCE: See KOKUTSU-DACHI.

BACK THROW: See URA-NAGE.

BACK THRUST KICK: See USHIRO-GERI.

BACK-UP MASS (EP) The assistance of body weight used directly behind the action employed. For example, a punch delivered when the

Backward Sweep

elbow is directly behind the fist, or the bracing of one finger directly behind the other in delivering a two-finger chop.

BACKWARD BREAKFALL: See USHIRO-UKEMI.

BACKWARD SWEEP In Chinese boxing, the spinning of the body in a full circle from a crouched position while extending one leg to sweep an opponent or temporarily offset his or her balance.

BADIK A Malayan dagger shaped like a butterfly whose straight blade bears one sharp edge. It is more often referred to as a butterfly knife.

BAEKJUL BOOLGOOL (bayk'jul bul'gool) *Kr.* "indomitable spirit" In tae kwon do, an attitude of extreme confidence and fearlessness when engaged in combat.

BAJAWAH BOX: See MAIN TINDJU.

BAJUTSU (baw-jut-suh) *Jp.* "art of horsemanship" A method of combat on horseback developed by bushi (warriors) of feudal Japan. Known also as jobajutsu.

BAKAT MAKGI; BAKAT MARKI (bawk'awt maw'kee; bawk'awt mawr'kee) *Kr.* "outside block" A tae kwon do block directed at the outer portion of an attacker's arm or foot. Known also as bakkat-makki.

BAKKAT-CHIGI: See BAKURO TAERIGI.

BAKKAT-MAKKI: See BAKAT MAKGI.

BAK-SING CHOY-LI-FUT *Ch.* A kung-fu system combining two Chinese martial arts, Choy-Li-Fut and northern Shao-lin. It is primarily a long-arm style employing a strong horse stance, and makes use of many of the tactics seen in other Choy-Li-Fut styles, namely, the quick turning from side to side and shifting of the shoulders and hips to whip the arms around.

BAKURO CHAGI: See NOOLLO CHAGI.

BAKURO MAKGI: BAKURO MARKI (bah-kaw'roh maw-gee; baw-kaw'roh mawr'kee) *Kr.* "outward block" A tae kwon do block in which the hand moves from an inward position outward.

BAKURO TAERIGI (baw-kaw-roh' tay'ree-gee) *Kr.* "outward strike" A tae kwon do strike whereby the attacking weapon reaches its target by moving from an inward position outward. Known also as bakkat-chigi.

BAL (bawl) *Kr.* "foot."

BALANCE BREAKING: See KUZUSHI.

BALDEUNG: See BALDUNG.

BAL DUL GI (bawl dool gee) *Kr.* "foot lifting" A dodging tactic used in tae kwon do to avoid a sweeping technique.

BALDUNG (bawl'doong) *Kr.* "instep" A tae kwon do striking point or target area. Known also as baldeung and baltung.

BAL GURUM (bawl gu-rum') *Kr.* "footwork" Offensive and defensive footwork patterns of tae kwon do.

BALISONG A fan knife produced in the Philippines.

BALKAL (bawl'kawl) *Kr.* "footsword" The outer edge of the foot used in tae kwon do kicking techniques. Also known as jokdo and balnal.

BALKUT (bawl'koot) *Kr.* "toes."

BALL OF THE FOOT Part of the anatomy used as a striking point for numerous types of kicks.

BALNAL: See BALKAL.

BALTUNG: See BALDUNG.

BAL TWIKUMCHI (bawl twee-koom'chee) *Kr.* "heel of the foot."

BANDAE CHIRUGI (bawn'day chee-ru'gee) *Kr.* "reverse punch" A tae kwon do punch delivered from the side of the body opposite the forward leg. Known also as bandae jireugi and bandae jirugi.

BANDAE DOLLYO CHAGI (bawn'day dool'yoh chaw'gee) *Kr.* "reverse turning kick" A tae kwon do kick used against an opponent to the side or rear. Known also as momdollyo-chagi.

BANDAE DOLLYO GORO CHAGI (bawn'day dool'yoh goh'roh chaw'gee) *Kr.* "reverse hooking kick" A tae kwon do kick which moves in the opposite direction of the roundhouse kick. See also ROUNDHOUSE KICK.

BANDAE JIREUGI: BANDAE JIRUGI: See BANDAE CHIRUGI.

BANDAL CHAGI (bawn'dawl chaw'gee) *Kr.* "crescent kick" A tae kwon do kick that travels in a wide circular motion and strikes with the sole of the foot.

BANDAL JIRUGI (bawn'dawl jee-ru-gee) *Kr.* "crescent punch" A tae kwon do punch in which the fist travels in a semicircle or circle from the waist to the target.

BANDAL SON (bawn'dawl sawn) *Kr.* "arc hand" A tae kwon do strike using the area between the forefinger and the thumb. Known also as ageum-son.

BANDESH (ban desh) *Ind.* An ancient form of Indian fighting whose principal tenet is to defeat an armed enemy without killing him.

BANDO (bawn'doh) *Burmese* "way of discipline," "systems of defense," or "art of fighting" A Burmese method of armed and unarmed combat composed of karatelike striking and kicking techniques, judolike throws, stick fighting, swordplay, and knife and spear fighting. There are many subdivisions and styles of bando. The most popular is known as Burmese boxing and is one of the world's most brutal combat sports.

Bando is classified into three distinct forms. The hard style, often referred to as Burmese boxing or bando boxing, is one of the world's most brutal combat sports. Similar to Thai boxing, it is conducted in a ring and the only illegal techniques are finger-thrusts to the eyes, throat, and groin. The combatants can fight bare-fisted for either three of four rounds of three minutes duration. The middle style, often referred to as the bando defensive system, is similar to light-contact karate sparring. Here, all of the offensive and defensive techniques are practiced against one or more opponents. The high style of bando is its most advanced form, combining training in mind, bodycand spirit. It is similar to some Chinese internal systems and Japanese aikido.

BANG-AU (bawng'au) *Kr.* "defense."

BANJANG (bohn-yohn) A West Javanese style of gulat.

BAN JAYOO DAERYON (bawn jeye'yoo day'ryawn) *Kr.* "semifree sparring" The stage between prearranged sparring and free sparring in tae kwon do. The distance between players, the weapons used, the method of attack and defense, and the number of steps are all optional, except that players alternate between being the attackers and the defenders.

BANKYUK (bawn-kyook') *Kr.* "counter" or "counterattack."

BANSHAY A Burmese martial art, influenced by both Chinese and Indian sources, which embraces the use of such weapons as the sword, staff, and spear.

BAN MA BU *Ch.* "half-horse stance" In kung-fu, a combination of the horse and cat stances in which 60 percent of the body weight is supported by the back foot.

BARAI: See HARAI.

BARO-JIREUGI; BARO-JIRUGI (both: baw'roh jee'roo'gee) *Kr.* "obverse punch" A tae kwon do punch delivered from the same side of the body as the forward leg.

BARU SILAT (bar-oo see-laht) *Indo.* "new place" An eclectic form of Sumatran pentjak-silat based on sterlak silat, but relying on principles found in karate and jujutsu.

BASE LINE (EP) Imaginary line(s) used to illustrate the direction and execution of a basic technique.

BASHO (baw'shoh) *Jp.* Grand sumo tournaments scheduled six times each year throughout Japan. Each event lasts fifteen days and ends with the presentation of the Emperor's Cup.

BASICS Fundamental techniques taught to martial arts novices as a foundation for advanced techniques.

BASIC SPARRING: See YAKUSOKU KUMITE.

BASSAI (baw-seye') *Jp.* "to penetrate a fortress" or "thrust asunder" A karate kata formulated in the shorin-ryu school of Okinawa.

BASTON (bos-ton) *Phil.* "stick" A wooden stick or rattan cane of varied lengths used in arnis de mano.

BASTONERO (bos-ton-arow) *Phil.* Students and practitioners of arnis de mano.

BAT-SAI: See BASSAI.

BATTOJUTSU (bawt-toh-jut'suh) *Jp.* "sword-cutting technique" An expression equivalent in meaning to iaijutsu (sword-drawing art), but more clearly akin to striking instantly with the sword when dealing with an enemy.

BAYAN SILAT (bah-yan sea-lot) A form of Malayan bersilat.

BEAR One of the five animals whose movements composed the basis of Hua To's exercises and which are extent today in various Chinese boxing schools. See also FIVE ANIMALS.

BEAR CLAW: See TIGER CLAW.

BEAR HAND The palm with the fingers slightly bent and used to rake the opponent's face, used in karate and kung-fu.

Baston

BELADAU A Sumatran curved dagger with a convex cutting edge.

BELO; BELO-LEONG: See PARANG.

BELT A cloth belt of different colors worn around the waist to denote a level of achievement in most martial arts. In Japanese, it is called an obi; in Korean, a ti. The color of the belts varies according to style. The predominant colors are: white, yellow, gold, orange, blue, green, purple, red, brown, and black. Some systems use colored stripes across the tip of the belt to denote the various ranks. At one time a white stripe running the entire length of the belt was used to distinguish females, especially in judo.

BELT SHOULDER THROW In judo, a variation of seoi-nage (shoulder throw) in which the loose ends of the belt are grasped in place of the more orthodox hold on the lapel.

BENGKONG (ben-kong) A belt worn in bersilat with different colors denoting the wearer's rank.

BENT-WRIST BLOCK: See KAKUTO; DUNG SONMOK.

BEOM-SEOGI: See DWIT BAL SOGI.

BERSILAT (bear-sea-lot) *Malaysian* "to do fighting" A native Malayan martial art reputedly founded by Huang Tuah of Malacca in the 15th century A. D. Bersilat embraces both empty-hand and weapons techniques and is practiced in two forms. Silat pulot is purely the exhibition at weddings and other public celebrations, while silat buah is the serious combative. Silat buah techniques are classified into a salutation, bodily movement in which weapons are employed, evasive tactics, side-striking techniques, warriorship, techniques of stabbing, and kicking and falling. Because of a growing emphasis on sport, the use of weapons has declined.

BINOT (bee-noh) *Ind.* An ancient Indian form of weaponless fighting that employed wrestling techniques against both armed and unarmed assailants.

BIRD One of the five animals whose movements composed the basis of Hua To's exercises. See also FIVE ANIMALS.

BISENTO (bee-sehn-toh) *Jp.* A spearlike weapon with a blade resembling a scimitar affixed to its end. It was used by the ninja of feudal Japan.

BITURO CHAGI (bee-too'roh chaw'gee) *Kr.* "twisting kick" A tae kwon do kick that approaches the target area vertically in an arc traveling from the inside to the outside.

BLACK BELT A rank designating a high level of achievement in a martial art. Most styles recognize ten degrees of black belt, running upward from first degree to tenth degree. See also DAN.

BLACK CRANE: See CRANE.

BLOCKING Any technique that hinders, checks, neutralizes, or nullifies an opponent's attack, using any part of the body.

BLUE BELT A rank designation symbolizing a level of achievement below black belt. In karate, a blue belt normally represents sixth kyu (grade); in tae kwon do, third gup (grade). Some systems use a purple belt to indicate the same level.

BLUE CRANE: See CRANE.

BO (boh) *Jp.* "staff," "stave," or "stick" A wooden staff approximately six feet long. It is one of the five weapons systematized by the early Okinawan developers of te (hand), and originated with the poles used by farm people to balance heavy loads across the shoulders.

BODHIMANDALA: DOJO.

BODY COMMUNICATION (EP) The giving and receiving of information by body movements, mannerisms, expressions, gestures, habits, and so on. Each of these characteristics can be used by the experienced and intelligent fighter as a means of anticipating the opponent's strategy and thus defeat him or her with appropriate countermeasures.

BODY DROP: See TAI-OTOSHI.

BODY DROPPING: See MOM NACHUGI.

BODY LANGUAGE (EP) The ability to use body movements, mannerisms, expressions, gestures, habits, and so on in relaying either true or misleading information.

BODY MOVEMENT: See PHIHAGI.

BODY STYLE That particular characteristic which distinguishes the performance of one practitioner from another, even when executing the identical technique. The difference is a matter of personal interpretation and body shape.

BODY TRANSLATION (EP) The decoding of body movements, which provides clues to an opponent's true intentions.

BOGU (boh'goo) *Jp.* "protective equipment" Protective equipment of nonmetallic materials used in several styles of Japanese karate, primarily for competitive sparring. Such equipment was derived from kendo (way of the sword).

BOGU KUMITE (boh'ghoo koo'mee-teh) *Jp.* "sparring with armor" A method of contact sparring in karate in which participants wear protective body equipment to avoid injury.

BOJUTSU (boh-jut'su) *Jp.* "art of the staff" An armed system of combat centering around the use of a long wooden staff called a bo. The staff is employed with a two-handed gripping action and kata is its sole training method. Techniques include striking, thrusting, blocking, parrying, deflecting, sweeping, and holding. By quick changes in the grip, the length of the weapon can be varied for long-range or close-quarter combat.

The art of using the staff was developed from Japanese spear and lance techniques. The common weapon learned in most schools of martial arts in feudal Japan, it became popular in Okinawa, where edged and metal weapons were outlawed by the ruling Shimazu clan.

BOKBOO (bawk'boo) *Kr.* "abdomen" In tae kwon do, a target area or the point from which ki (spirit) is derived.

BOK MEI P'AI *Ch.* The Cantonese word for Pat Mei P'ai. See PAT MEI P'AI.

Bojutsu

BOKKEN (boh'kehn) *Jp.* "wooden sword" A wooden staff resembling the contours of the forged katana. As used by the Japanese feudal warrior, the bokken proved combat efficient and greatly increased the range of kenjutsu (art of the sword) practices before coming into its own as a weapon of lethal possibilities. Today the bokken is mainly used as an instrument for safely practicing techniques of the sword.

BOKUTO: See BOKKEN.

BONG The Korean term for the wooden bo, or long staff.

BO-SAI KUMITE (boh-seye koo'mee-teh) *Jp.* "staff and short weapon with 2 prongs sparring" A weapons kata of isshin-ryu karate in which the wielder of the bo plays the aggressor and the sai handler is the defender.

BOT JUM DO *Ch.* "butterfly knives" In wing-chun kung-fu, short knives used in pairs that represent one of only two weapons common to this style.

BOW To bend the head or body in greeting or respect, a traditional practice indigenous to almost all martial arts. In Japanese, it is called rei; in Korean, kunyeh.

BOWING: See REI.

BOW STANCE A kung-fu stance in which one faces one's opponent sideways, keeping one leg straight while the other is bent almost halfway. The toes are pointed at a forty-five degree angle toward the opponent.

BOXING, CHINESE: See GWO SHU; KUNG-FU; WUSHU.

BOXING, GREEK A pre-Christian Olympic sport and form of pugilism using both the clenched-fist and open-hand techniques. It is the only pre-Christian form of open-handed fighting to have been documented visually, through vases and paintings, and descriptively, through records of the early Olympic Games. Greek boxing is the forerunner of pankration, an early striking and kicking combative that spread to India and China and could have been integrated with embryonic kung-fu practices.

BREAKFALL: See UKEMI.

BREAKING The practice of destroying bricks, boards, and other resistant materials with empty-hand and foot techniques of the martial arts, usually as a test of power or display of showmanship. In Japanese, it's called tameshiwara; in Korean, kyupka.

BREATHING A significant martial arts exercise used in three ways: for the purpose of meditation, in conjunction with the execution of a technique, and, most importantly, for developing and generating the internal force called ki (spirit) in Japanese and chi (vital energy) in Chinese. While breathing techniques vary, most subscribe to inhaling deeply through the nose and into the abdomen, where ki originates. Exhalation is either through the nose or mouth, depending on the sect practicing it.

BRIDGE (EP) To close the gap between oneself and one's opponent.

BROADSWORD A large curved, single-edged sword used as a chief weapon of kung-fu.

BROKEN RHYTHM (EP) A deliberate interruption of action used to deceive an opponent. It is related to deceptive timing.

BROWN BELT A grade designation indicating a level of achievement directly below first-degree black belt. In the Okinawan and Japanese arts, a brown belt normally represents the third to first kyu (grade); while in tae kwon do, a belt of light red denotes second and first gup (grades).

BU (boo) *Jp.* "military" A concept denoting the entire military dimension of feudal Japan. It is used in compounds such as bushi, budo, and bujutsu.

BUCKLE (EP) A method used to force the opponent's legs to bend in or out, or forward and back. Its use can unbalance, twist, sprain, or even break an opponent's leg.

BUDDHISM A religious doctrine, one branch of which—the Chan school, or Zen—is closely connected to the practice of kung-fu through the Buddhist monks who helped develop the art. As Chan Buddhism emerged in the 6th century A. D., its influence on martial arts was unmistakable.

In the 6th century, the monk Ta-Mo (Bodhidharma in Sanskrit), whose legends in Chinese mythology are elaborate, is said to have arrived at the Shao-lin Temple in the Shao-Shi mountains of Hunan province. He presumably developed a series of eighteen exercises, which he documented in a manuscript called the *I-Chin-Ching (Muscle Change Classic)* and which eventually became the Shao-lin method of Chinese boxing. This

Breaking

development, however, has been challenged by many authorities and it should thus be viewed cautiously. The method that eventually did emerge from the Shao-lin Temple was called the wai-chia, or external schools of Chinese boxing.

BUDO (boo'doh) *Jp.* "military way" or "way of fighting" Spiritually related systems, not necessarily designed by or for warriors, for self-defense. Budo is a generic term encompassing all of the Japanese do (way) arts, which are largely 20th-century offspring stemming from concepts that can first be positively identified about the mid-18th century.

Some of the more predominant budo practices today are judo, karate-do, aikido, kendo, kyudo, and iaido. Budo subscribes to creating the ideal psychological state by removing the fear of death and excessive self-consciousness so its user can freely and completely make use of the acquired physical techniques.

BUDOKA (boo-doh'kaw) *Jp.* "military art person" Any follower of the budo doctrine belonging to such arts as aikido, judo, kendo, karate-do, iaido, and kyudo.

BUDOKAN (boo'doh-kawn) *Jp.* "hall of martial ways" A large indoor arena specially constructed in Tokyo for the 1964 Olympics. It often serves as the site of various martial arts competitions.

BUGEI (boo'gay) *Jp.* "martial arts" A generic term encompassing the older Japanese jutsu (arts) which were in practice before the mid-18th century and were the predecessors of budo. Ideally, bugei applies specifically to those principles used by the samurai, or bushi, whose occupation was called bugei. It includes strategy, fortifications, and tactics.

BUGEI-SHA (boo-gay shuh) *Jp.* "martial arts person" The formal name for exponents of bujutsu.

BUJIN (boo'jeen) *Jp.* "military person" A name for the martial arts expert; same as bugeisha.

BUJUTSU (boo-jut'soo) *Jp.* "military art(s)" A collective term for all of the Japanese jutsu (arts) extant before the mid-18th century and practiced almost exclusively by the samurai warrior. These combatives, whose main use was to overcome a foe in combat, were the forerunners of the modern do (way) systems. Thus, judo evolved from jujutsu, kendo from kenjutsu, karate-do from karate-jutsu, kyudo from kyujutsu, and so on.

BUKE (boo-keh) *Jp.* "person of military class" Samurai.

BUKI-HO: See KOBUDO.

BUNKAI (bun-keye') *Jp.* "analysis" The detailed study of martial arts techniques and practical kata applications.

BURMESE BOXING: See BANDO.

BUSHI (boo-shee) *Jp.* "military person," "warrior," or "samurai" A generic term for the Japanese warrior that was changed to samurai after the 15th century A. D. The bushi functioned as armed bodyguards for the feudal lords and followed with unswerving allegiance the code of bushido; same as buke.

BUSHIDO (boo-shee'doh) *Jp.* "way of the warrior" A strict code of ethical behavior followed by the samurai. Bushido was formulated during the Tokugawa Era (1603–1868) of Japan, surprising perhaps, in peaceful times. The premise of the code was to advise a samurai how to conduct himself in battle and how to find a meaningful place in a peacetime society.

Its main tenets were loyalty to one's lord and dutiful service. To die in the service of one's lord was viewed as the ultimate expression of this loyalty.

Bushido's ethical basis is applied in modern martial arts through the endorsement of virtues such as pride in duty, discipline in conduct, and humility in oneself.

BUSHI NO TE (boo-shee noh teh) *Jp.* "warrior's hand(s)" A nebulous term used in Okinawa in the 1920s to represent karate.

BUTJABA MAKGI: See GRASPING BLOCK.

BUTJAPGO CHAGI *Kr.* "grasping kick" An acrobatic tae kwon do technique against two opponents whereby one opponent is kicked with one or both feet while the second is grabbed. Known also as japko-chagi.

BUTOKUDEN; BUTOKUKAI: See DAI NIPPON BUTOKUKAI.

BUTOKUKAN (boo-toh-ku-kan) *Jp.* "martial virtues" An unusual style of karate founded in 1961 by Reichi Keichi. It emphasizes speed, lightness, and the concept of circular movement.

BUTSUKARI (bu-tsu-caw'ree) *Jp.* "clashing" A judo exercise of applying repeatedly a throwing technique to an unresisting partner without actually throwing him or her to the ground.

BUTTERFLY KICK In kung-fu forms, the successive execution of two crescent-type kicks, the second usually slapped against the kicker's own open hand at its uppermost peak.

BUTTERFLY KNIFE A short-bladed weapon of southern Chinese origin normally used in pairs. Known in Chinese as Bot Jum Do.

Butterfly Knives

C

CADENCE The method in which a fighter coordinates his tempo and rhythm to establish the overall timing pattern movements.

CAPOEIRA (ka-po-era) A Brazilian form of combat adapted by African slaves to fight oppression. In it, the foot is considered the strongest weapon while the head represents the weakest target area. Thus, bringing the foot to the opponent's head, the strongest to the weakest point, is at the heart of its strategy. This involves not only kicking, but also somersaulting and handsprings.

CASCADE DROP: See TAKI-OTOSHI.

CAT STANCE: See NEKO-ASHI-DACHI.

CENTERING The total concentration of ki or chi at the point approximately two inches below the navel, which is considered to be the location of the body's center when relaxed.

CENTER LEVEL The area of the body encompassing the neck to the waist. It is generally used as a subdivision for the explanation of target areas.

CENTER LINE The center of the body encompassing some of the weakest parts, including the nose, chin, solar plexus, and groin.

CENTER OF GRAVITY A central point in the body, approximately at the navel, around which weight is evenly balanced. Balance and stability are acquired through understanding of its concept since anatomical movements shift its location.

CHA BAPGI (chaw bawp'gee) *Kr.* "stamping kick" A tae kwon do kick thrust downward on an opponent's instep. Usually used while being held from behind.

CHA BUSIGI (chaw boo-see'gee) *Kr.* "smashing kick" A collective term for six tae kwon do kicking techniques: apcha busigi (front snap kick), dwitcha busigi (back snap kick), dollyo chagi (turning kick), bandae dollyo chagi (reverse turning kick), bandae dollyo goro chagi (reverse hooking kick), and cha bapgi (stamping kick).

CH'A CH'UAN *Ch.* A northern Chinese form of kung-fu developed from the 14th to the 17th century by Muslims of Sinkiang, Chinghai, and Kansu, in the west and south of China, and primarily practiced by this group today. In this system, the practitioners fight from long range using high, long leaps to close the gap.

CHAGI (chau'gee) *Kr.* "kicking" An encompassing term for the wide variety of kicks used in tae kwon do.

CHAIN In China, any one of various weapons approximately twelve feet in length attached to a one-pound metal weight with metal rings crowning its egg-shaped base. Ordinarily, this version of the Chinese chain was swung around in a variety of unpredictable patterns and at tremendous speed. Defensively, it was used to keep enemies at bay while plotting a strategy against overwhelming odds or in an individual encounter. In Japan, the kusari, a similar chain, was used connected to a pick or sickle. Because of the inherent danger in mastering this weapon, modern versions feature a rope in place of the traditional chain.

CHA JIRUGI (chaw gee-roo'gee) *Kr.* "piercing kick" A collective term for two types of tae kwon do thrust kicks: the dwitcha jirugi (back piercing kick) and the youcha jirugi (side piercing kick).

CHAKURIKI (chaw-koo-ree'kee) *Jp.* A karate training theory in which strength is borrowed from another source. See also CHA-RYWK.

CHAMPAKA PUTIH *Indo.* "white flower" A form of pentjak-silat from

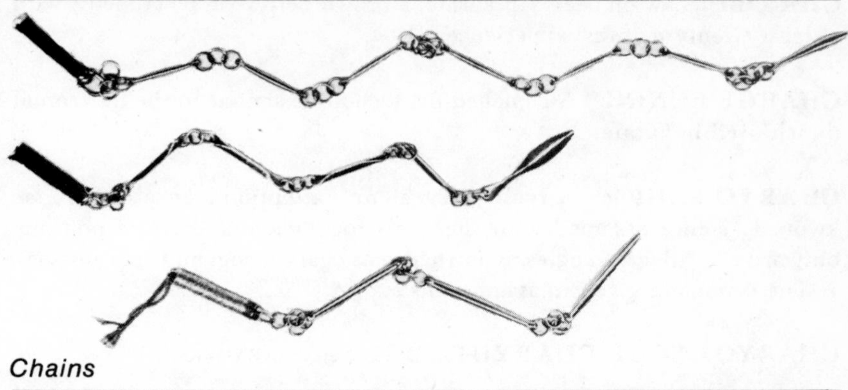

Chains

Central Java in which the practitioners crouch low to the ground and make use of spinning leg sweeps.

CHA MUM CHAGI (chaw moom chaw'gee) *Kr.* "checking kick" A tae kwon do blocking technique using the feet.

CHANAN: See HEIAN.

CHANG CH'UAN *Ch.* "long fist" A style of Chinese boxing originating in northern China. This long-arm style is quite often found mixed with others. It was chosen by the People's Republic of China as a compulsory set performed in competition. See also WUSHU.

CHANG-HON YU (chawng-hawn yoo') *Kr.* "blue cottage school" A style of tae kwon do founded by General Choi Hong Hi and bearing his pen name, Chang-hon. It is one of the three main schools from which numerous hyung (forms, patterns) have been derived. Chang-hon is characterized by a combination of fast and slow, light and forceful movements together with extensive footwork. It contains twenty hyung of historical or symbolic significance.

CHANG KWON (chawng kwawn') *Kr.* "heel of the hand" A striking point used in tae kwon do and other Korean martial arts.

CHANG MU KWAN (chawng'moo kwawn) *Kr.* "propagation of military arts training hall" A Korean martial art founded by Byung In Yoon in 1946. It did not conglomerate with the Korean styles that synthesized under General Choi Hong Hi to become tae kwon do.

CHA-OBI (chaw oh'bee) In karate, a brown belt worn by students with at least twenty months' experience.

CHARGE PUNCH A clenched-fist technique similar to the horizontal punch used in karate.

CHARYO-SOGI (chaw-ryoh' soh'gee) *Kr.* "attention stance" 1. A tae kwon do stance assumed with the heels together and the toes pointing outward at 45-degree angles. Known also as charyot-sogi and charyut-sogi. 2. The command given to assume this stance.

CHARYOT-SOGI; CHARYUT-SOGI: See CHARYO-SOGI.

CHA-RYWK *Kr.* "borrowed strength" One of two special training systems developed by ancient Korean warriors to increase proficiency in farando. While the term "cha-rywk" indicates the taking of strength from another source and adding to it one's natural strength, it actually means increasing bodily power through artificial devices, medicines, and training. There are three training methods in cha-rywk: spiritual, physical, and medicinal. Known also in Japanese as chakuriki.

CHASHI (cha'see) *Ch.* A Chinese exercise tool once made of iron and more recently of cement. These blocklike objects, with handles, are used in one- and two-hand exercises to strengthen the wrists and arms.

CHATAN-YARA BO KATA (chaw-tawn yaw-raw boh kaw-taw) *Jp.* "Chatan Yara's staff form" A kata centering around the use of the bo (staff). Stemming from Chatan Yara, a famous Okinawan karate master, the form is structured to encourage empty-hand combat in the ensuing close-range struggle.

CHAUSSON: See SAVATE.

CHEAT (EP) Refers to the execution of a deceptive move prior to the one intended. It includes the use of both the hands and the feet.

CHECK (EP) To restrain, hinder, or repress an opponent from taking action; accomplished by pinning, pressing, or hugging, usually at the joints, so that leverage is minimized thus nullifying the opponent's actions.

CHECKING BLOCK: See MOMCHAU MAKGI.

CHECKING KICK: See CHA MUM CHAGI.

CHEENA ADI (chee'nah a-dee) A Singhalese combative art practiced in secrecy until recently. It includes empty-hand and weapons techniques.

CHEKAK (chee-kak) *Ind.* A form of Indonesian bersilat emphasizing breathing and restrained use of strength.

CHEONKWON (chung'kwan) *Kr.* "sky" A tae kwon do poomse (form) whose pattern consists of twenty-seven movements.

CHI (chee) *Ch.* "spirit," "air," "breath," or "vital energy" A biophysical energy generated through breathing techniques studied in kung-fu. Ideally, chi can infuse a person with tremendous vitality and make him or her extremely powerful in action, much more so than the power developed purely through the muscular system alone. The methods of developing and controlling this force are numerous, but all of them include, in addition to meditation and concentration, the fundamental exercise of abdominal breathing. Known also in Japanese as ki.

CHIANG *Ch.* "spear" One of the major Chinese weapons practiced in wu shu.

CHIAO-TI *Ch.* An ancient form of Chinese wrestling practiced about 500 B.C. Participants wore horned headgear with which they attempted to gore one another.

CHIBURI (chee-boo'ree) *Jp.* "removing blood from sword" In iaido (way of the sword), a sharp downward stroke of the sword done in such a way as to shake off the blood accumulated from previous cutting actions. This action is traditionally done before returning the blade to its scabbard. Chiburi is one of the four phases of study in all Japanese iai (sword) techniques, whether a jutsu (art) or do (way) form.

CHI-CHUNG *Ch.* "control of breath" A series of exercises developed by Hua To, according to some authorities, and based on the movements of five animals: the bear, bird, deer, monkey, and tiger. These exercises served as the basis for the Chinese internal systems of kung-fu.

CHICKEN BEAK A kung-fu hand technique in which the tips of the fingers are held firmly together and used in a thrusting or snapping motion, usually to a target area of the face. This technique is also used in numerous styles of karate.

CHICKEN-HEAD WRIST The top of the wrist, used when the hand is bent downward. It is employed in different styles of karate and kung-fu.

CHI DO KWAN (chee doh kwawn) *Kr.* "wisdom way training hall" A Korean martial art founded by Yoon Kue Pyang. Chi do kwan joined the tang soo do organization but broke away, then in 1965 rejoined the group. Known also as jee do kwan.

CHIEN *Ch.* The double-edged sword used in many styles of kung-fu. Known also as the gim or jyan.

CHIEN-SHU *Ch.* "art of the sword" A term used in reference to the techniques of the Chinese double-edged sword.

CHI GERK *Ch.* "sticking legs" A wing-chun kung-fu exercise similar to chi sao (sticking hands) whose objective is to gain a superior position while maintaining constant contact with one of the opponent's legs. It includes blocks and attacks with the legs, knees, and feet.

CHIGIRIKI-JUTSU (chee-gee-ree-kee joo-tsu) *Jp.* A method of armed combat centering around a metal ball and chain attached to a short stick. It was used by the Japanese bushi and samurai.

CHI GUAN *Ch.* "sticking stick" A wing-chun kung-fu exercise with sticks of about nine feet in length. Similar to other "sticking" exercises, the object is to maintain contact with an opponent's stick as a means of eventually defeating him or her.

CHI HSUAN MEN *Ch.* "unusual style" A defensive method centering around the white jade fan, a fanlike metal weapon, with which an opponent's sword could be taken by a scissors motion. It also teaches vital-point techniques to be used after the disarmament. Chi hsuan men was founded by an Indian named Han Lo-ming in about the 5th century B.C..

CHI HSUAN SHO *Ch.* "unusual hand" A modern form of kung-fu combining elements of chi hsuan men and tamo sho.

CHI-JIREUGI: See OLLYO JIRUGI.

CHIKAMATO (chee'kaw-maw-toh) *Jp.* In kyudo, a close-range type of target shooting.

CHIKARA (chee-caw'raw) *Jp.* "strength" or "power."

CHIKARAISHI (chee-kaw-raw-shee) *Jp.* "power stone" A one-foot wooden stick embedded in a round stone weighing about ten pounds and used as a training device by Okinawan karateka. Its exercises help strengthen the arms and abdominal muscles.

CHIKARA KURABE (chee-kaw-raw ku-raw-beh) *Jp.* "power comparing or competition" An early Japanese combative art that came to be known as kumiuchi (inner grappling).

CHI KUNG *Ch.* "breath exercise" A breathing exercise that cultivates chi and transmits it to all the bodily organs. Known in ancient China as "the method to repel illness and prolong life."

CHIKUTO: See SHINAI.

CHILDAN (chill'dawn) *Kr.* "seventh rank" Seventh-degree black belt in tae kwon do.

CHILGUP (chill'goop) *Kr.* "seventh class" An elementary rank of tae kwon do at which most students wear an orange belt.

CHIMGOO SUL PUP *Kr.* In hwarang-do, the term representative of

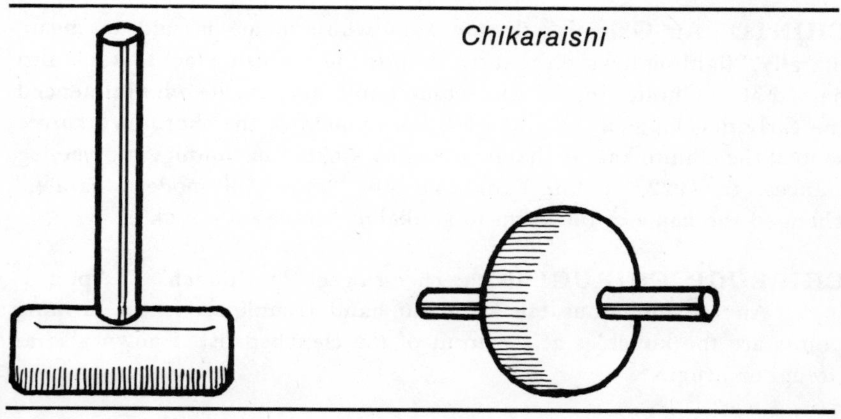
Chikaraishi

acupuncture. Known as kookup hwal bob when used specifically to revive an injured person.

CHIM-KIU *Ch.* One of the three kuens of wing chun kung-fu.

CHIMPAN (chim-pan) *Jp.* "judge" or "referee" The referee of a match. Also shinban, sinban, shimpan.

CHINA-HAND ART One translation of karate-jutsu, or tode. The Japanese translation is "empty-hand."

CHINESE GOJU A style of karate founded by the American karate practitioner Ron Van Clief. The essence of Chinese goju is circular motion combined with the more direct karate kicking and punching techniques.

CHINESE KARATE: See CH'UAN FA.

CHING-LO *Ch.* Acupuncture's twelve meridians of the body on which the key points of treatment lie and which are associated with the vital organs. Each meridian is either yin, for organs with mainly storage functions, or yang, for actively working organs.

CHING-SHEN *Ch.* Spirit or vivacity in the Chinese martial arts.

CH'IN-NA *Ch.* "art of seizing" An ancient Chinese fighting method for splitting tendons, dislocating joints, and attacking vital points of the body. It is thought to be the forerunner of jujutsu and aiki-jutsu. Known also as the bone-twisting art.

CHINTO An Okinawan karate kata whose name is said to mean, literally, "fighting toward the east," despite the confusing fact that it is also named after Chinto, the famous Chinese military attaché who influenced the early development of te (hand). Formulated in the shorin-ryu karate school, the Chinto kata is characterized by kicking techniques and one-leg stances. In 1922, Gichin Funakoshi, the "father of modern karate," changed the name of this form to gankaku ("crane on a rock").

CHIREUGI; CHIRUGI (both: chee-ru'gee) *Kr.* "punch" or "punching" Any of numerous tae kwon do hand techniques whose striking points are the knuckles at the front of the clenched fist. Known also as jireugi or jirugi.

CHI SAO *Ch.* "sticking hands" A wing-chun kung-fu exercise that

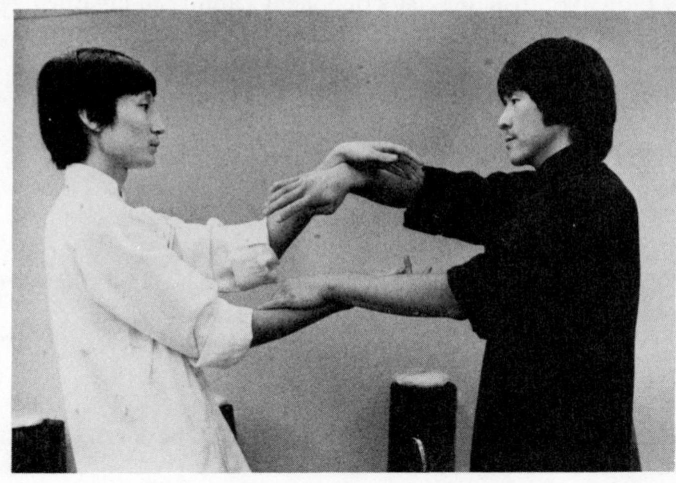

Chi-Sao

develops sensitivity to the hands and arms of its user. With their hands and wrists lightly touching, two people balance each other's forward motions with a rocking movement. Neither person can project his hands forward without telegraphing his intention. The user thus learns to detect an opponent's intentions by touch.

CHITO-RYU (chee'toh-ryoo) *Jp.* A minor style of Japanese karate founded by Tsuyoshi Chitose, after whom it was named. It is a combination of goju-ryu and shorin-ryu karate.

CH'O CHIAO *Ch.* A northern Chinese style of kung-fu specializing in high kicks.

CHODAN (choh'dawn) *Kr.* "first rank" First-degree black belt in tae kwon do.

CHOGUP (choh'goop) *Kr.* "first class" First-degree brown belt in tae kwon do.

CHOI-YONG (choy yawng) *Kr.* A tae kwon do hyung (pattern) named after General Choi Yong, a 14th-century commander-in-chief of the Korean armed forces. It consists of forty-five movements.

CHOJUM: See FOCUS.

CHOKE Any form of obstructing one's opponent's ability to breathe by using various types of arm and leg leverage to pinch the air passage or a blood vessel close to the head, causing loss of consciousness. It is most often employed in jujutsu and judo.

CHOKELOCKS In judo, an attack on the neck or throat by strangulation to produce choking or unconsciousness. See also SHIME-WAZA.

CHOKU-ZUKI (choh-koo zoo'kee) *Jp.* "straight punch" Any karate thrust punch delivered at a target directly forward. See also SEIKEN.

CHOMO HANAGI: See TODE.

CHONG BONG (chawng bawng) *Kr.* The Korean name for the long staff. See also BO.

CHONGUL (chawn'jool) *Kr.* "front stance" A tae kwon do stance assumed with one foot placed forward and the body weight equally distributed.

CHON-JI (chawn-je) *Kr.* "heaven and earth" A tae kwon do hyung (pattern) whose name is interpreted in the Orient to represent the creation of the world or the beginning of human history. Consisting of nineteen movements divided into two similar forms, one each to represent heaven and earth.

CHOOKYO MAKGI: See CHUKYO MARKI.

CHOOMUK: See AP CHOOMUK.

CHOONGDAN (choong'dawn) *Kr.* "middle" or "center" The area of the body encompassing the neck to the waist. It is used in tae kwon do as a subdivision for the explanation of target areas.

CHOONG-JANG (choong'jawng) *Kr.* A tae kwon do hyung whose name derives from the pseudonym given to Kim Duk Ryang, a 15th-century Korean general. It consists of fifty-two movements.

CHOONG-MOO (choong'moo) *Kr.* A tae kwon do hyung named after Admiral Yi Sun-Sin, reputedly the inventor of the armored battleship. It consists of thirty movements.

CHOONG-SIM (choong'sim) *Kr.* "center of gravity."

CHOP: See SHUTO; KARATE CHOP.

CHOSHI: See RHYTHM.

CHO-WA (choh waw) *Jp.* "harmony" In the Japanese martial arts, the harmonious mental and physical reaction while at practice.

CHOWASURU (choh-wah-soo-ru) *Jp.* "to catch harmony with opponent" or "to harmonize" In the Japanese martial arts, to harmonize movements in kata demonstrations and in training.

CHOW-GAR *Ch.* The Chow family style of kung-fu founded by Chow-Lung in the Kwang-Tung province of southern China. A unique blend of the Hung-Kuen and Choy-Gar (Choy family style) kung-fu systems, Chow-Gar was said to have had the head of Hung and the tail of the rat from the Choy-Gar footwork.

CHOY *Ch.* One of the five basic southern styles of Shao-lin kung-fu whose ingredients are the five animal styles, intricate hand techniques, circular motion, and a powerful horse stance. Choy, the monk who originated this system, is honored in the Choy-Li-Fut style of kung-fu.

CHOY-GAR: See CHOW-GAR.

CHOY-LI-FUT *Ch.* One of the most popular of the Southern Chinese kung-fu systems. Derived from the Shao-lin Temple of 6th-century A.D. China, it was created in 1836 by Chan Heung. Choy-Li-Fut is essentially a long-range form of Chinese boxing that relies heavily on strong horse stances and graceful yet dynamic long-handed techniques. Free-swinging roundhouse blows, overhead foreknuckle thrusts, backfist strikes, and uppercuts make it one of the more aggressive systems of kung-fu practiced today. Weapons used in this system include the Pa-kua lance, willow leaf double swords, and "eighteen" staff.

CH'UAN *Ch.* "fist" or "boxing" A general term used loosely to refer to a system of boxing, although it does not apply to any specific style. Known also as chwan or kuen.

CH'UAN FA *Ch.* "way of the fist" The major Chinese precursor of karate. Most forms of 20th-century ch'uan fa are said to be descendents of

Ch'ueh Yuan's "170 hand-and-foot positions." Although they have undergone a steady evolution, some sources claim they still can be traced to Bodhidharma's embryonic "eighteen positions." Known as ken fat in the Cantonese language, and kempo in Japanese.

CH'UAN SHU *Ch.* "art of the fist" An encompassing term for certain empty-hand Chinese martial arts. Kung-fu, Wushu, Gwo Shu, Gwo Chi, Chung Kuo Ch'uan, Ch'uan Shu can more or less be considered synonymous, although none is specific enough to denote a particular style. All of them are more or less generic terms.

CH'UAN-TE *Ch.* "first principle in action" The kung-fu set or form.

CHUDAN (choo'dawn) *Jp.* "middle level" or "center level" The term used in Japanese martial arts to represent the middle part of the body, or trunk area, which is often used to designate a target area for techniques. In Japanese karate this word is sometimes affixed to the title of a technique, for instance, yoko-geri-chudan, meaning a side kick to the trunk. Known as choongdan in tae kwon do.

CHUDAN-NO-KAMAE (choo'dawn noh kaw-meye) *Jp.* "middle level guard" Most common posture in kendo, with the point of one's weapon aimed to the opponent's throat or eye level.

CHUDAN-TSUKI (choo-dawn skee) *Jp.* "middle level strike" A karate fist blow directed to the middle of an opponent's body.

CHUDAN-UKE (choo-dawn oo'keh) *Jp.* "middle level block" A collective term for karate blocking techniques that safeguard the middle area of the body.

CHUGAERI (choo-gaw-uh-ree) *Jp.* "middle turn" or "middle twist" In judo, the forward rolling breakfall. See also UKEMI.

CHU-GOSHI (choo goh'shee) *Jp.* A judo posture in which one is half-sitting and half-rising.

CHUI (choo-ee) *Jp.* "warning" Admonition by a referee in a match; short of an actual penalty.

CHUJO-RYU (choo-joh ryoo) *Jp.* One of the earliest schools of Japanese swordsmanship, believed to have originated near the end of the 13th-century A.D. However, because there is no positive evidence that its rise was regular or systematic, kendo historians favor the Nen-ryu as having been the first transmitted school of swordsmanship.

CHUKEN (choo kehn) *Jp.* "middle sword" The middle of five players on a kendo team.

CHUKYO MARKI (chook'yoh mawr'kee) *Kr.* "rising block" A tae kwon do blocking technique used to safeguard the head from a downward strike.

CHUNG DO KWAN (chung'do kwawn) *Kr.* "blue wave school" A Korean form of empty-hand fighting founded by Won Kook Lee in 1945.

CHUNG-GA (chung gaw') *Kr.* "augment."

CHUNG-GUN (choong goon') *Kr.* A tae kwon do hyung named after a 19th-century Korean patriot. It consists of thirty-two movements.

CHUNG-JANG (choong jang') *Kr.* A tae kwon do hyung whose name was derived from the name of Kim Dok-Ryong, a 16th-century Korean general.

CHUNG-KUO CH'UAN *Ch.* "Chinese fist" One of the numerous terms used to designate Chinese boxing. See also KUNG-FU; WUSHU.

CHUNG KWON (choong kwawn') *Kr.* "fore-knuckle" A tae kwon do hand technique in which the fingers are bent inward until the tips just touch the palm. It is used to strike the point between the nose and the upper lip, or between the ribs. Known also as pyon-joomeok (fore-knuckle fist).

CHUNG-MU (choong'moo) *Kr.* A tae kwon do hyung consisting of thirty movements. It was named after Yi Sun-Sin, a 16th-century admiral.

CHUNIN (choo-neen) *Jp.* "middle person(s)" The second of three ninja military ranks designating the leader of a group of ninja on assignment. Those led by chunin were the genin; those who obtained the assignment were the jonin.

CHUSOKU: See KOSHI.

CHWA *Kr.* "left" or "left side."

Claw

CHWAN: See CH'UAN.

CIRCLE/WHIRLWIND: See ITSUTSU-NO-KATA.

CIRCULAR BLOCK A method of redirecting or neutralizing an opponent's attack by employing circular hand movements. In tae kwon do it is called dolli myo makgi.

CIRCULAR MOVEMENTS (EP) Moves that loop or follow an oval. Such moves can be used either offensively or defensively and can orbit in a single direction or divert into multiple directions.

CIREUM *Kr.* A collective term for all Korean wrestling. Practiced as a sport today, it derives from Chinese and Mongolian forms of grappling and very much resembles Japanese sumo. A second type, tong-cireum, found predominately in the northern areas, is closer to Mongolian wrestling.

CLASSICAL 1. (EP) A term used to describe the so-called pure systems of karate. Many of the movements associated with these systems are not practical in our present environment since the methods were created for the types of defense needed during ancient times. 2. A term designating techniques and/or philosophies conforming to certain standards of tradition.

CLASSICAL STYLES OF KARATE: See KARATE-DO.

CLAW (EP) 1. A pulling and tearing action utilizing the fingertips that results in scratching and/or ripping. 2. The claw-hand techniques in kung-fu encompass a wide variety of techniques differing, sometimes dramatically, from style to style. One therefore finds whole systems built around the particular use of the claw techniques, as in the eagle claw style, or simple additions to those constructed around nonclaw techniques. The training used to develop a formidable weapon of the claw-hand has been a closely guarded secret. In the uppermost training levels, a master of the claw-hand could crush a thick glass bottle with the bare hand.

CLOCK PRINCIPLE (EP) A teaching system that helps students to imagine visually the direction they are to follow. Students are told to think of themselves as being in the middle of a clock facing twelve, with six o'clock to the rear, three and nine o'clock to the right and left respectively, and all other numbers in their respective positions.

CLOSE PUNCH: See URA-ZUKI.

CLOSE-RANGE TECHNIQUES Maneuvers suitable for close-quarter fighting relying especially on the use of the hand, elbow, and knee.

CLOSE STANCE: See MOA-SEOGI.

CODE OF BUSHIDO The samurai's moral code of honor. See BUSHIDO.

COLLAR SHOULDER THROW In judo, a variation of the seoi-nage (shoulder throw) in which the hold on the lapel is restrained and the thrower's arm is bent and placed under the armpit of the opponent. Known also as the lapel shoulder throw.

COLLAR WHEEL CHOKE A judo grappling technique of shime-waza (strangling techniques) in which an opponent's collar is used to choke him.

COMBINATION Any series of techniques executed successively.

COMBINATION KICK: See RENZOKU-GERI.

COMBINED PALM HEEL BLOCK: See PALM HEEL BLOCK.

COMMITTED ACTION (EP) To move in such a manner as to bind oneself to a certain line of action.

COMPOUND TECHNIQUES Any combat technique that utilizes more than one simple technique in rapid succession without returning to full guard.

CONSECUTIVE KICK: See YONSOK CHAGI.

CONTINUITY (EP) The principle that no move passes from one position to another without being utilized effectively. It is a counterpart of economy of motion.

CONTINUOUS TECHNIQUES A method of attacking an opponent with a specific technique continuously and with proper timing to effect its execution.

CONTINUOUS WEAPONS (EP) The employment of a series of multiple natural weapons when involved in combat or freestyle.

CONTROL (EP) The regulation of force to produce accuracy but not injury. For example, a punch delivered at a specific target but does not hurt or injure. It may or may not make contact with the intended target.

CONTROLLED CONTACT Another term for semi-contact karate competition. See also SEMI-CONTACT.

CONTROLLED RESPONSE (EP) The regulation of one's actions so that one does not react prematurely, unnecessarily, or foolishly. This is especially true if the opponent should employ deceptive action.

COORDINATION (EP) The synchronization of one's moves with the moves, timing, and direction of an opponent, in order to attack advantageously. This also can refer to movements brought into order to act as a whole.

CORKSCREW PUNCH (EP) A twisting punch that makes contact at the time the clenched fist is facing palm down.

CORNER DROP: See SUMI-OTOSHI.

CORNER THROW: See SUMI-GAESHI.

CORNO-BRETON Also known as Cornish wrestling, this form of grappling practiced in Cornwall, England, for fifteen centuries is very similar to Japanese judo. The most significant difference is that a wrestler is not permitted to go to the ground with an opponent, but must make the throw while standing. Should any part of the body other than the feet touch the ground, the hold must be broken and the players shake hands and begin anew. All holds must be applied above the waist with strangulations forbidden. Each bout is ten minutes in duration.

COTTON NEEDLE A high form set of white crane kung-fu, which is performed slowly.

COUNTER; COUNTERATTACK Any retaliatory technique instantaneously executed in opposition to an opponent's initial attack.

COUNTERBALANCE (EP) Opposed forces that enhance the effectiveness of a particular blow, maneuver, or move.

COVER-OUT (EP) A single crossover and a step back to increase the distance between oneself and an opponent and to place oneself in a safe cover position.

COVER STEP (EP) The first step of a front crossover that aids in concealing the groin area.

CRAB'S CLAW A kung-fu technique using the thumb and forefinger pressed together as in the pincer of a crab.

CRANE Called ho in Chinese, one of the more popular animals of kung-fu. Traditionally, there are four kinds of crane: black, yellow, white, and blue. Cranes can represent longevity or agility and were formerly embroidered upon the court robes of civil officials of the fourth grade. See also PAK-HOC.

CRANE'S BEAK 1. A hand technique used in many martial arts that employs the compressed tips of the fingers as the striking point. 2. The traditional white-crane hand.

CRANE STANCE A defensive stance of both karate and kung-fu in which the supporting leg is bent at the knee while the raised foot is held at or behind the knee for protection against a sweep, or while executing a low block. It very much resembles the standing posture of a crane. Known as tsuruashi-dachi in Japanese. See also ONE-LEG STANCE.

CRANE STYLE The name for two different styles of kung-fu. One, originating in Tibet, was taught to the royal family and royal guards during the Ching dynasty. The other derives from Fukien province and is of an altogether different background.

Although both styles were inspired by the crane, neither system has an overabundance of movements characterized by cranelike stances or hand maneuvers.

CRESCENT KICK A straight-legged, circular kick executed with either the front or rear foot. The crescent kick starts from the floor and passes across the front of an opponent at head level in either a clockwise or counterclockwise direction. The striking point is usually the instep or sole of the foot. Known in Japanese as mikazuki-geri; in Korean as bandal chagi.

CRESCENT-KICK BLOCK The act of using the crescent kick to parry a center- or upper-level attack, usually with a slight bending at the knee. Known in Japanese as mikazuki-geri-uke.

CRESCENT PUNCH: See MAWASHI-ZUKI; BANDAL JIRUGI.

CROSS-CHEST CHOKE A judo technique employing a combination of immobilization and choking.

CROUCHING STEP One of the eight basic postures of Shao-lin boxing.

CUTTING KICK A variation of the side thrust kick used in karate to attack an opponent's leg or instep. Known in Japanese as fumikiri.

D

DA SUM SING *Ch.* A Shao-lin kung-fu exercise used to strengthen the forearms. It is performed by two opponents throwing full power blows at each other and alternately blocking with the forearm.

DAAB (Daw'b) *Thai.* A Thai sword used in the art of krabi-krabong.

DACHI (daw'chee) *Jp.* "stance" or "position."

DAEBEE (daw'bee) *Kr.* "guard."

DAEBI MARKI (daw'bee mawr'kee) *Kr.* "guarding block" A tae kwon do block performed with both hands in front of the chest.

DAERYON (daw'ryawn) *Kr.* "sparring" The tae kwon do counterpart to karate kumite.

DAH JONG *Ch.* A kung-fu exercise used to strengthen the forearms, palms, and fists. In dah jong, the different parts of the arm are repeatedly struck against hard, immovable objects after which they are treated with various herbal ointments that work to heal and then strengthen the arm.

DAI KISSAKI (deye kee-saw-kee) *Jp.* Enlarged point on a Japanese sword, a style more commonly found on swords from the 1700's on. Not to be confused with mond uchi, which is the cutting portion of the blade, approximately six to seven inches from the tip down. Always proportionate with overall length of the sword.

DAI NIPPON BUTOKUKAI (deye nee-pohn boo-toh-koo-keye) *Jp.* "Great Japan Martial Virtues Association" An organization founded in 1895 for the purpose of preserving and propagating the various Oriental martial arts both in Japan and abroad.

DAINI SEISAN (deye-nee say-sawn) *Jp.* A karate kata practiced in Uechi-ryu. It is a combination of the sanchin and Seisan katas.

DAISAN (deye-sawn) *Jp.* The completed drawing phase of kyujutsu (art of the bow).

DAISENSEI (deye-sehn'say) *Jp.* "great teacher" A polite title for a teacher of Japanese martial arts holding tenth-degree black belt rank.

DAI-SHARIN (deye shaw-reen) *Jp.* "great wheel" A judo throwing technique in which the opponent is thrown in the fashion of a large wheel.

DAISHO (deye'shoh) *Jp.* "big and small" Two swords, one long and the other short, worn by the samurai class in feudal Japan.

DAITO (deye'toh) *Jp.* A long sword, whose cutting edge was over 24 inches in length, as contrasted with such shorter swords as the wakizashi (eighteen inches).

DAKI-AGE (daw-kee aw'gay) *Jp.* "hugging lift" 1. A judo technique used to raise an opponent from the mat in groundwork. 2. In a judo match, to score a point by lifting the opponent from the ground to shoulder height.

DAKIKOMI-JIME (daw-kee-koh-mee jee-meh) *Jp.* "hugging choke" In judo, a choking technique.

DAKI-SUTEMI (daw-kee soo-tehm'ee) *Jp.* "hugging sacrifice throw" A judo sacrifice technique usually employed against a shorter opponent.

DALE DROP In judo, a sacrifice technique of koshiki-no-kata (kata of the antique forms).

DALLYON JOO *Kr.* "forging post" A tae kwon do training device similar to the karate makiwara. See also MAKIWARA.

DAN (dawn) *Jp.* "rank" or "degree" A term used in the Japanese martial arts for anyone who has achieved the rank of at least first-degree black belt. The dan ranks are as follows:

shodan—first degree
nidan—second degree
sandan—third degree
yondan—fourth degree
godan—fifth degree
rokudan—sixth degree
shichidan—seventh degree
hachidan—eighth degree
kudan—ninth degree
judan—tenth degree

DAN-GUN (dawn-gun) *Kr.* A tae kwon do hyung consisting of twenty-one moves and named after the legendary founder of Korea.

DANJUN (dawn-jun) *Kr.* Part of the body just below the navel which is believed to be the source of ki (spirit) in tae kwon do.

DANJUN KI (dawn-jun kee) *Kr.* A method of developing ki in hwarang-do, the essence of which is controlled breathing.

DAN-ZUKI: See CONSECUTIVE PUNCH.

DARI PYOGI (daw-ree pyoh'gee) *Kr.* "leg stretching" A series of tae kwon do exercises performed to develop flexibility in the legs.

DARUMA: See BODHIDHARMA.

DAYANG (Daw-yang) *Phil.* The female black belt ranks in the Filipino art of arnis de mano. These ranks range from first to tenth degree.

DDEE (dee) *Kr.* "belt."

DDUIYO CHAGI (dee'yoh chaw'gee) *Kr.* "jumping kick."

DE (deh) *Jp.* "advancing."

DEASHI-HARAI (deh-aw'she-haw-reye') *Jp.* "advanced foot sweep" A judo foot technique often referred to by judoka as ashi-barai (foot sweeping). Deashi-harai is the first technique of the go kyo no waza (five stages of techniques).

DEATH TOUCH: See DELAYED DEATH TOUCH.

DEBANA-O-KUJIKI (deh-baw'naw oh koo-jee'kee) *Jp.* "unnerve at the outset" Winning a contest in the opening seconds, whether it is in sports, warfare, debate, and so on. For example, psyching out an opponent before the start of a bout, or overwhelming the opponent with one's reputation.

DECEPTIVE ACTION (EP) The utilization of feinting movements or gestures to deceive an opponent.

DECEPTIVE RHYTHM (EP) A planned sequence of an irregular flow of action used to deceive an opponent.

DECISION: See YUSEI-GACHI.

DEE JEEA JIRUGI (dee-jee-aw jee'roo-gee) *Kr.* "upset punch" A short tae kwon do punch performed with either a single or double fist against a close-range opponent.

DEER One of the five animals whose movements comprise the basis of Hua To's exercises.

DEEYMYUN BANDAE DOLLYO CHAGI (dee-myun ban-day dohl-yoh cha'gee) *Kr.* See FLYING REVERSE TURNING KICK.

DEEYMYUN BITURO CHAGI: (dee-myun bee-too-roh cha'gee) *Kr.* See FLYING TWISTING KICK.

DEEYMYUN CHAGI (dee-myun cha'gee) *Kr.* "flying kick" An encompassing term for the many types of airborne kicks of tae kwon do.

DEEYMYUN DOLLYO CHAGI: (dee-myun dohl-yoh cha'gee) *Kr.* See FLYING TURNING KICK.

DEEYMYUN IJUNG YOP CHAGI: (dee-myun ee-juhng yohp cha'gee) *Kr.* See FLYING DOUBLE SIDE KICK.

DEEYMYUN YOPCHA JIRUGI: (dee-myun yohp'cha gee'ru-gee) *Kr.* See FLYING SIDE PIERCING KICK.

DEFENSE 1. (EP) A protective move designed to safeguard against injury. 2. Protection against attack.

DEFENSIVE OFFENSE (EP) The execution of a move both protective to oneself and simultaneously injurious to one's opponent.

DEFENSIVE PERSUASION (EP) Refers to the forcing of an opponent to defend a particular area, thus creating an opening elsewhere.

DEFENSIVE POSTURE: See JIGO HONTAI.

DEFLECT (EP) To deviate the course of an attacking weapon.

DELAYED DEATH TOUCH A Chinese martial arts technique known as dim mok, which reputedly enables its user to slay an opponent days, weeks, or even months after the technique has been applied to the victim. Many kung-fu exponents claim to possess this knowledge, but to date no proof of its existence has surfaced.

DELETE (EP) The elimination of a weapon and target within a technique sequence.

DERU-PON (day'roo pohn) *Jp.* A term used to denote the winning of a judo contest in the opening seconds before a contestant has had time to adjust her or himself or even grasped the opponent's jacket.

DESHI (day'shee) *Jp.* "disciple" or "trainee".

DIAGONAL STANCE A position in which one leg is held forward with the body weight evenly distributed and the legs spread approximately twice the width of the shoulders. Known in Korean as sasun sogi.

DIAGONAL STRADDLE LEG STANCE: See FUDO DACHI.

DIGUTJA CHIRUGI: "u-shape punch" See U-PUNCH.

DIM MOK *Ch.* "touching of nerve points" A Chinese system of kung-fu based on the science of striking pressure points on the body at a specific time of day. See also DELAYED DEATH TOUCH.

DISCIPLE A pupil or follower of a particular teacher or school. A term commonly used in place of student in pre-modern martial arts, when teachers were highly selective and chose students carefully.

DISCIPLINE Training that develops self-control and character. It is proclaimed to be an additional virtue inherent in the martial arts.

DISTRACTION (EP) Intentional move or moves used in freestyle or in combat to bewilder an opponent. Such moves will create an opening for a score or a damaging blow.

DIT DA JOW: See TIEH DA JYOU.

DIVERSIFIED ANGLE OF ATTACK (EP) The ability to attack from one angle and switch to another without any loss of motion, especially when using only one hand. When using two hands, alternate action from two or more angles while striking to the same target is still considered a diversified angle of attack; for example, a punch to an opponent's jaw that changes into a lifting punch under his chin.

DIVERSIFIED ANGLE OF COVER (EP) Refers to the changing of directions while covering out; not getting into the habit of covering out in one direction.

DIVERSIFIED ANGLE OF RETREAT (EP) Another phrase describing the diversified angle of cover.

DIVERSIFIED TARGETS (EP) The striking of varied targets to ensure multiple effect.

DIVISION A specific category according to rank, weight, sex, and/or age frequently used in karate tournaments, or judo contests, and less often in some other types of martial arts competition.

DJUROES (joo'rohs) *Indo.* Dancelike fighting movements used in the Indonesian martial arts, similar to karate katas.

DO (doh) *Jp.* "way" or "path" When this term is used as a suffix to a particular style of the Japanese martial arts, it is indicative of more than just a means of combat. Do indicates a discipline and philosophy with moral and spiritual connotations, the ultimate aim being enlightenment, personal development, and so forth. The most common do practices are karate-do, kendo, judo, and aikido.

DO (doh) *Jp.* "torso" or "trunk of the body" In kendo, do refers to both the trunk of the body and the protective equipment covering it. The left side of the do is rarely a valid target.

DOBOK (doh'bawk) *Kr.* "uniform" The uniform worn in tae kwon do. It is similar to that worn by karateka but may have a colored stripe running down the collar and edge. The dobok is usually white.

Dobok

DOGI (doh'gee) *Jp.* "martial arts uniform."

DOGU (doh'goo) *Jp.* "tools," "equipment," or "instruments" All the pieces of equipment used in martial arts practice.

DOHYO (doh-hyoo) *Jp.* A circular ring, fifteen feet in diameter, in which sumo contests are conducted. The edge of the ring is marked with straw bags and the surface is covered with smooth earth.

DOHYO IRI (doh-hyoo e-ree) *Jp.* The ceremonial entry of the sumo champions into the arena.

DOJANG (doh'jawng) *Kr.* "training hall" or "gymnasium" Any facility in which the Korean martial arts, especially tae kwon do, are practiced.

DOJO (doh'joh) *Jp.* "the place of the way" A training hall or gymnasium where karate, judo, aikido, and other Japanese martial arts are practiced.

DOJO ETIQUETTE The rules of conduct traditionally observed in the dojo that center around the virtues of humility and respect. Among the most common of these is the series of traditional bows performed upon entering and leaving the premises.

DOLGI (dul'gee) *Kr.* "turning."

DOLLI MYO MAKGI: See CIRCULAR BLOCK.

DOLLYO CHAGI (dul'yoh chaw'gee) *Kr.* "turning kick" A tae kwon do kick in which the snapping motion of the knee and the turning of the hips are used simultaneously to attack a frontal opponent. Known widely as the roundhouse kick.

DOLLYO JIREUGI (dul'yoh jee-roo'gee) *Kr.* "turning punch" A tae

Double-Bladed Hook Sword

kwon do punch in which the fist is launched in a semicircular fashion from the hip.

DOOL (dul) *Kr.* "two."

DOO PALMOK (du pawl'mawk) *Kr.* "double forearm" A tae kwon do block in which the blocking arm is augmented with the opposite fist near the elbow.

DOO SANKARAK CHIRUGI: See TWO-FINGER SPEAR HAND.

DORA (du'raw) *Kr.* "turn" A Korean command used in formal tae kwon do classes.

DORMANT STRENGTH Strength not properly applied to its maximum limits.

DORO CHAGI *Kr.* "waving kick" A tae kwon do block in which the foot is used to redirect an attack to the groin or the leg.

DO SAN *Kr.* A tae kwon do hyung consisting of twenty-four movements.

DOSHU (doh'shoo) *Jp.* "master" or "master of the way."

DOUBLE-BLADED HOOK SWORD A Chinese weapon resembling a crooked staff, with the end pointed and a blade resembling a sickle attached to the side.

DOUBLE BLOCK The act of simultaneously parrying or nullifying two distinct techniques, a defensive maneuver often contained in kata.

DOUBLE CHECK (EP) A single, simultaneous, or dual delivery that restrains, hinders, or represses an opponent from taking action from more than one leverage point.

DOUBLE FACTOR (EP) Entails a dual movement of defense that can incorporate any combination of blocks, parries, and checks. It also refers to sophisticated moves that are both defensive and offensive.

DOUBLE-FIST PUNCH A karate punching technique in which both fists strike the same target simultaneously. It can also refer to a number of different punches in which both fists strike the target at the same time, such as the u-punch, scissors punch, and parallel punch. Known in Japanese as the morote-zuki.

DOUBLE FOREARM: See DOO PALMOK.

DOUBLE-HANDED NECKLOCK A judo strangulation technique in which both hands are used to apply pressure to the carotid arteries with the object of rendering the opponent unconscious.

DOUBLE KICK The act of performing two simultaneous or consecutive kicks.

DOUBLE PALM CHANGE One of the several basic actions of pa-kua kung-fu.

DOUBLE STEPPING: See OMGYO DIDIGI.

DOUBLE SWORD A Chinese weapon that appears to be a single sword until the opponent is at close range, at which time the user separates the two swords for combat.

DOWNWARD BLOCK Any act of neutralizing an opponent's low-level attack. Known in Japanese as gedan-barai; in Korean as naeryo marki.

DOWNWARD HOOKING BLOCK A karate blocking technique in which the arm is swung downward in a wide circle to block and grab an opponent's leg and unbalance him or her. Known in Japanese as gedan-kake-uke.

DOWNWARD PUNCH A tae kwon do punch delivered vertically toward an opponent on the ground. Known in Korean as naeryo jireugi.

DOWNWARD X BLOCK A low-level parry augmented by crossing one arm over the other.

DOZUKIRI (doe-zoo-care'ee) *Jp.* The second stage of kyudo (way of the bow and arrow) in which the archer sets his body into a firm stance.

DRAGON'S HEAD FIST 1. A kung-fu technique in which the middle joint of the third finger is extended to form a striking area. It is used against a vulnerable target area such as the solar plexus. 2. A kyokushinkai karate technique in which the middle knuckles of the forefinger and

Drop Kick

middle finger are extended and used as the striking point. Known in Japanese as ryutoken.

DROP (EP) The execution of moves that employ "marriage to gravity" when the body weight drops with the intended action.

DROP KICK The act of dropping to the floor and delivering a kick upward. Commonly used by many karate practitioners.

DROPPING BLOCK A karate blocking technique in which the forearm is brought straight down from above the head to an opponent's attacking arm. Known in Japanese as otoshi-uke.

DRUNKEN MONKEY: See MONKEY STYLE.

DRUNKEN STYLE Kung-fu movements characterized by the deceptive instability of the practitioners. They often appear to wobble unsteadily as if drunk, and will purposely stumble to the ground from where they proceed to attack with a surprising variety of foot and leg techniques. The moves of this style are both beautiful and humorous to watch, but very difficult to learn.

DUE BACK One of the eight directions of unbalance in judo. Known in Japanese as ma-ushiro.

DUE FRONT One of the eight directions of unbalance in judo. Known in Japanese as man-mae.

DUMOG (doo-mog) *Phil.* An early form of wrestling practiced by Filipino natives.

DUNG JOOMUK: See BACKFIST.

DUNG SONKAL: See RIDGE HAND.

DUNG SONMOK (dung sawn'mauk) *Kr.* "reverse wrist" A tae kwon do blocking technique applied with the wrist.

DURO MARKI (doo'roh mawr'kee) *Kr.* "scooping block" A tae kwon do hand-blocking technique of circular motion used to nullify an opponent's kick and unbalance her or him.

DWI CHAGI (dwee chaw'gee) *Kr.* "back kick."

DWIKUMCHI (dwee-kum'chee) *Kr.* "back sole" A term used in tae kwon do to represent the bottom of the foot.

DWIT BAL SOGI (dwit bawl soo'gee) *Kr.* "rear foot stance" A tae kwon do stance in which the heel of the front foot is off the ground and the majority of body weight is distributed to the rear leg.

DWITCHA BUSIGI (dwit'chaw boo-see'gee) *Kr.* "back snap kick" A tae kwon do kick directed to the rear in which the kicking foot is quickly withdrawn to its original position.

DWITCHA JIRUGI (dwit'chaw jee-roo'gee) *Kr.* "back piercing kick" A tae kwon do kick directed to the rear, using the heel in a thrusting manner.

DWIT KOASEOGI: See KOA-SEOGI.

DWITKOOCHI: See L-STANCE.

EAGLE CLAW SYSTEM A style of kung-fu properly known as xing-chiao and characterized by clawlike attacks to the eyes and throat; and high leaps and kicks. This system was popularized by grandmaster Liu Fa Mang, who taught the style for the famous Ching Wu (Jing Mo in Cantonese) Athletic Association based in Shanghai, China.

EBI-GARAMI (ay'bee gaw-raw'mee) *Jp.* "lobster entanglement" A judo strangulation technique.

ECONOMY OF MOTION (EP) Any movement that takes little time to execute but still causes the intended effect. Failure to cause the intended effect will only categorize the move as being wasted motion. It must be short and effective to be considered economical.

EDGE OF FOOT The lateral side of the foot used as a striking point for numerous kicks in karate. Known in Japanese as sokuto and in Korean as balkal.

EDGE OF HAND The fleshy outer edge of the hand used as the striking point for the knife-hand technique often called the karate chop. Known in Japanese as shuto and in Korean as sonkal.

EIGHT DIRECTIONS OF UNBALANCE In judo the eight most advantageous directions in which to throw an opponent: due front, right, front corner, right side, right rear corner, due back, left rear corner, left side, and left front corner. See also KUZUSHI.

EISHIN RYU (ay-shin ri-yu) The original style of iaijutsu (sword drawing art) that embraces numerous kata and is combat-, not sport-oriented.

EKU *Okinawa* "oar" A weapon developed by Okinawan fishermen. Today it is a training weapon common to Okinawan karate. It is employed somewhat like the bo (staff) and the broad, flat end is used to deliver the decisive blow.

ELBOW Used as a striking point in close-quarter combat or as a target area in applying arm locks. Known in Japanese as empi or hiji and in Korean as palkoop or palkumchi.

ELBOW STRIKES: See EMPI-UCHI.

EMBUJO (ehm-boo'joh) *Jp.* A place of exhibition or athletic performances where martial arts events are often staged.

EMBU SEN (ehm-boo sehn') *Jp.* The footwork patterns or floor patterns that one follows when performing karate katas. Often called predetermined performance lines, they vary from the straight line to the T and I execution patterns.

EMPI: See ELBOW.

EMPI (em'pee) *Jp.* "flying swallow" A kata formulated in the shorin-ryu karate school of Okinawa, though the Okinawans call this form Wanshu or Wansu, after the great Chinese martial artist. When Gichin Funakoshi introduced the Wanshu kata to Japan, the Japanese, with Funakoshi's approval, changed all Okinawan terminology to their native language. With the absence of a Japanese equivalent for Wanshu they chose to use the word "empi."

There are two variations of the empi kata. The Japanese practice the longer, more complex form, especially in Shotokan karate. The kata is performed with swift ascending and descending movements similar to that of a swallow in flight. Also known as en-bi.

EMPI-UCHI (ehm'pee oo'chee) *Jp.* "elbow strikes" Karate attacking techniques in which the elbow is used to strike forward, sideward, backward, upward, or downward. Elbow techniques are chiefly used in

Empi Uchi (Upward Elbow)

close-quarter combat to the chin, solar plexus or ribs. The six major elbow techniques are:

1. Forward elbow strike (mae empi-uchi or mae hiji ate)
2. Side elbow strike (yoko empi-uchi or yoko hiji ate)
3. Back elbow strike (ushiro empi-uchi or ushiro hiji ate)
4. Side elbow strike (yoko mawashi empi-uchi or yoko mawashi hiji ate)
5. Upward elbow strike (tate empi-uchi or tate hiji ate)
6. Downward elbow strike (otoshi empi-uchi or otoshi hiji ate)

EMPTY HAND One translation of the word "karate": kara = "empty"; te = "hand."

EMPTY-HAND ART One translation of "karate-jutsu."

EMPTY PUNCHING The practice of punching alternately with the right and left hands at an imaginary opponent.

EN BI: See EMPI.

ENERGY/ACTION: See ITSUTSO-NO-KATA.

ENCHO (ehn-choh) *Jp.* "continuation" or "extension" 1. The overtime period(s) of a match 2. The referee's announcement of the beginning of the overtime period.

ENSHO (en'show) *Jp.* "round heel" The heel of the foot used in kicking, especially backward. Known also as kakato.

ENTEKI (ehn-teh-kee) *Jp.* The art of long-distance archery.

ENVIRONMENTAL CONDITIONS (EP) Existing conditions of combat or freestyle that include rules of a particular tournament, weather conditions, time of day, number of persons involved, general surroundings, layout, terrain, and so on.

EOTGEOREO MAKKI *Kr.* "x fist" A tae kwon do block requiring both hands, usually employed in blocking a downward strike. Known also as gyocha joomuk.

ER LIANG MEN *Ch.* "two elements boxing" A style of kung-fu that bases its philosophical structure as well as its techniques on the theories of yin/yang duality.

ERI (eh'ree) *Jp.* "lapel."

ERI KATSU (eh'ree kat'su) *Jp.* The lapel method of resuscitation used in judo.

ERI-SEOI-NAGE (eh'ree see-oy naw'geh) *Jp.* "lapel shoulder throw" A judo throw using the opponent's collar.

ESCRIMA: See ARNIS.

ESTOCADOR (es-to-ka-door) *Phil.* A practitioner of escrima.

EUI AM (oo awm) *Kr.* A tae kwon do hyung consisting of forty-five movements.

EXPLOSIVE PRESSURE (EP) Bursting aggressive action that keeps constant force on an opponent, thus preventing the opponent from setting up to retaliate.

EXTENDED KNUCKLE FIST: See ONE-KNUCKLE FIST.

EXTENSION The full extent or range of a technique.

EXTENSION OF THE BODY A doctrine common to the art of weaponry indicating that the weapon should not be manipulated as an extraneous unit, but as a part of the entire body.

EXTERNAL POWER Power generated through external sources or muscular power as in most so-called "hard" karate systems.

EXTERNAL SYSTEM Any Chinese kung-fu style that emphasizes the training of bones and muscles, exercise of chi-kung, and defeating an opponent at the instant of attack. Known in Chinese as wai-chia.

FADE OUT (EP) To move back from an action.

FALLING THROWS Judo techniques coming under the category of sacrifice throws. See also SUTEMI-WAZA.

FARANDO: See CHA-RYWK.

FARI GATKA *Hind.* An Indian form of fencing centered around shields (fari) and swords (gatka). The gatka is a three-foot, leather-covered stick. The fari, nine inches in diameter, is also leather bound. To score points the stick must simply touch the vital points designated on an opponent's body.

FEEL (EP) A word to describe the use of the foot in moving backward. When moving back, the foot should lightly slide so that it literally feels its way back to sense possible obstacles.

FENG-CHIU SHU *Ch.* "muscle-splitting skill" One of the original names for Chinese wrestling, or chin-na.

FINGER-LOCKING In judo or jujutsu, the act of using locking techniques on the fingers with the intention of gaining a submission from an opponent.

FIST Area of the hand most commonly employed as a striking point for punching. Specifically, the first knuckles of the index and middle fingers.

In martial arts, it is also referred to as the forefist. See also SEIKEN; AP CHOOMUK.

FISTHOOK A punch delivered in an arc that is snapped inward and downward following impact. Often used in kung-fu.

FIVE ANIMALS The tiger, bear, monkey, deer, and bird; the animals whose movements were transformed into exercises by Chinese surgeon Hua To (A.D.190–265).

FIVE POWER RULE In goju-ryu karate, a method of grading the intensity with which a blow is delivered. A slight blow would register at one or two degrees by this scale, while a powerful blow would reach five.

FIVE STAR BEAT One of the rhythms played on the large Chinese drum during the ceremonial lion dance.

FIVE-STEP SPARRING In karate, a method of prearranged practice fighting in which the attacker takes five steps forward to deliver a series of attacks, while the defender retreats and blocks and then executes a counter to the final attacking technique. Known in Japanese as gohon kumite.

FLOATING HIP THROW: See UKI-GOSHI.

FLOATING HOLD An immobilizing technique used in judo.

FLOATING LEG In judo, the leg that is not supporting the weight of the body; the active leg in executing sweeps and other leg throws.

FLOWING PUNCH A karate technique that jointly blocks and counters in the same motion. Known in Japanese as the nagashi-zuki.

FLUIDITY That property of smoothly mixing sustained movements with sudden bursts of power. This quality is particularly evident in a fine kata performance.

FLURRY (EP) In karate, a fast, explosive exchange of techniques.

FLYING BACK KICK In karate, a linear thrust kick directed backward and launched with a jump.

FLYING CRESCENT KICK A circular karate and tae kwon do

kicking technique launched with a jump in which the foot travels to the target in either a clockwise or counterclockwise direction.

FLYING DOUBLE SIDE KICK A tae kwon do technique with which high and low targets are attacked in succession from an airborne position. Known in Korean as the twimyo ijung yop chagi.

FLYING FRONT KICK In karate, a linear snap or thrust kick directed forward while airborne. Known in Japanese as the mae-tobi-geri.

FLYING KICK Any kick in which the movement is characterized by leaping in conjunction with the execution of the technique. Known in Japanese as tobi-geri and in Korean as twimyo chagi.

FLYING REVERSE TURNING KICK A tae kwon do technique in which the body is rotated 360 degrees in midair to add momentum to the kick. Known in Korean as the twimyo bandae dollyo chagi.

FLYING ROUNDHOUSE KICK A roundhouse kick executed in midair. Known in Japanese as the mawashi-tobi-geri.

FLYING SIDE KICK A side kick executed in midair. Known in

Flying Side Kick

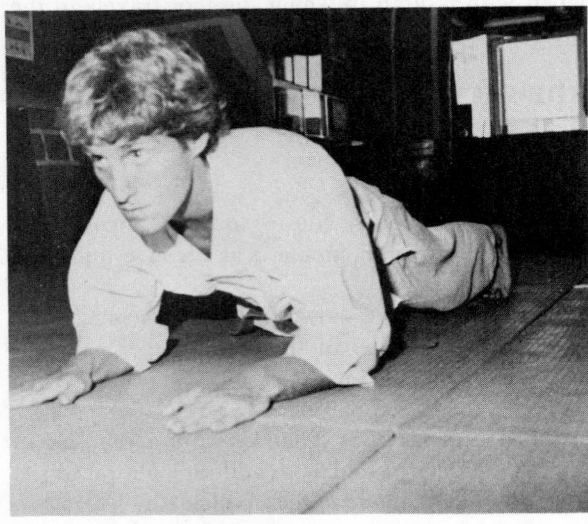

Forward Breakfall

Japanese as the yoko-tobi-geri, in Korean as the twimyo yopcha jirugi (flying side piercing kick).

FLYING SIDE PIERCING KICK: See FLYING SIDE KICK.

FLYING TURNING KICK A tae kwon do turning kick delivered in midair and delivering the kick backwards. Known in Korean as the twimyo dollyo chagi.

FLYING TWISTING KICK A tae kwon do kick executed to the front while in midair. Known in Korean as the twimyo bituro chagi.

FOCUS In karate, the act of concentrating complete mental and physical force into a single striking point. Known in Japanese as kime, the concept is common to all martial arts.

FOLLOW THROUGH To continue execution of a technique to its absolute completion. See also ZANSHIN.

FOLLOW UP A technique that immediately follows another as a repetition or addition.

FOOT MANEUVERING SEQUENCE Movements that help one move toward or away from an opponent.

FOOTSWORD Another name for the edge of the foot.

FOOT THROW A judo throwing technique done from a standing position in which the action of the foot is used in the delivery. Known in Japanese as the ashi-waza.

FOOTWORK The act of using the feet for offensive or defensive mobility when fighting.

FOREARM Part of the body often used in blocking. Known in Japanese as the ude and in Korean as the palmok.

FOREARM BLOCK A karate blocking technique used to nullify an attack to the body or face. There are two types of forearm blocks: those directed from the outside to the inside, and vice versa. Known in Japanese as the ude-uke.

FOREARM PRESSING BLOCK A karate block in which the arm is bent 90 degrees in front of the body and the forearm is used to block an opponent's attack by pressing the attacking hand downward.

FORE KNUCKLE A semiclenched fist technique in which the second knuckles of the four fingers are used as a striking point. Known in Japanese as the hiraken.

FORGING POST: See MAKIWARA.

FORM 1. An expression used in martial arts to describe the manner in which one executes techniques. Good form consists of proper posture, balance, coordination, timing, and the controlled use of speed and power. 2. A predetermined pattern of movement synomymous with almost every martial art. Known in Japanese as kata (formal exercise), in Korean as hyung (pattern), and in Chinese as kuen. See also KATA; HYUNG; KUEN.

FORMAL EXERCISE(S): See KATA; HYUNG; KUEN.

FORMS OF FIVE A form of five judo techniques developed by Professor Jigoro Kano to represent the soul of Japan. Left unnamed upon his death, it came to be called the kata of the five principles.

FORWARD BREAKFALL A method of falling in which one falls face down and strikes the mat with the hands and forearms to avoid injury to the face and chest.

FORWARD ELBOW STRIKE: See EMPI-UCHI.

FORWARD STANCE A karate stance in which one foot is placed forward, with the knees bent over the toes, while the back foot remains relatively straight. The body weight is distributed with the front leg bearing 60 percent of the weight. Known in Japanese as the zenkutsu-dachi.

FORWARD SWEEP In Chinese boxing, the swinging of one extended leg in a circle while keeping the center of gravity low. The opponent is knocked off balance with the inner side of the extended leg, which usually strikes the opponent's lower legs.

FOUNDATION A strong base of fundamental techniques upon which progress can best be achieved.

FOUR-STEP SPARRING A method of prearranged practice fighting in which the attacker takes four steps forward to deliver a series of attacks and the defender blocks throughout the sequence and counters the final technique.

FOU-TOU-OU *Ch.* A sword used in kung-fu, known as the hook and crescent sword.

FREESTYLE SPARRING 1. Usually the most advanced stage of martial arts training in which two opponents fight against one another without predetermined variables. Known in judo as randori, in kendo as jigeiko, and in aikido as jiyuwaza, in Japanese karate as jiyu kumite, and in Korean as jayoo daeryon (free sparring). 2. In karate, the main objective in freestyle sparring, commonly called freestyle, is to find or create an opening in the opponent's defense and then deliver a decisive blow. In its most basic form, freestyle techniques are pulled just short of contact.

Freestyle puts students under actual combat conditions and thus forces them to perfect fighting abilities without any injury to either participant. The practice has now gained popularity as a sport in which there is a free exchange of blows, blocks, and counterattacks until one of the players scores a cleanly executed attack to a vital point of the opponent's body.

FRICTIONAL PULL (EP) The multiple effects caused by scraping, hooking, and pulling; the result causes pain to an opponent

FRONT BLOCK: See APMAKGI.

Front Kick

FRONT KICK A kick delivered forward with the rear foot, using the ball, heel, or instep of the foot as the striking point. There are two types of front kicks: the front snap kick (mae-geri-keagi), which uses the snapping motion of the knee to kick an opponent; and the front thrust kick (mae-geri-kekomi) in which the ball of the foot or the heel is thrust in a straight line into the target area. Known in Japanese as mae-geri.

FRONT LEG KICK A karate kick executed with the front leg and similar to the front snap kick, which is done with the rear leg. Known in Japanese as mae-ashi-geri.

FRONT RISING KICK: See AP CHA OLLIGI.

FRONT SNAP KICK: See FRONT KICK.

FRONT STANCE: See FORWARD STANCE.

FRONT STRIKE: See AP TAERIGI.

FRONT THRUST KICK: See FRONT KICK.

FU *Ch.* The battle axe.

FU-ANTEI *Jp.* A judo term denoting instability or lack of balance.

FUCHI (foo'chee) *Jp.* "rim," "edge," or "metal sleeve" The metal sleeve located at the base of the handle next to the guard of a samurai sword. It is usually made as part of a matched set with the kashira or pommel cap.

FU-CHIAO-PAI *Ch.* A tiger claw system of kung-fu, supposedly developed at the Shao-lin Temple. The essence of the style is to simulate the speed and grace of a fighting tiger.

FUDO-DACHI (foo'doh daw'chee) *Jp.* "immovable stance" In karate, a combination of the forward and horse stances. In this stance, both knees are bent so as to make it an effective posture against a powerful attack.

FUGUL (foo'gul) *Kr.* "back stance" A tae kwon do stance in which 70 percent of the body weight is distributed to the rear foot. See also KOKUTSU-DACHI.

FUJOSHI-YO-GOSHIN-NO-KATA (fu-joh-shee yoh goh-sheen noh kaw-taw) *Jp.* "the self-defense form for women's use" The judo kata of self-defense employed exclusively by female practitioners.

FU JOW PAI: See FU-CHIAO-PAI.

FUKAI (foo-keye') *Jp.* To hold strongly.

FUKI BARI (foo-kee baw-ree) *Jp.* "needle blowing" A technique of blowing small needles from the mouth. The needles were sometimes spit into the opponent's face at very close range to create an opportunity to attack or escape. Longer needles were shot from a short blowgun. It was a weapon commonly used by ninja and commoners.

FUKIYA (foo-kee-yaw) *Jp.* Pins and poison darts shot through a blowgun, weapons used extensively by the ninja.

FUKIYU (foo-kee-yoo) *Jp.* A karate kata of the Okinawan shorin-ryu school.

FUKUBU (foo-koo-boo) *Jp* A target area in sport karate that includes the diaphragm, abdomen, and side chest area.

FUKUMI BARI (foo-koo-mee baw-ree) *Jp.* Tiny, pin-sized dirks held in the mouth and blown out at the enemy's eyes, weapons commonly used by the ninja. Same meaning as fuki bari.

FUKURO-GAESHI NO JITSU (foo-koo-roh geye-eh-shee noh juh-tso) *Jp.* "owl return technique" A tactic used by the ninja through which he seemingly betrayed his own lord by escaping to an enemy camp. He would then betray the enemy lord at a time of crisis and return to his allied camp.

FUKURO-GAESHI ZEN JITSU (foo-koo-ro geye-eh-shee zen juh-tso) *Jp.* An infiltration tactic used by the ninja to create dissension between the enemy lord and one of his relatives. Same as fukuro-gaeshi no jitsu.

FUKURO-KENSUI (foo-koo-roh ken-swee) *Jp.* "hanging bag" A judo necklock performed while the opponent is on the ground.

FUKUSHIN SHUGO (foo-koo-shin shu-go) *Jp.* A term used in competition signaling the corner judges to come together for a decision.

FUGYUGATA (foo-gyo-ga-tah) *Jp.* A set of two basic kata practiced by Okinawan karate stylists.

FU JYA *Ch.* A style of kung-fu that employs both hard and soft techniques. In the hand techniques, which outnumber those of the foot, the palm often replaces the fist when striking. There are both northern and southern styles of fu jya. Known also as fut gar or fut ga.

FULL-CONTACT KARATE A contest whereby two players engage in full-contact bouts with protective hand and foot pads, with the object of rendering one another unconscious. Fighters are permitted to use both hand and foot blows, according to predetermined rules, and must deliver a minimum number of kicks per round. Championship contests range from nine to twelve rounds, depending on the sanctioning body's regulations, for world titles. Amateur bouts are three rounds in duration. All rounds are two minutes in length, with a one minute rest period in between.

Full contact karate was inaugurated on September 14, 1974, at the Los Angeles Sports Arena, where fourteen fighters from eight countries competed for four world titles, under Professional Karate Association sanction.

FUMI-ASHI: See SUIEI-JUTSU.

FUMIKIRI: See CUTTING KICK.

FUMI-KOMI (foo'mee koh'mee) *Jp.* "step in" A karate stamping kick usually applied to the knee, shin, or instep of an opponent.

FUMI-WAZA (foo'mee waw'zaw) *Jp.* "stamping techniques" One of the broad categories into which karate techniques are divided.

FUNDOSHI (fun-doh-shee) *Jp.* A loin cloth; the traditional Japanese male undergarment. It is still worn by many men for its comfort.

FUSEN-GACHI (foo-sehn gaw'chee) *Jp.* "win by default" A term denoting a default in a judo contest or in a Japanese-style karate match. Known also as fusensho.

FUSENSHO: See FUSEN-GACHI.

FUTARI (ftaw'ree) *Jp.* "two people" Two opponents meeting in a Japanese-style karate match.

FUT GA; FUT GAR: See FU JYA.

GADKA: See GATKA.

GAIWAN (geye-wawn') *Jp.* "outer arm" Part of the forearm located on the side opposite the thumb. Often used in karate blocking tactics.

GAKE (gaw'kay) *Jp.* The hooking action used in some judo ankle and sacrifice throws.

GAKKO (gawk'koh) *Jp.* "school."

GAKU (gaw'koo) *Jp.* "frame" A framed photograph of the founder, a great instructor, or a philosophical text, that hangs at the kamiza (instructor's or upper side) of most martial arts schools.

GANKAKU (gawn-kaw'koo) *Jp.* "crane on a rock" A kata formulated in the shorin-ryu karate school of Okinawa. Originally, it was known as Chinto. Gichin Funakoshi changed the name after his arrival in Japan. See also RO-HAI.

GANMEN (gawn-mehn) *Jp.* A target area referred to in sport karate. It includes all of the head and face area.

GANSEKI-OTOSHI (gawn-seh'-kee oh'toh'shee) *Jp.* "stone drop" A judo hand technique, rarely used by modern judoka.

GARAMI (gaw-raw-mee) *Jp.* "entanglement."

GARI (gaw'ree) *Jp.* A reaping action with the leg commonly used in judo.

GASSHUKU *Jp.* A training camp.

GATAME (gaw-ta-may') *Jp.* "locking" or "holding."

GATKA An Indo-Pakistan martial art that resembles European saber fighting except that a gatka, or wooden stick, replaces the sword.

GEDAN (gay'dawn) *Jp.* "lower" or "lower level" A term often used in karate to pinpoint an area to be attacked. Usually refers to the lower trunk area.

GEDAN BARAI: See DOWNWARD SWEEP.

GEDAN KAKE UKE: See DOWNWARD HOOKING BLOCK.

GEDAN-TSUKI (gay'dawn tskee) *Jp.* "downward thrust" A karate punch, usually directed to the groin area.

GEDAN-UKE (gay'dawn oo'kay) *Jp.* An encompassing term used to represent karate blocks that protect the lower area of the body.

GEKIGAN-JUTSU (geh-kee-gawn juts-uh) *Jp.* A combat system centered around the use of the ball and chain.

GEKKEN (gehk'kehn) *Jp.* "severe sword" A name often used in place of kendo during the Meiji era (1868–1912), especially by the military.

GENIN (gay-neen) *Jp.* "low person" Ninja of the lowest rank who were often responsible for carrying out dangerous assignments.

GENKOTSU (gehn-koh-tsu) *Jp.* "attacking vital points" A system of combat used in feudal Japan.

GENSEIRYU (gehn-say-ryoo) *Jp.* A style of karate characterized by tumbling and somersaults.

GERI (gay'ree) *Jp.* "kick."

Gi

GETA (gay'taw) *Jp.* "clogs" Japanese wooden shoes. Geta have two "heels" running across the width of the sole. These vary in height depending on the conditions, i.e., mud, dirt, for which the geta were made.

GI (ghee) *Jp.* "uniform" or "suit" The traditional uniform worn in many Japanese martial arts. It normally consists of pants and a loose jacket, tied with a belt, and is most often white in color. The karate-gi is made of a light cotton material, while the judo-gi is of a much heavier double-woven fabric because of the throwing and grappling involved.

GI (ghee) *Kr.* In Korean martial arts, "spirit" or inner strength.

GIM: See CHIEN.

GO (goh) *Jp.* "five."

GODAN (goh'dawn) *Jp.* "fifth rank" A fifth degree black belt.

GOHON KUMITE: See FIVE-STEP SPARRING.

GOJU-RYU (goh'joo ryoo) *Jp.* "hard-soft way" A style of karate originated in Okinawa and Japan. Practitioners learn how to combine soft blocking tactics with quick, strong counterattacks. Much emphasis is placed on speed so that blows are delivered in rapid succession. Goju-ryu employs very dramatic breathing exercises as well as dynamic tension katas. It is among the foremost karate systems extant in modern Japan.

GOJU-SHIHO (goh-joo shee'hoh) *Jp.* "fifty-four steps" A kata formulated in Okinawan Shuri-te karate. Some authorities attribute techniques of this kata to the moves of the legendary phoenix, whereas other katas are derived from the movements of the crane, eagle, and so on.

GOKAKUGEIKO (goh-kaw'koo-gay'koh) *Jp.* A method of practice in which two equally skilled opponents attempt to defeat one another. It is used by kendo and judo practitioners. See also KEIKO.

GOKYO; GOKYO NO WAZA (goh-kyoh noh waw-zaw) *Jp.* "five stages of techniques" Known also as Kodokan gokyo, a systematic guide for teaching judo established by Jigoro Kano in 1896 and revised in 1920. The five stages, or kyo, are arranged from easy to difficult according to a very complex study of the dynamics and skills necessary to perform each throw.

The gokyo are practiced throughout the world as the basis for teaching judo. They are as follows:

First Kyo
1. deashiharai
2. hizaguruma
3. sasae-tsuri-komi-ashi
4. ukigoshi
5. osotogari
6. ogoshi
7. ouchigari
8. seoi-nage

Second Kyo
1. kosotogari
2. kouchigari
3. koshiguruma
4. tsurikomi-goshi
5. okuriashibarai
6. tai-otoshi
7. haraigoshi
8. uchimata

Third Kyo
1. kosotogake
2. tsurigoshi
3. yoko-otoshi
4. ashiguruma
5. hane-goshi
6. haraitsurikomiashi
7. tomoe-nage
8. kata-guruma

Fourth Kyo
1. sumigaeshi
2. taniotoshi
3. hanemakikomi
4. sukuinage
5. utsuriogoshi
6. oguruma
7. sotomakikomi
8. ukiotoshi

Fifth Kyo
1. osotoguruma
2. ukiwaza
3. yokowakare
4. yokoguruma
5. ushirogoshi
6. uranage
7. sumiotoshi
8. yokogake

GOKYU (goh'kyoo) *Jp.* "fifth class" A beginner or intermediate student, depending on the style, of Japanese and Okinawan karate. In judo, usually a yellow belt.

GOLCHO CHAGI (gohl-choh chaw'gee) *Kr.* "hooking kick" A tae kwon do block using the side instep, in a semicircular movement. It is used against the elbow joint or against the Achilles heel of the opponent.

GOLCHO MAKGI (gol'cho mawk'gee) *Kr.* "hooking block" A tae kwon do block using the hands to hook the opponent's attacking weapon.

GOLD BELT Color of the belt worn in the beginning level of study in the Korean martial arts. Usually about eighth gup.

GOMAN (goh'mawn) *Kr.* "end" A Korean command used in tae kwon do.

GOMSON (gum'sawn) *Kr.* "bear hand" A semiclenched hand used to attack in tae kwon do.

GONG GYUK (gawng gyuk') *Kr.* "attack."

GONG GYUK GI (gawng gyuk gee') *Kr.* "attacking techniques."

GO-NIN-GAKE (goh nin kah-keh) *Jp.* "five person attack" A judo contest in which one competitor is pitted against five opponents who have to be defeated successively in a given time period.

GO-NO-SEN (goh noh sehn') *Jp.* A term in which a judo competitor, realizing that the attempted technique has failed, tries to maintain composure, but is defeated when the opponent takes advantage of the disturbed balance to execute a successful technique.

GO-NO-SEN-NO-KATA (goh no sehn noh kaw'taw) "forms of counterthrowing" The third kata of judo, which embraces twelve attacking techniques and twelve counters to them.

GO-NO-SEN-NO-KATA	*COUNTERATTACKS*
osotogari	osotogari
hizaguruma	hizaguruma
ouchigari	deashiharai
deashiharai	deashiharai
kosotogake	tai-otoshi

GO-NO-SEN-NO-KATA	*COUNTERATTACKS*
kouchigari	sasae-tsuri-komi-ashi
kubinage	ushirogoshi
koshiguruma	ukigoshi
hane-goshi	sasae-tsuri-komi-ashi
haraigoshi	ushirogoshi
uchimata	sukuinage
kataseoinage	sumigaeshi

GORO CHAGI (goh'rah chaw-gee) *Kr.* "sweeping kick" A tae kwon do takedown technique whose objective is to sweep an opponent off balance or throw him or her to the ground.

GOSHI (goh-shuh) *Jp.* "hip."

GOSHIN-JUTSU (goh-sheen juts'-uh) *Jp.* "art of self-defense" Self-defense aspect practiced in numerous Japanese martial disciplines as opposed to kata, sparring, and freestyle training.

GOSOKU (goh-soh-koo) *Jp.* A modern system of karate founded by Tak Kubota of Los Angeles, California.

GO-TI *Ch.* An ancient form of Chinese wrestling.

GOTON NO JUTSU (go-tun no joo-tsu) *Jp.* "five escape techniques" Escape methods used by the ninja of feudal Japan. They included environmental ploys of escape through trees, tall grass, the bare ground, walls, large stones, water, and the use of metal and fire for distraction. Each of these techniques involved a specialization at which the ninja became expert.

GOYANGHEE SOGI (goh-yawng'hee soh'gee) *Kr.* "cat stance" Stance in which the body weight is 90 degrees on the rear foot with the front toes touching the ground only.

GRADING An examination in the physical and theoretical skills used in many martial arts with the purpose of determining whether a student shall advance in rank.

GRAPPLING TECHNIQUES A composite group of judo techniques with which the competitors attempt to achieve victory while on the ground. Known in Japanese as katame-waza, or more often as ne-waza (ground techniques), grappling techniques fall into three major categories:

osae-waza (pinning techniques), shime-waza (choking techniques), and kansetsu-waza (joint-locking techniques).

GRASPING BLOCK A karate blocking technique in which the attacking foot or hand is seized and the opponent's balance is broken. Known in Japanese as the tsukami-uke, in Korean as the butjaba makgi.

GRASPING KICK: See BUTJAPGO CHAGI.

GRAVITATIONAL MARRIAGE: See MARRIAGE TO GRAVITY.

GREEN BELT Color of the belt worn in the intermediate level of study in most Japanese and Okinawan martial arts.

GROUNDWORK A term often used in judo when referring to techniques performed while on the ground. See also GRAPPLING TECHNIQUES.

GUARD The position of the hands and legs when squaring off to fight, or between the execution of techniques.

GUJARI DOLGI (ghoo-jar-ee dol-gee) *Kr.* "spot turning" A tae kwon do method of defensive turning to meet an oncoming attacker.

GULAT: See BAJANG.

GUMTOO (gum'too) *Kr.* A check in tae kwon do.

GUNBAI (gun-beye) *Jp.* "war fan" A rigid iron or wooden fan carried by generals in battle and used today by sumo referees as a symbol of their authority.

GUNG-FU (gung foo') *Ch.* The Cantonese pronunciation of kung-fu. See also KUNG-FU.

GUNGUL SOGI (jun-gul soh'gee) *Kr.* "walking stance" A tae kwon do stance in which the front foot is forward and the rear is turned outward at a 25-degree angle.

GUN SHIN PUP (gun sheen pup) *Kr.* The hwarangdo techniques of concealment, deception, and camouflage. It is very similar to Japanese ninjutsu.

GUNTO SOHO (gun-toh soh-hoh) *Jp.* A method of using the Japanese army sword. It was formerly known as Toyama Ryu Iai.

GUP (gup) *Kr.* "grade" or "class" A Korean grade designating a level of achievement below black belt. In America, the most popular belt colors representing the gup classes are white, gold, orange, green, blue, and red.

GWANG-GAE (gwawng-gay) *Kr.* A tae kwon do hyung (pattern).

GWO SHU; See KUNG-FU.

GYAKU (gyaw'koo) *Jp.* "reverse" or "opposite."

GYAKU-JUJI-JIME (gyaw'koo joo-jee jee-may) *Jp.* "reverse cross necklock" The tenth judo technique of katame-no-kata.

GYAKU-MAWASHI-GERI: See REVERSE ROUNDHOUSE KICK.

GYAKU-SANKAKU-JIME (gyaw-koo sawn-kaw-koo jee-may) *Jp.* "reverse triangular necklock" A judo necklock.

GYAKU-TE (gyaw'koo-tay) *Jp.* "reverse hand" The art of locking joints and arm bars, used in judo, jujutsu, and aikido. It can also refer to a countermove or attack.

GYAKU-TEDORI (gyaw-koo teh-adh-ree) *Jp.* "reverse twisting" A wrist-locking technique used in judo and aikido.

GYAKU-YONO-JUJI-JIME (gy-aw-coo yoh-noh joo-gee gee-may) *Jp.* The lateral cross necklock, a judo choking technique.

GYAKU ZUKI: See REVERSE PUNCH.

GYOCHA JOOMUK: See EOTGEOREO MAKKI.

GYOJI (gy-oh'gee) *Jp.* The referee of a sumo match.

HABAKI (ha-ba'kee) *Jp.* The collar around the blade of a samurai sword. It is located just below the guard for the purpose of assuring a tight fit between scabbard and blade.

HACHI (ha'chee) *Jp.* "eight."

HACHIDAN (ha'chee-dan) *Jp.* "eighth rank" An eighth-degree black belt in the Japanese and Okinawan martial disciplines.

HACHIJI-DACHI (ha-chee'jee da'chee) *Jp.* "open-leg stance" A natural position used in karate in which the feet are spread shoulder width and the toes point outward at 45-degree angles.

HACHIKYU ha'chee-kyoo) *Jp.* "eighth class" A white belt, or beginner, in the Japanese and Okinawan martial disciplines.

HACHIMAKI (ha-chee-ma'kee) *Jp.* "head wrapping" A light cotton towel, also known as the tenugui, wrapped around the forehead to restrict perspiration from running into the eyes and face. It is worn by kendoka underneath the men and also by some karate players as a sweat band.

HADAKA-JIME (ha-da-ka jee-meh) *Jp.* "naked necklock" A judo stranglehold categorized as the seventh technique of katame-no-kata.

HA'I (heye) *Kr.* The pants worn in tae kwon do practice.

HAIBU (heye-boo) *Jp.* Back area. A primary target area in sport karate.

HAIRIKATA (heye-ree-ka'ta) *Jp.* Judo methods of entry into throwing or groundwork.

HAISHU (heye'shoo) *Jp.* "backhand" The back of the stiffened hand, used mostly in delivering a strike.

HAISHU-UCHI (heye'shoo oo'chee) *Jp.* "backhand strike" A karate strike delivered with the back of the open hand, usually while in a horse stance.

HAISHU-UKE (heye'shoo oo'keh) *Jp.* "backhand block" In karate, the back of the open hand used with a snapping motion of the forearm to block an opponent's punch.

HAISOKU (heye-soh'koo) *Jp.* "instep" Part of the foot used as the striking point for several karate kicks.

HAITO (heye'toh) *Jp.* "ridge hand" In kendo, the command to hold the shinai at a level just below the waist, which corresponds to the position where a sword would be worn in its scabbard.

HAITO-UCHI (heye'toh oo'chee) *Jp.* "ridge-hand strike" An open hand karate strike using the inside edge of the palm. It is usually aimed at the neck, temple, or ribs.

HAIWAN (heye'wan) *Jp.* "back arm."

HAIWAN NAGASHI UKE (heye'wan na-goh'shee oo'keh) *Jp.* "back-arm sweeping block" A karate blocking technique using the rear arm to nullify a punch to the head.

HAJIME (ha'juh-may) *Jp.* "begin" Referee's command used to start a Japanese martial arts match.

HAKAMA (ha'kuh-muh) *Jp.* "divided skirt" The skirtlike trousers or culottes primarily worn in kendo, aikido, iaido, and sometimes in the upper ranks of judo and in some styles of jujutsu. The traditional garb of the samurai class.

HAKKO-RYU (hak'koh ryoo) *Jp.* A form of jujutsu in which atemi (striking) techniques are emphasized.

Hakama

HAKTARI-SEOGI (hak-ta'ree soh-gee) *Kr.* A cranelike stance used in tae kwon do in which the edge of the working leg is placed on the knee joint of the supporting leg.

HAKUTSURU (haw-coo-tsu-roo) *Jp.* The white crane or stork techniques of Okinawan karate.

HALBERD A shafted weapon with an axelike cutting blade, sometimes used to describe the Chinese quando.

HALF-MOON STANCE: See HANGETSU-DACHI.

HALF SIDE CHOKE A judo choking technique executed from the side. It is classified under shime-waza, the grappling techniques employed to choke the neck or body.

HAM-BO (ham'boh) *Jp.* A wooden staff of regulation size used in bojutsu (art of the staff).

HAMMATO: See KYUDO.

HAMMER FIST The bottom of the clenched fist, used primarily for striking in karate. Known in Japanese as kentsui.

HANA (han'a) *Kr.* "one."

HANARE (ha-na-reh) *Jp.* The final stage of shooting an arrow in kyudo (art of the bow). Hanare occurs when the arrow is actually released.

HAN-BAL SOGI (han'bal soh'gee) *Kr.* "one-leg stance." See also CRANE STANCE.

HAND CONDITIONING The act of striking, rubbing, or grinding the hands against an abrasive surface to toughen the skin and bone by building callouses and/or producing calcium deposits. It is chiefly practiced by karate and kung-fu practitioners. While the result is supposed to lead to stronger techniques and protection of the hands from injury, serious or even permanent damage could be a byproduct of this training.

HANDO-NO-KUZUSHI (han-doh noh kuh-zoo-shee) *Jp.* In judo, the breaking of an opponent's balance by making use of the motion in reaction to a feint.

HANDSWORD Another name for the knife hand.

HANE-GOSHI (ha-neh gohsh) *Jp.* "springing hip throw" A judo hip throw in which the opponent is thrown over the hip with the aid of the thrower's bent leg, which helps to lift the opponent off the ground.

HANE-MAKI-GOSHI (ha-neh ma-kee gohsh) *Jp.* "winding springing hip throw" A judo sacrifice technique.

HANEMAKIKOMI (ha-neh-ma-kee-koh-mee) *Jp.* "outer winding springing hip throw" A judo hip technique.

HANGETSU (han-geht'soo) *Jp.* "half moon" A kata formulated in the shorei-ryu karate school of Okinawa. Many of the movements of this kata are carried out in the form of an arc, which symbolizes a half moon. See also SEISAN.

HANGETSU-DACHI (han-geht'soo da'chee) *Jp.* "half-moon stance" A defensive karate stance in which the feet are placed as in the front stance, but not quite so far apart, and the knees are forced inward.

HANGING CHOKELOCK A judo technique in which the user is kneeling between an opponent's legs, whose lapel is clutched with both hands, and the lower part of one of the opponent's legs is used to apply pressure to the neck.

HANMI (han'mee) *Jp.* "half-body" A posture relative to an opponent in which one foot is placed forward in relation to the opponent.

HAN MU KWAN (han moo kwan) *Kr.* "miliary arts school" A style of Korean karate.

HANSHI (han'shee) *Jp.* "master" A respected master, of Japanese martial disciplines, who is of eighth- to tenth-degree black belt rank, although not all masters receive this title. The term finds its origin in fencing, where it is used as "fencing master."

HANSOKU-GACHI (han-soh'koo ga'chee) *Jp.* "winner by violation" The decision awarded in a match when an opponent has violated the rules.

Hane-Goshi

HANSOKUMAKE (han'soh'koo-ma'keh) *Jp.* "loser by violation" A verdict against the loser when there has been a violation of the rules of a match.

HAN SONGARAK CHIRUGI (han sohn-ga'rak chee'roo-gee) *Kr.* "one-finger strike" A tae kwon do technique used to attack the eyes or throat.

HAN SONDUNGBYO CHIRUGI *Kr.* "one-knuckle strike" A tae kwon do technique used to attack the face and temple.

HANSOO (han'soo) *Kr.* "water" A tae kwon do hyung (form).

HANTEI (han-tay) *Jp.* "judgment" or "decision" A command by the referee to the judges to choose the winner of a match when neither contestant has scored or if the score is tied.

HAN UCHI KEN: See FORE-KNUCKLE.

HAO CH'UAN *Ch.* Another name for white crane kung-fu.

HAPKIDO (hap-kee'doh) *Kr.* "way of coordinated power" A Korean martial art characterized by kicking without retraction and composed of three primary skills: nonresistance when meeting force, circular motion in countering and attacking, and the water principle—total penetration of an enemy's defenses.

Hapkido emphasizes a nonviolent code of counterdefense. If the force of an attacker's blow is strong, it must be met with soft reception and countermoves. If the force is soft, it must be countered with a powerful defense. This approach leads to the fluid circular motion and constant mobility which sets hapkido apart from any other art and makes it extremely difficult to master.

HAPPO-NO-KUZUSHI (hap-poh noh koo-zoo-shee) *Jp.* The eight directions of unbalance in judo. See also KUZUSHI.

HARA (hah-rah) *Jp.* "abdomen" Gravity and mass in the human body, traditionally considered in Eastern thought to be the seat of the soul and center of ki. Means the same as tanden.

HARA-GATAME (ha-rah gah-tah-meh) *Jp.* A type of arm-bar locking the opponent's arm against the stomach.

HARA-GATAME-UDE-KUJIKI (ha-ra ga-ta-meh oo-deh koo-jee-kee)

Jp. A judo dislocation technique in which the stomach is used to apply pressure to an opponent's elbow.

HARAGEI (ha-ra-gay) *Jp.* "stomach arts" The art of concentrating ki in the abdomen; disciplines focusing on developing the tanden.

HARAI (ha-reye') *Jp.* "sweep" or "sweeping."

HARAI-GOSHI (ha-reye gohsh') *Jp.* "sweeping hip throw" The fifth judo technique of nage-no-kata. It is performed by using the back as a lever against the opponent's forward hip, then sweeping up the forward thigh with one leg and throwing the opponent.

HARAIMAKIKOMI (ha-reye'ma-kee-koh'mee) *Jp.* "sweeping winding throw" A judo sacrifice throw.

HARAI-TSURI-KOMI-ASHI (ha-reye tsu-ree ko-mee ash) *Jp.* "sweeping drawing ankle throw" A judo foot technique used to sweep an opponent's ankle.

HARA-KIRI (ha-ra kee'ree) *Jp.* "belly cutting" Ritual Japanese suicide with a sword, practiced by the samurai warrior. This phrase is the informal word for seppuku.

HARDAN (har'dan) *Kr.* "low" or "low level."

HARDAN KYOCHA MARKI (har'dan kyoh'cha mar-kee) *Kr.* "downard X block."

HARDAN MARKI (har'dan mar'kee) *Kr.* "downward block."

HARD STYLE 1. In Chinese boxing, representative of an external system. 2. A contemporary term denoting a system that primarily employs hard, powerful techniques executed in linear patterns, such as in Japanese karate or Korean tae kwon do.

HARNESSING THE FORCE (EP) To capitalize and bring into condition the production of maximum power. In short, teaching a student how to obtain 100 percent power related to one's body structure.

HASAMI-ZUKI (ha-sa-mee soo-kee) *Jp.* "scissors punch" A karate double-fist technique in which the front and back of the opponent is attacked simultaneously.

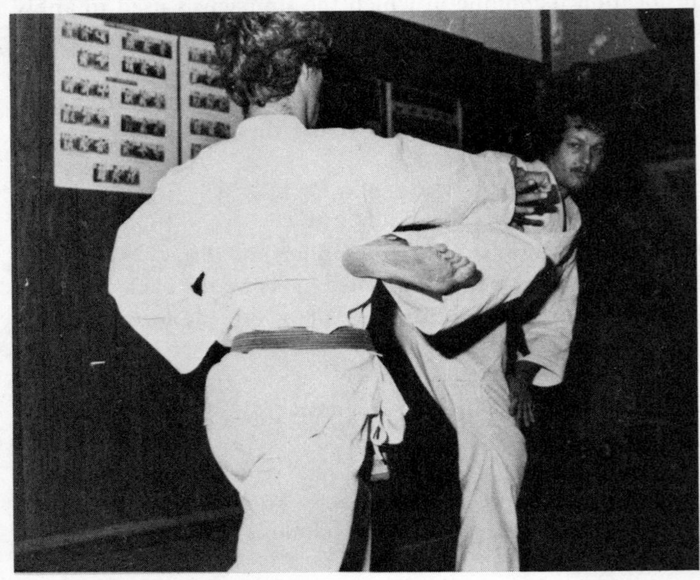

Heel Kick

HASAMU (ha'sa-moo) *Jp.* "to hold between" To hold an opponent between the legs in judo groundwork.

HASHI (ha'she) *Jp.* "border" or "edge" The boundary line of a contest area.

HASSHAKU-BO (has-sha-koo boh) *Jp.* "eight-foot staff" The wooden spear used in bojutsu (art of the staff).

HATA (ha-ta) *Jp.* "flag" The flag used by referees or lines persons to indicate scores, decisions, or jogai.

HAURI (ha'ree) *Kr.* "hip."

HAYAGAKE-JUTSU (ha-ya-ga-keh juts-uh) *Jp.* "speed technique" A technique to improve speed in running and walking.

HED OT DEW: See TIEH DA JYOU.

HEEL KICK Any kicking technique delivered in a hooking motion with the heel as the striking point.

HEEL OF THE FOOT Part of the foot commonly used as a striking point for martial arts kicking. Known in Japanese as the kakato.

HEEL OF THE HAND Another name for the palm heel.

HEIAN (hay'an) *Jp.* "peace" or "tranquility" A set of five kata formulated in the shorin-ryu karate school of Okinawa by Yasutsune Itosu in 1903–06. The heian kata are called pinan (peaceful mind) in Okinawa, while Japan uses the original name.

HEIKO-DACHI (hay'koh da'chee) *Jp.* "parallel open stance" A basic karate stance with the feet spread shoulder width and the toes pointing forward.

HEIKO-ZUKI: See PARALLEL PUNCH.

HEISOKU-DACHI: See INFORMAL ATTENTION STANCE.

HENKA (hehn'ka) *Jp.* Variations or mutations in judo techniques.

HERBOLOGY The Chinese science of plant pharmaceutics.

HIDARI (hee-da'ree) *Jp.* "left" or "left side."

HIDARI-ASHI-GURUMA (hee-da'ree aw-shee goo-room'aw) *Jp.* "left-hand leg wheel" A judo throw. The left-sided version of ashi-guruma.

HIDARI-ATO-SUMI: See KUZUSHI.

HIDARI-JIGO-TAI (hee-da'ree jee'goh teye) *Jp.* "left defensive posture" A judo position in which the hips are lowered by bending the knees, the feet are spread about thirty inches apart, and the left foot is placed approximately twenty-four inches forward.

HIDARI KOTE (hee-dar'ee koh-teh) *Jp.* "left forearm" In kendo, a cut aimed at the left wrist or lower forearm. This cut cannot be scored in a match unless the left hand is above the shoulder as in the jodan-no-kamae.

HIDARI-MAE-ERI (hee-dar'ee ma-eh eh-ree) *Jp.* "left front collar" Term used to describe part of the judo uniform.

HIDARI KUZUSHI: See KUZUSHI.

HIDARI-MAE-SUMI: See KUZUSHI.

HIDARI-MEN (hee-da'ree-men') *Jp.* In kendo, an oblique cut to the left side of the opponent's head. It is only scored within 45 degrees of the center, an area roughly defined by the center strip of the men-gane (mask) and the left men himo (cord).

HIDARI-SHIZENTAI (hee-dar'ee-shee'zen-teye) *Jp.* "left natural position" A judo position in which the body is relaxed and the left foot is placed approximately twelve inches forward.

HIDARI-SOTO-NAKA-SODE (hee-dar'ee soh-toh na-ka soh-deh) *Jp.* Left outer middle sleeve of the judo-gi.

HIDARI-SOTO-UE-SODE (hee-dar'ee soh-toh oo-eh soh-deh) *Jp.* Left outer upper sleeve of the judo-gi.

HIDARI-UCHI-UE-SODE (hee-dar'ee oo'chee ooh-eh sod-deh) *Jp.* Left inner upper sleeve of the judo-gi.

HIDARI-UE-SODE (hee-dar'ee ooh-eh soh-deh) *Jp.* Left upper sleeve of the judo-gi.

HIDARI-USHIRO-SUMI-KUZUSHI: See KUZUSHI.

HIDARI-YOKO-ERI (hee-dar'ee yoh'koh eh'ree) *Jp.* The left side collar of the judo-gi.

HIDDEN MOVES (EP) Transitory moves that have meaning and purpose, yet remain obscure to the eyes of the observer or practitioner. Until they are actually used, they remain hidden and obscure.

HIGH FORM A specialized aspect of a kung-fu system in which the techniques strongly depend on timing and positioning rather than on speed and power.

HIGH-LINE GUARD Any guard position where the lead hand is raised to shoulder level.

HIGH STANCE A position facilitating mobility in which the center of gravity remains high off the ground by less bending of the knees and the assuming of a narrow stance.

HIJI (hee'gee) *Jp.* "elbow" The same meaning as "empi," which is of native Okinawan derivation.

HIJI-ATE: See EMPI-UCHI.

HIJI-MAKIKOMI (hee'jee ma-kee-koh'mee) *Jp.* "winding elbow lock" An immobilization technique used in judo.

HIJI-OTOSHI (hee'jee oh-toh'shee) *Jp.* "elbow drop" A judo technique using hand and arm movements to throw the opponent.

HIJI-TSURI-UKE: See ELBOW SLIDING BLOCK.

HIJI-WAZA (hee'jee wa'za) *Jp.* "elbow techniques" A series of judo immobilizing locks against the elbow classified under kansetsu-waza (grappling techniques).

High Stance

HIKI-KOMI-GAESHI (hee'kee koh'mee ga-eh-shee) *Jp.* "pulling-in throw" A judo sacrifice technique classified under ma-sutemi-waza, throws executed with the back touching the ground.

HIKI-OTOSHI (hee'kee oh-toh'shee) *Jp.* "drawing drop" The sixth judo technique of koshiki-no-kata (kata of the forms antique).

HIKI-TAOSHI (hee'kee ta-oh'shee) *Jp.* "pull down" A judo technique of hiji-waza (elbow techniques).

HIKITATE GEIKO (hee-kee-ta-teh gay-koh) *Jp.* In kendo, training practice in which a senior-level kendoka works with a lower-level student while free fighting.

HIKIWAKE (hee-kee-wa-keh) *Jp.* "draw" or "tie" Referee's term denoting a draw in a match.

HIMM *Kr.* "force" or "power."

HIP ROTATION A torquing motion common to almost all martial arts, which is used in conjunction with the execution of certain techniques to generate power. It is especially valuable when delivering a punching technique from the rear side.

HIPS Part of the anatomy believed to be the center of power for all karate techniques. The hips are used to drive the force of all hand techniques, as well as many foot techniques.

HIP THROW A throwing technique delivered from a standing position using primarily the hips. The techniques classified under the general term of koshi-waza (hip techniques).

HIRAKEN (hee-ra-kehn') *Jp.* "flat fist" or "level fist." See also FOREKNUCKLE.

HIRAKEN-ZUKI (hee-ra-kehn' zoo'kee) *Jp.* "foreknuckle fist punch."

HIRATE (hee-ra'tay) *Jp.* "foreknuckle."

HISHIGI-HIZA-GATAME (hee-she-gee hee-za ga-ta-meh) *Jp.* "arm-knee lock" A judo armlock in which the knee is used to apply pressure to the elbow joint.

HITOSASHIYUBI IPPONKEN (hee-toh-sa-she-yoo-be eep-pohn-kehn) *Jp.* "forefinger one-knuckle fist" See also ONE-KNUCKLE FIST.

HIZA (hee'za) *Jp.* "knee" or "lap."

HIZA-GATAME (hee'zah gat-ah-may') *Jp.* "armlock with knee" The fourteenth judo technique of katame-no-kata. Known also as the ude-hishigi-hiza-gatame.

HIZA-GATAME-UDE-KUJIKI (hee-zah-gah-tah-mee oo-deh koo-jee-kee) *Jp.* "knee-set arm breaking" A judo technique of kansetsu-waza in which the knee is used to apply pressure to the elbow joint to cause pain or dislocation.

HIZAGURUMA (hee-zah-goo-room'ah) *Jp.* "knee wheeling" A judo leg technique in which the opponent is thrown in a circular wheel-like motion.

HIZA-JIME (hee'za jee-may') *Jp.* "chokelock with knee" A judo choke.

HIZA-SEOI (hee'zah seh-oh) *Jp.* A judo technique and variation of seoi-nage.

HIZA-WAZA (hee'za-wa'za) *Jp.* "knee techniques" Judo kneelocking techniques in which the objective is to wrench the knee joint by bending or twisting. These techniques are prohibited in sport judo.

HO-GOO (hoh'goo) *Kr.* "safeguard" Protective equipment worn by tae kwon do competitors to minimize injury while sparring.

HOHUP (hoh'hoop) *Kr.* "breathing."

HOHUP CHOJUL (hoh'hoop choh'jool) *Kr.* "breath control" See also BREATHING.

HOJO-JUTSU (hoh'joh jut-soo) *Jp.* "art of tying" Techniques used to tie and immobilize a victim by means of a cord. It was practiced extensively by the Japanese samurai and is today part of the training given to Japanese policemen.

HOJUTSU (hoh-jut'soo) *Jp.* "art of firearms" or "gunnery."

HO JYA: See HOP GAR.

HOKKA NO JUTSU (hohk-ka noh juts) *Jp.* The practice of setting fires to spread confusion in time of battle. Used frequently by the ninja.

HOLD-DOWN A series of judo immobilization techniques carried out on the ground with the objective of controlling an opponent's limbs or body for thirty seconds to score one point. Known as osae-waza or osaekomi-waza in Japanese.

HOMBU (ham'boo) *Jp.* "Headquarters" 1. This term can be used to define any headquarters for a martial arts school. The Kodokan, for example, is the hombu for judo. 2. A seventy-five-mat dojo located in the Shinjuku section of Tokyo, which serves as the official aikido headquarters.

HON-GESA-GATAME (han geh-sa ga-ta-meh) *Jp.* "regular scarf hold" A hold-down technique employed in judo. Often referred to as the kesa.

HONORARY DEGREE Designates rank given to someone who has not otherwise earned it through normal channels. Often, advanced ranks of seventh- to tenth-degree black belt are honorary degrees awarded for years of devotion and study.

HOOKING BLOCK The act of neutralizing an opponent's center-level attack by hooking the wrist over the opponent's wrist at the point of contact.

HOOKING KICK: See GOLCHO CHAGI.

HOOKING KNIFE HAND BLOCK A karate blocking technique using the edge of the hand. Known in Japanese as the kake-shuto-uke.

HOOK PUNCH A punch executed from the hip toward the inside of the body, primarily used to strike an opponent's center level from close quarters. A technique commonly used in the naihanshi kata.

HOOK SWORD A traditional Chinese weapon the size of a conventional sword with a sharp double-edged blade and a hook protruding off to one side at the pointed end.

HOP GAR A style of Chinese kung-fu, also known as Lama, which is composed of twelve short-hand and twelve long-hand maneuvers, with eight forms employing both empty-hand and weapon techniques. The most important aspect of this system is its footwork, called kay-men-bo, which was developed for use atop the mui-fa-jeong, a series of stumps driven into the ground.

No less significance can be attributed to its philosophy, which expounds the importance of understanding one's own inner limits, fears, and capabilities. Technique and form, according to Hop-Gar philosophy, are a means to an end, but not the end itself.

Hop Gar came into prominence during the Ching dynasty as the official martial system used by the Manchu emperor and his royal guard. It was, and still is, a style designed for fighting, as opposed to those styles designed for health or dancing. Known as ho jya in Mandarin.

HORANG YI APBAL: See TIGER CLAW.

HORANG YI YIP: See TIGER MOUTH.

HORIZONTAL PUNCH A fist strike delivered straightforward from the hip with a torquing motion. The movement terminates with the fist in a horizontal position.

HORIZONTAL ZONES (EP) Another of the categorical zones of protection. It basically entails the protection of three horizontal or height levels: the solar plexus to the top of the head; the groin to the solar plexus; and the feet to the groin.

HORSE STANCE A position in which the legs are spread approximately twice the width of the shoulders, the body weight is evenly distributed, and the toes are pointed straight forward. The horse stance is a position common to many martial arts.

In karate, it is also referred to as the straddle-leg stance. Known in Japanese as the kiba-dachi.

HOSIN SUL (hoh'sin sul) *Kr.* "self-defense techniques."

HOUR-GLASS STANCE A position in which the knees and feet are tensed inward, the feet are spread approximately shoulder width, and the body weight is evenly distributed. This stance is chiefly employed while performing the sanchin kata of karate. Known in Japanese as the sanchin-dachi.

HSING-I *Ch.* "form of mind" An internal system of kung-fu emphasizing linear movement.

HUA CH'UAN *Ch.* "flowery hand system" A northern Chinese style of kung-fu.

HUA-TO: See FIVE ANIMALS.

HUG (EP) Keeping close to or up against a key area on an opponent's body, thus minimizing the possibilities for leverage and action.

HU KOU *Ch.* "tiger mouth."

HULLYO MARKI (hul'yoh mark'ee) *Kr.* "sweeping block" A tae kwon do block that uses the hands to disturb an opponent's balance.

HUNG-GAR *Ch.* A major style of southern Chinese kung-fu characterized by very hard, strong techniques and stable horse stances.

HUNG-KUEN: See CHOW-GAR.

HUNG SING *Ch.* The founder of the Choy Li Fut style of kung-fu. 2. A particular variation or style of Choy Li Fut kung-fu.

HWA-RANG (wa-rang') *Kr.* 1. A band of Korean warriors who, much like the Japanese samurai, adhered to strict philosophical and moral codes. 2. A Korean hyung named after the hwa-rang warriors which originated in the Silla dynasty about A. D. 625.

HWARANG-DO (wa-wrang'doh) *Kr.* "way of the flower of manhood" A native Korean philosophical code similar to Japanese bushido and possessing a structured series of physical techniques that were advocated by warriors known as the hwa-rang. Modern hwarang-do includes both hard and soft techniques and combines circular and linear movements. Besides fundamental maneuvers, hwarang-do includes some spectacular spinning and jumping kicks, as well as throws, locks, chokes, and matwork. The weaponry phase of training includes stick, spear, sword, and knives.

HYUNG (hyung) *Kr.* "pattern," "form," or "mold" A series of prearranged offensive and defensive tae kwon do movements executed against imaginary attacking opponents. It is similar to Japanese karate katas. Known also as poomse (form).

I (ee) *Ch.* "will," "mind," or "intent."

IAI (ee'eye) *Jp.* "swordplay" 1. A sword exercise or kata employing a series of thrusting and cutting techniques while drawing and returning the blade. 2. A form of sparring used in classical karate in which both the attacker and defender begin by sitting and facing one another.

IAIDO (ee-eye'doe) *Jp.* "way of the sword" The modern art of drawing the samurai sword from its scabbard. It is based on an earlier practice called iai-jutsu (sword-drawing art).

IAI-JUTSU (ee-eye-jut'sue) *Kr.* "sword-drawing art" The classical method of Japanese swordsmanship based on the perfection of the initial movement of the sword and the striking of the enemy instantly. This art was synonymous with the samurai warrior.

IBUKI (ee-boo'kee) *Jp.* "breath control" Isotonic breathing exercises based on dynamic tension principles practiced in conjunction with, and also separate to, the execution of karate techniques.

ICHI (ee-chi) *Jp.* 1. "one" 2. "position" or "posture."

I-CHIN-CHING *Ch.* "Muscle Change Classic" A work on the martial arts purportedly written by Bodhidharma.

I-CHING *Ch.* "Book of Changes" An ancient Chinese book of divination that served as the philosophical basis of the internal boxing systems of China.

I-CHIN SUTRA *Ch.* A book attributed to Bodhidharma which set down the tenets of Chan Buddhism.

I CH'UAN *Ch.* "will fist" One of several names for hsing-i.

IDORI (ee-doh-rhee) *Jr.* "seated defense" In judo, the first series of techniques in the kime-no-kata, the kata of self-defense or combat.

IJUNG CHAGI (ee'jung cha'gee) *Kr.* "double kick."

IKI-KOMI (ee-kee-koh'mee) *Jp.* In judo, the act of pulling an opponent into groundwork before a throw has been attempted.

IKKYU (ee'kyoo) *Jp.* "first grade" First-level brown belt in Japanese and Okinawan martial arts. The grade just prior to shodan or first-degree black belt.

ILBO DAERYON: See ONE-STEP SPARRING.

ILGOPE (eel'gohp) *Kr.* "seven."

ILGUP (eel'gup) *Kr.* "first class" First level red belt in tae kwon do, the grade just prior to first-degree black belt.

ILL (eel) *Kr.* "first."

IMMOBILIZATION TECHNIQUES: See HOLD-DOWN.

INAGASHI: See KYUDO.

INATOBI: See SUIEI-JUTSU.

INFORMAL ATTENTION STANCE A natural position used in karate in which the body is held erect but relaxed and the feet are placed together. Known in Japanese as heisoku-dachi.

IN-IBUKI (in ee-boo-kee) *Jp.* "passive" or "internal breathing" A soft but firm type of breathing that stems from deep in the abdomen. It is common to many different martial arts, particularly goju-ryu karate.

INITIATIVE The ability to make the first threatening attack on an opponent's centerline in any given exchange. Finding ways to obtain the initiative is the key to successful timing, and therefore strategy, in positional theory.

INJI CHOOMUK (in'jee choo'muk) *Kr.* "foreknuckle fist."

INNER KNIFE HAND: See RIDGE HAND.

INNER POWER: See CHI; KI.

INNER WINDING THROW A judo sacrifice technique in which one winds the opponent's body around one's own to take the opponent to the ground.

INSERT (EP) The addition of a weapon or move simultaneous with, or sandwiched in between, the base moves.

INSIDE BLOCK Any block executed from inside the boundary of the body to the outside.

INSIDE SNAPPING BLOCK The act of snapping the foot upward and inward to parry a low-level attack.

INSTEP Part of the foot commonly used as a striking point for various martial arts kicking techniques. Known in Japanese as the haisoku and in Korean as the baldung.

INSTRUCTOR: See SENSEI; SABOM; SIFU.

INTERNAL POWER Power generated from internal sources, as in the Chinese internal systems. This term is rather difficult to classify by style since some hard systems also use internal power. In other cases, both internal and external sources are tapped for overall strength. See also CHI; KI.

INTERNAL SYSTEM Any kung-fu system that emphasizes the regulation of breath, the toughening of bones and muscles, the ability to advance and retreat, and the unity of hard and soft. These systems usually advocate a defensive, circular approach to combat. Among the most popular internal systems are t'ai-chi ch'uan, pa-kua, and hsing-i.

INVERTED FIST Another name for the back knuckle, or uraken.

Ippon-Seoi-Nage

INWARD BLOCK Any karate block executed from outside the boundary of the body to the inside.

IPPAN-YO-GOSHIN-NO-KATA (ip-pawn yoo goh-shin noh kah-tah) *Jp.* The judo kata of self-defense for men.

IPPON (ee'pawn) *Jp.* "one point" 1. A term used primarily to denote a full-point scoring technique in a Japanese-style match. 2. "one of them"; used when counting items characterized by length such as shinai. 3. In judo, a referee's term used when a clean throw has been executed, when a player has submitted. The term thus represents the winning of the match in these situations.

IPPON-KEN: See ONE-KNUCKLE FIST.

IPPON KUMITE: See ONE-STEP SPARRING.

IPPON NUKITE: See ONE-FINGER SPEAR HAND.

IPPON-SEOI-NAGE (eep'pan-say-oh-na'geh) *Jp.* "one-arm shoulder throw" A judo technique in which the opponent is thrown over one shoulder. A frequently used tournament technique. See also SEOI-NAGE.

IPPON-SHOBU (eep'pan-shoh'p') *Jp.* "one-point throw" A term indicating a one-point match.

IRO-OBI *Jp.* In karate a colored belt; usually an experienced student.

IRON PALM A method reputedly enabling one to produce a psycho-physical heat internally, which, with control, can be made to project into the palms of the hands or to any area of the body. The training necessary to manifest this method is so rigorous that there is doubt as to whether or not practitioners have been able to achieve the real iron palm. Today, any practitioner who achieves "a hand like iron," as the saying goes, is credited with possessing an iron palm. This technique belongs almost exclusively to the domain of kung-fu.

ISOMETRICS A set of body-building exercises performed by pushing or pulling against an immovable opposing force. These exercises are chiefly practiced by judoka for improving pushing/pulling power.

ISSHI KEN (eesh'shee kehn') *Jp.* "extended index finger." See also ONE-KNUCKLE FIST.

ISSHIN-RYU (eesh'sheen ryoo) *Jp.* "one-heart method" A hybrid form of unarmed combat based on several Okinawan karate systems and founded by Tatsuo Shimabuku in 1954.

ITAMI-WAKE (ee-ta-mee wah-keh) *Jp.* "break by injury" A term used to denote the loss of a contest owing to injury.

ITSUTSU-NO-KATA (eet-sut'soo no ka'ta) *Jp.* "kata of five principles" or "forms of five" Though not actually named by judo founder Jigoro Kano, these five principles are generally considered to be energy/action, reaction/nonresistance, circle/whirlwind, pendulum/motion, and void/inertia.

IWA-NAMI (ee'wa na'mee) *Jp.* "waves on the rock" In judo, the twenty-first technique of koshiki-no-kata, the forms antique.

J

JAJUN BAL (ja-jun bal) *Kr.* "foot shifting" A tae kwon do method of dodging one step away in any direction.

JAJUNBAL OMGYO DIDIGI (ja-jun-bal ohm-gyoh dee-dee'gee) *Kr.* "shift stepping" A tae kwon do method of stepping, which follows a shifting motion.

JAMMING A term denoting any forward motion used to neutralize a

Jamming

kick or punch by pressing into a close or tight position relative to the opponent.

JAPKO-CHAGI: See BUTJAPGO CHAGI.

JAYOO DAERYON: See FREE-SPARRING.

JEE DO DWAN: See CHI DO KWAN.

JEET KUNE DO (jeet koon doh') *Ch.* "way of the intercepting fist" A collection of basic mental and physical concepts, observations of combat maneuvers, and philosophies of attitude gathered and developed by the late Bruce Lee.

JEJA (jay'ja) *Kr.* "student."

JIBON-NO-TSUKURI (jee-bohn noh tsu-koo-ree) *Jp.* In judo, the preparation of oneself in preliminary action before executing a throw.

JIGEIKO: See FREESTYLE SPARRING.

JIGO-HONTAI (jee'goh han-teye') *Jp.* A judo defensive posture in which the feet are positioned approximately thirty inches apart and the hips are lowered by bending the knees. Known also as jigo-tai.

JIGO-TAI: See JIGO-HONTAI.

JIKAN (jee'kan) *Jp.* "time" A term used by the timekeeper at the beginning and the end of a Japanese-style match.

JIMAN (jee'man) *Jp.* In kyudo (way of the bow), the fifth stage of firing an arrow. Jiman is the holding of the fully drawn bow in preparation for release.

JION (jee'an) *Jp.* A kata formulated in the shorei-ryu school of Okinawan karate. It also is practiced in Japanese Shotokan karate. This form is believed to be named after Jion-ji, a famous Buddhist temple.

JIP JOONG (jip'joong) *Kr.* "concentration."

JIPTJUNG (jipt'joong) *Kr.* "power gathering" The act of breathing while meeting an opponent's attack in order to unify one's internal and external forces. This term is common to tae kwon do.

JIREUGI: See CHIREUGI.

JIRUMYO CHAGI (jee-roo-myoh cha-gee) *Kr.* "punching kick" A tae kwon do technique performed against two opponents while in midair. One opponent is punched while the other is kicked.

JIRUGI (jee-roo'gee) *Kr.* "punch" The encompassing term used in tae kwon do to represent striking with the fist.

JITTE: See JUTTE.

JITAE *Kr.* "earth" A tae kwon do hyung (form).

JIU-JITSU: See JUJUTSU.

JIYU (jee'yoo) *Jp.* "freedom" (of movement, et al).

JIYU-IPPON KUMITE (jee-yoo eep'pan koo'mee-tay) *Jp.* "semifree one-blow sparring."

JIYU KUMITE: See FREE-SPARRING.

JIYU RENSHU (jee-yoo ren-shoo) *Jp.* Free practice in kendo.

JIYU WAZA: See RANDORI.

JO (joh) *Jp.* "staff" or "stave" A four-foot long, two-inch thick wooden staff used in jojutsu (art of the staff).

JOBAJUTSU (joh'ba-jut'soo) *Jp.* "art of riding" A method of military riding skills as practiced by the samurai of feudal Japan.

JODAN (joh'dan) *Jp.* "upward" or "upper level" A compound word affixed to the name of techniques in Japanese karate, such as yoko-geri-jodan, a side kick to the upper level.

JODAN-KAMAE; JODAN-NO-KAMAE (joh'dan-ka-maw'eh; joh'dan noh ka-maw'eh) *Jp.* "high-level posture" A posture in which one holds a weapon, such as a sword or shinai, with one or both hands over the head.

JODAN-UKE: See UPWARD BLOCK.

JODO (joh'doh) *Jp.* "way of the stick" The Japanese method of stick

Various Shots of Judo

fighting using a stick approximately four feet long. It derived from jojutsu and is practiced today chiefly as an art form.

JOGAI (joh'geye) *Jp.* "out of bounds" A term used by a referee to denote that either or both contestants are out of bounds. The action of the match stops until both have returned.

JOGAI NAKAE (joh'geye na-ka-eh) *Jp.* A term used in karate tournaments by the referee to indicate that a contestant has stepped out of the match area and should return.

JOJUTSU (joh-jut'soo) *Jp.* "art of the stick" The Japanese art of stick fighting, which was developed about four hundred years ago. Today the art is known as jodo and has been adopted by the police who refer to it as keibo soho (police stick art).

JOKDO (jok'doh) *Kr.* "edge of the foot."

JOK GI (jok'gee) *Kr.* "foot techniques."

JOKGI DAERYON (jok'gee dar-yon) *Kr.* "foot technique sparring" A prearranged form of tae kwon do sparring in which the feet are used exclusively.

JONIN (joh'nin) *Jp.* A ninja leader.

JOOMUK (joo'muk) *Kr.* "fist."

JOONG BONG (joong bang) *Kr.* A medium-sized staff.

JOSEKI (joh'seh-kee) *Jp.* "upper side" In a traditional Japanese dojo, the area where instructors often times line up and face the students at the beginning and end of each practice session. It is located just left of the kamiza (upper seat) where the honored guests and officials sit.

JOU FA *Ch.* An ancient form of Chinese combat that emphasized close-range grappling techniques.

JOZA (joh'za) *Jp.* "high seat" The upper seat in a judo dojo. This term sometimes replaces the word kamiza (upper seat).

JU (joo) *Jp.* "gentle," "supple," or "soft" 1. The principle of suppleness, adaptation, and nonresistance recognized in aikido and judo. 2. The number ten.

JUDAN (joo'dan) *Jp.* "tenth rank" Tenth-degree black belt in the Japanese and Okinawan martial arts.

JUDO (joo'doh) *Jp.* "gentle way" A Japanese art of self-defense and a sport with Olympic recognition, judo is now practiced in almost every country in the world. Like jujutsu, its forerunner, judo is a method of turning an opponent's strength and overcoming by skill rather than sheer strength. Judo in its present form was founded by Jigoro Kano in 1882 who gave the sport its name.

Judo techniques are divided into three categories: tachi-waza (standing techniques), ne-waza (ground techniques), and atemi-waza (vital point techniques).

Tachi-waza, also called nage-waza (throwing techniques), are subdivided into te-waza (hand throwing techniques), koshi-waza (hip techniques), ashi-waza (foot and leg techniques), and sutemi-waza (sacrifice techniques) in which one throws one's opponent from a supine position.

Ne-waza is a method of fighting an opponent on the ground and is divided into osaekomi-waza (holding techniques), shime-waza (strangling techniques), and kansetsu-waza (locking techniques).

Atemi-waza includes methods of striking the opponent with either hand or foot. It is practiced only for self-defense and is prohibited in competition.

In a judo contest, only one point is needed to defeat an adversary. Points are awarded for a clean throw; for controlling an opponent on the ground for thirty seconds; or for obtaining surrender by applying either a stranglehold or an arm lock. If neither opponent obtains a point in the given time, the referee may award the decision due to the aggressiveness of one fighter over the other.

Grading in judo is based on both proficiency in contest and on one's knowledge of the art. Designations in rank are shown by the different colors of the belt. Beginners start with a white belt and are gradually promoted to yellow, orange, green, blue, and brown belt. Ultimately, the student advances to black belt. The dan ranks range from first-degree black belt, the lowest, to tenth-degree, the highest level of achievement.

Judo is practiced in a dojo (the place of the way), or training hall, which is covered by mats. The participants wear a gi (uniform) consisting of a loose jacket, pants, and a belt.

Training in judo consists of randori (free exercise), kata (formal exercise), and uchikomi (inner winding), or stationary exercise.

Etiquette plays an important role in judo. It is customary for all judoka to bow toward kamiza both when entering and leaving the dojo. A bow is also exchanged between judoka at the beginning and end of each practice session, and formal classes always begin with the students bowing to the sensei (teacher).

JUDOGI (joo-doh-gee) *Jp.* "judo uniform" The uniform worn for judo. It consists of a jacket and trousers and a belt. Traditionally, the uniform is white.

JUDOKA (joo-doh'ka) *Jp.* "judoperson" A practitioner of judo.

JUDOSHUGYOSHA (joo-doh-shoo-gyo-shah) *Jp.* A judo term for any black belt below the rank of fourth-degree.

JUICHIDAN (joo-ee'chee-dan) *Jp.* "eleventh rank" In judo, an eleventh-degree black belt. Only the founder, Jigoro Kano, has ever reached this level.

JUJI-GATAME (joo-jee ga-ta-meh) *Jp.* "cross armlock" A judo armlock in which the legs are placed crosswise over an opponent's body, trapping the opponent's arm between the thighs. When the hips are slightly raised, the elbow joint is bent backward, causing pain. Juji-gatame is the twelfth technique of katame-no-kata. It is also known as the ude-hishigi-juji-gatame.

JUJI-JIME (joo'jee jee-may') *Jp.* "cross lock" or "strangle-cross choke" A group of judo choking techniques in which the arms are crossed while gripping the opponent's collar on both sides.

JUJI-UKE (joo'jee-oo'keh) *Jp.* "cross block." See also X BLOCK.

JUJUTSU (joo-jut'soo) *Jp.* "art of gentleness," "art of suppleness," or "art of pliancy" Literally, the technique or art of suppleness, flexibility, pliancy, gentleness—all varying renditions of the ideogram "ju." All of these terms, however, represent a single principle, a general method of applying a technique, of using the human body as a weapon in unarmed combat.

Jujutsu techniques include methods of striking, kicking, kneeing, throwing, choking, and in particular, joint-locking. Weaponry, as well as holding and tying an adversary, is also part of this popular Japanese system.

According to certain authorities, jujutsu appeared during the 13th century. Among many others, the following are mentioned prominently in martial chronicles as having been notable jujutsu schools: the Tenjin-Shinyo-ryu, the Takenouchi-ryu, the Sosuishitsu-ryu, the Kito-ryu, and the Sekiguchi-ryu. Together with a number of others, these schools formed a modified synthesis in the school of judo founded by Jigoro Kano in the 19th century. Almost all of these methods of combat developed through the skilled adaptation of the principle of ju to their techniques.

More than 725 jujutsu systems developed in Japan. Today, the art has spread worldwide, but it is not as popular as karate. It is probably more popularly known as either jujitsu or jiu-jitsu, two variations of the word whose accuracy is questionable.

JUKEN-DO (joo-kehn doh) *Jp.* "way of the bayonet" A modern armed martial art developed from juken-jutsu (art of the bayonet) which was practiced by Japanese feudal warriors. Juken-do is followed by exponents who wear protective armor since the attacks are made with wooden rifles and simulated bayonets. In contest, one of three targets must be struck: the heart, the lower left side, or the throat.

JUKEN-JUTSU (joo-kehn jut'oo) *Jp.* "art of the bayonet" A technique of using the bayonet that was practiced when modern rifles were adopted. The art came to be practiced as juken-do (way of the bayonet) and is still practiced today in Japan as a competitive sport.

JUMPING SPINNING BACK KICK A back kick in which the

Jumping Spinning Back Kick

delivery is characterized by an initial leap and the turning of the body 180 degrees.

JUMPING SPINNING CRESCENT KICK A crescent kick in which the delivery is characterized by an initial leap and the turning of the body 180 degrees. Synonymous with tae kwon do, it is often classified under the so-called "flying" kicks.

JUNBI SOGI (joon'bee soh'gee) *Kr.* "ready stance."

JUNIDAN (joo-nee'dan) *Jp.* "twelfth rank" Twelfth-degree black belt, the highest rank attainable in judo. To date, only Professor Jigoro Kano, judo's founder, has held this rank.

JU-NIN-GAKE (joo-neen ga-keh) *Jp.* A contest that pits one judoka against ten opponents who are to be defeated successively in a given time.

JU-NO-KATA (joo'no ka-ta) *Jp.* "forms of gentleness or suppleness" The sixth kata of judo, which is composed of fifteen techniques divided into three phases:

First Series
1. tsuki-dashi (hand thrusting)
2. kata-oshi (shoulder push)
3. ryote-dore (two-hand seizure)
4. kata-mawashi (shoulder turning)
5. ago-oshi (jaw twisting)

Second Series
6. kiri-oroshi (direct hand cut with weapon)
7. ryo-kata-oshi (pressing on both shoulders)
8. nanami-uchi (diagonal strike)
9. katate-dori (single hand hold)
10. katate-age (raising the hand for striking)

Third Series
11. obi-tori (belt seizure)
12. mune-oshi (chest punch)
13. tsuki-age (uppercut)
14. uchi-oroshi (direct head strike)
15. ryogan-tsuki (both eyes poke)

The ju-no-kata techniques are composed of gentle movements designed to teach body control when attacking or defending, and also how to employ one's strength most effectively. In the days when women were barred from shiai, ju-no-kata was considered their especial province. It is also favored by elders of advanced rank.

JU-NO-MICHI (joo'no mee'chee) *Jp.* "the gentle way" Proper and effective judo, from the most skillful application of the exponent's mental and physical qualities.

JU-NO-RI (joo'no ree) *Jp.* "principle of gentleness" In judo, the art of dealing with an opponent's power and turning it to effect a victory.

JUN-TEDORI (joon tay-doh'ree) *Jp.* "normal twist" A judo technique of kote-waza, the wrist-locking techniques.

JUSHIN (joo'sheen) *Jp.* "center of gravity."

JUTSU (ju'tsoo) *Jp.* "art" A term linking a fighting method with the bugei, or martial disciplines of war, rather than with the sporting or aesthetic practices of modern Japan. The philosophic and aesthetic sects are generally connected to the do (way) methods developed after the mid-18th century. See also BUGEI.

JUTTE (ju'tay) *Jp.* "ten hands" 1. A kata formulated in the shorei-ryu karate school of Okinawa. 2. A forked iron truncheon that can parry an attack by a sword. It was used by Japanese warriors and commoners and later by Japanese police who used it to overcome assailants or make arrests. It derives its name from the fact that its original form resembled the Chinese character for the number ten and was a hand weapon.

JUTTE-JUTSU (ju'tay jut'soo) *Jp.* "art of the iron truncheon" A method of combat using the jutte, a short metal truncheon also known as the jitte.

JYAN: See CHIEN.

KABUTO (ka-boo-toh) *Jp.* The helmet worn by the Japanese samurai. It was made of iron or lacquered leather, and was secured to the head by a series of silk cords.

KACHI (ka'chee) *Jp.* (a) "win" or "victory."

KACHINUKI-SHIAI (ka-chee-noo-kee shee-eye) *Jp.* A type of contest in which one contestant takes on each opponent in succession without rest between matches until he or she is defeated. Each win counts as one, and a draw counts as one-half but eliminates both contestants. Also known as kachinuki taikai.

KAE-BAEK *Kr.* A tae kwon do hyung named after Kae-Baek, a famed general of the Paekchae dynasty (A.D. 660).

KAESHI (ke-eh'shee) *Jp.* "counter" The countering of an opponent's offensive action in judo.

KAESHI-KATA (ka-eh-shee ka-ta) *Jp.* In the grappling phase of judo, methods of countering an opponent's attempt to hold one down.

KAGAMIBIRAKI (ka-ga-mee-bee-rah-kee) *Jp.* "mirror opening" or "rice-cutting ceremony" An annual celebration among all martial artists in Japan, held in mid-January. It is an old military custom in which students bring mochi (rice cake) from New Year's Day through the first week in January and, on a given day, everyone gathers in the main dojo to eat rice and bean soup in the tradition of the samurai.

KAGI-YARI (ka'gee ya'ree) *Jp.* "key spear" A hooked spear used for parrying and hooking an opponent's weapon. Like the jutte, it was useful to the police in making arrests.

KAGI-ZUKI: See HOOK PUNCH.

KAHO (ka'hoh) *Jp.* A method of practice in bujutsu (military arts) and budo (military ways) in which kata is emphasized.

KAIKEN (kai'ken) *Jp.* "short knife" A six-inch knife used by women of the samurai class. Women of the buke or warrior class always carried this weapon as men carried the sword. It was used for jigai (suicide).

KAISHO (keye'show) *Jp.* "open hand" An encompassing term for the open-hand techniques of karate.

KAJUKENBO (ka-joo-kehn'boh) A hybrid method of combat founded in Hawaii in 1947 by five experts: Walter Choo (karate), Joseph Holke (judo), Frank Ordonez (jujutsu), Adriano Emperado (kenpo), and Clarence Chang (Chinese boxing). The name "kajukenbo" was derived from the five martial disciplines of its founders: *ka* from karate, *ju* from judo and jujutsu, *ken* from kenpo and *bo* from Chinese boxing.

KAKARI GEIKO (ka-ka'ree gay'koh) *Jp.* 1. A type of judo practice in which the student and instructor work together and the former attempts to throw the latter under any circumstances. 1. A basic training method of kendo in which practitioners execute continuous attacks in short bursts of fifteen to thirty seconds. This builds both physical endurance and speed of technique. Although all kenshi practice kakari geiko, beginners do not have the skill in timing and movement needed to act as receivers for this practice.

KAKATO (ka-ka-toh) *Jp.* "heel of the foot."

KAKATO-GAESHI (ka-ka-toh geye-shee) *Jp.* "heel overturning" A judo technique in which the heel of the opponent is swept away with the hand.

KAKATO-GERI (ka-ka'toh gay'ree) *Jp.* "heel kick" A karate stomping kick.

Kakiwake-Uke

KAKE (ka'kay) *Jp.* The completion of a judo throw.

KAKE-SHUTO-UKE: See HOOKING KNIFE-HAND BLOCK.

KAKE-UKE (ka'kay oo'kay) *Jp.* "hooking block" A karate blocking technique using the wrist to hook and block an opponent's punch.

KAKIWAKE-UKE (ka'kee-wa'kay oo'kay) *Jp.* "wedge block" A two-handed karate block using the outer surface of the wrist to neutralize a two-handed attack, such as a grab.

KAKUP (kay'cup) *Kr.* "rank."

KAKUTO (ka-koo'toh) *Jp.* "bent wrist" Part of the wrist that forms the bend and is used as a karate striking point to attack an opponent's arm or armpit.

KAKUTO-UKE (ka-koo'toh oo'kay) *Jp.* "bent-wrist block" A karate block in which the bent wrist is used to deflect an opponent's attacking arm.

KALARI PAYAT (kal-a-ree pa-jat) *Ind.* An ancient form of Indian combat embracing hand-to-hand techniques and weapons such as the staff and daggers.

KALI (ka'lee) *Phil.* Filipino stick fighting, the foreunner of modern arnis.

KAMA (ka'ma) *Jp.* "sickle" One of the five systematized weapons used by the early te (hand) developers in Okinawa. The kama is a simple farming sickle that farmers converted to a weapon to combat the oppressing Japanese military. It is today practiced by Okinawan karate black belts, mostly in the form of kata.

KAMAE (ka-ma-eh) *Jp.* "attitude" or "posture" The stances, a general term found in all of the Japanese martial disciplines.

KAMA-YARI (ka'ma yar'ee) *Jp.* "sickle spear" A spear to which a single-edged, sickle-shaped blade is attached.

Kama

KAMI-UKE-GATAME (ka-mee oo-kay ga-ta-meh) *Jp.* The standing elbow lock in judo.

KAMIZA (ka-mee'zah) *Jp.* "divine seat" or "upper seat" The area at the front of the dojo where instructors and honored guests sit.

KANCHO (kan'choh) *Jp.* "master of the house" The senior karate instructor of a worldwide style.

KANG DUK WON (kang duk wan) *Kr.* "arena for the teaching of virtue" An early Korean martial art.

KANGEIKO (kan'gay-koh) *Jp.* "cold practice" In Japan, for two weeks during January, martial artists of all systems test their physical and mental endurance by working out in the cold and snow, often taking ice-cold showers under freezing waterfalls.

KANG-FA *Ch.* "hard method" An ancient art of Chinese boxing that concentrated on kicking and thrusting techniques.

KANI-BASAMI (ka-nee ba-sa-mee) *Jp.* "crab scissors" A judo throw that takes its movement from the crab grasping a prey in its pincers.

KANI WAZA (ka-nee wa-za) *Jp.* "scissor technique" A judo throw in which an opponent's leg is scissored and he or she is tossed to the rear.

KANKU DAI (kan-koo-deye') *Jp.* "looking at sky" A Shotokan karate kata derived from the Okinawan Kusanku form.

KANSETSU-WAZA (kan-seht-soo wa'za) *Jp.* "locking techniques" A collective term for techniques exerting pressure against various joints of the body—the arms, fingers, ankles, wrists, knees, and spine. In judo competition, only armlocks are permitted since an application of pressure against other joints is considered too dangerous.

KAN SHU *Ch.* "penetration hand" A Chinese training method in which a practitioner thrusts his or her hands into powder, then rice, sand, beans, and, finally, pebbles, to condition the limbs for striking.

KANZASHI (kan-za'shee) *Jp.* "hairpin" An ornamental hairpin used for self-protection by the women of feudal Japan.

KAPPO (kap'poh) *Jp.* A system of resuscitation used in Japanese martial arts. Known also as katsu (resuscitation).

KARADO-NO-HINERI (ka-ra-doh noh hee-nay-ree) *Jp.* In judo, the body twist required during the throwing stages of a technique.

KARA (ka'ra) *Jp.* "empty" or "China" Either of two ideograms, which, when compounded with another, to form karate (empty hand or China hand). The original character was t'ang, or China, pronounced "kara." In a move toward Japanese nationalism, Gichin Funakoshi changed the character to another one, also pronounced "kara," meaning "empty." He declared that the new concept was based on "hollowness," meaning unselfishness. Thus, the emptiness implied by the new ideogram refers to the state of rendering one's self empty, or egoless, for the purpose of unhindered development of spiritual insight.

KARATE (ka-ra'tay) *Jp.* "empty hand" or "China hand" An unarmed method of combat in which all parts of the anatomy are used to punch, strike, kick, or block. Karate originated in Okinawa as te (hand), and was directly influenced by earlier Chinese martial arts. The number of karate sects remains somewhere below one hundred.

Karate, like many other Oriental martial arts and ways, uses the belt system to indicate a practitioner's level. The ranks are divided into the kyu (grade) stages for students and the dan (rank; degree) classifications for advanced students and instructors. The requirements for each level varies according to style and instructor, as does the number of belts and colors.

In most Japanese systems, which are the most widespread, there are six grades rising from sixth to first kyu. Beginners always start with a white belt and work their way up to yellow, blue, green, brown, and black. The dan ranks range from shodan (first degree) to judan (tenth degree). Dan ranks of eighth degree and upward carry with them the title of shihan (doctor; master), and honorees usually wear a belt colored blood red, or some variation of red, white, and black.

Requirements for advancement include the basic movements, kata, and, for the more advanced, freestyle sparring. Karate is practiced in numerous ways, the most common being kihon (basic training), kata (formal exercises), and jiyu-kumite (freestyle sparring).

There are more than fifty kata in karate, all highly stylized. Each motion has a specific purpose and each sequence embodies the experience of numerous karate masters. The more sophisticated kata incorporate rapid changes of technique, slowness, speed, maintenance of balance, stretching and bending of the body, body shifting, correct breathing, combinations,

Various Shots of Karate

and quick tensing and relaxing of the muscles to facilitate the application of power.

Training in karate usually takes place in dojo, or training hall, which, unlike the judo dojo, does not require mats on the floor.

The traditional uniform, the karate-gi or just gi, consists of loose white trousers and a jacket. The jacket is fastened by a belt, called an obi, whose colors denote the practitioner's rank.

Karate competition is conducted on a number of levels. In noncontact, the traditional and most widely practiced method, attacks are stopped short of actual contact. Such competition prohibits contact to the face although body contact, if not excessive, is permissible. Semi-contact permits moderate contact to the face and body, but the contestants wear protective hand and foot padding so as to avoid injury. Lastly, full-contact karate is conducted in a ring strictly for professional fighters who attempt to win the contest by rendering one another unconscious.

Tameshiwara, the practice of breaking boards, bricks, and other materials, is another very popular aspect of karate. It is primarily used as a test of power to build self-confidence and confidence in one's techniques.

In karate, all parts of the body are used as weapons. Striking points of the hand and arm include the fist, the bottom fist, the edges of the hand, the palm, the wrist, the fingertips, the elbow, and the forearm. Striking points of the foot include the instep, heel, ball of foot, edge of foot, and the knee for close-range fighting.

KARATE CHOP A popular but erroneous name given to the open-hand strike with the outer edge of the hand used in karate and other Oriental combatives. While it has become synonymous with karate, it actually derived from Rikido-zan, the man most directly responsible for the popularity of professional wrestling in Japan, who used the karate shuto (knife hand) technique in his professional bouts. It caught on publicly and has since spread worldwide and is most universally recognized by non-martial-artists.

KARATE-DO (ka-ra-tay doh') *Jp.* "empty-hand way" A characteristically Japanese type of karate chiefly devoted to the study and practice of unarmed methods of empty-hand combat. Properly taught, it is a combination of spiritual discipline, physical education, self-defense, and competitive sport.

KARATE-GI (ka-ra-tay gee) *Jp.* "A karate uniform" See also DOGI.

KARATE-JUTSU (ka-ra'tay ju'tsoo) *Jp.* "China-hand art" "empty-hand art" The name chosen by Okinawan karate masters to replace the word "te" (hand). This was later changed to karate-do by Gichin Funakoshi, whose new connotation lent a spiritual and philosophical essence to what has been basically a physical art.

KARATEKA (ke-ra'tay-ka) *Jp.* "karate practitioner."

KASHIRA (ka-shee-ra) *Jp.* "pommel cap" or "ferrule" A metal cap covering the tip of the hilt of Japanese swords, daggers, and so forth. Frequently referred to as the pommel, it is usually made as part of a set with the fuchi.

KASUMI (ka-soo'mee) *Jp.* "fog," "mist" or "haze" In a judo contest, the meaning of a feint. Its purpose is to frighten, disturb, or distract an opponent to facilitate one's own attack.

KATA (ka'ta) *Jp.* "formal exercise" 1. A series of prearranged maneuvers practiced in many of the Oriental martial arts in order for one to become proficient in techniques. These prearranged moves can be practiced by oneself, as in karate, with a partner as in judo, or with a weapon as in iaido.

2. A series of prearranged karate maneuvers executed against one or more imaginary attacking opponents. In ancient times, kata served as a method of teaching and practicing karate when instructors were far removed from their disciples. It equally served as a means of practicing karate where it was otherwise outlawed.

These patterns of movements serve as a catalog for all techniques of the martial arts. Some systems emphasize a large number of them; some, a deep understanding of just a few. Many styles employ the same, or very similar, kata, sometimes with different names, sometimes in different order. In fact, two schools of the same style often show minor differences in the same kata.

Many kata, being very old, bear names whose meanings are obscure, so some names have been modernized. By the same token, some kata having the same name bear no resemblance to each other.

Most karate kata originated in Okinawa, and the original names, mainly Chinese, were transmitted by word of mouth. It is believed there existed thirty kata in Shuri-te (later, shorei-ryu) and Tomari-te (later, the matsubayashi-ryu sect of shorin-ryu), the principle Okinawan styles from which most kata derived. Most Okinawan and Japanese karate systems practice anywhere from twelve to nineteen of these original forms.

Some theories hold that the movements of kata derived from mimicking the movements of animals. Others speculate that they grew out of ancient dance forms. Because of the secrecy in which karate was originally practiced, there are no documented facts to support either view. Consequently, the method in which kata should be executed is open to a multitude of interpretations.

3. Graduated exercises in the prearranged forms of basic judo. This includes all of the forms of throwing, grappling, and attacking the vital points, together with the cutting and thrusting with dagger and sword. These prearranged techniques are performed by two people, one acting as the performer of the technique, called tori, the other as the receiver, called the uke.

The major judo kata are:

1 nage-no-kata (forms of throwing)
2. katame-no-kata (forms of grappling and holding)
3. go-no-sen-no-kata (forms of throw and counterthrow)
4. kime-no-kata (forms of self-defense)
5. itsutsu-no-kata (forms of the five principles)
6. ju-no-kata (forms of gentleness)
7. koshiki-no-kata (forms antique)
8. Kodokan-goshin-jutsu (Kodokan forms of self-defense)
9. Joshi judio goshin ho

KATA-ASHI-DORI (ka-ta a-shee doh-ree) *Jp.* "single leg hold" A judo countertechnique to ouchi-gari, the major inner reaping throw.

KATA GATAME (ka-ta ga-ta-meh) *Jp.* "shoulder hold" The second judo technique of katame-no-kata, the forms of grappling and holding in which the opponent is held securely by controlling his shoulders and also one of his arms.

KATA-GURUMA (ka'ta gu-roo'muh) *Jp.* "shoulder wheel" A judo throwing technique categorized as the third movement of the nage-no-kata, the forms of throwing. In this throw, the contestant literally lifts his opponent onto his shoulders and then throws him on his back.

KATA-HA-JIME (ka'ta ha jee'may) *Jp.* "single wing lock" A judo stanglehold categorized as the ninth movement of katame-no-kata, the forms of grappling and holding performed when the opponent is either seated or squatting and makes use of the lapel of the uniform to choke the opponent.

KATA-JUJI-JIME (ka'ta joo'jee jee'meh) *Jp.* "half-cross necklock" The sixth judo technique of katame-no-kata, the forms of grappling and holding. It is performed with one hand while lying on top of the opponent.

KATA-MAWASHI (ka-ta ma-wa'shee) *Jp.* "shoulder turning" The fourth technique of ju-no-kata, the forms of gentleness.

KATAME-NO-KATA (ka-ta'meh noh ka'ta) *Jp.* "forms of grappling and holding" The second judo kata consisting of fifteen techniques from the

Katana

art of grappling. Katame-no-kata is divided into three sets of techniques: osae-waza (holding techniques), shime-waza (stangling techniques), and kansetsu-waza (locking techniques), with five model techniques chosen from each set. These movements were selected as the most pertinent examples to explain the theory and practice of effective grappling

First Series: *Osae-Waza (Holding Techniques)*

1. kesa-gatame (scarf hold)
2. kata-gatame (shoulder hold)
3. kami-shiho-gatame (upper four-corner hold)
4. yoko-shiho-gatame (side four-corner hold)
5. kuzure-kami-shiho-gatame (broken upper four-corner hold)

Second Series: *Shime-Waza (Strangling Techniques)*

6. kata juji-jime (half-cross stanglehold)
7. hadaka-jime (naked chokelock)
8. okuri-eri-jime (sliding collar choke)
9. kata-ha-jime (single wing choke)
10. gyaku-juji-jime (reverse cross choke)

Third Series: *Kansetsu-Waza (Locking Techniques)*

11. ude-garami (entangled armlock)
12. juji-gatame (cross armlock)
13. ude-gatame (arm armlock)
14. hiza-gatame (knee armlock)
15. ashi-garami (entangled leglock)

KATAME-WAZA (ka-ta'may-wa'za) *Jp.* "grappling techniques" One of the three basic groups of techniques constituting judo. See also GRAPPLING TECHNIQUES.

KATANA (ka-ta'na) *Jp.* "sword" A Japanese sword, with a curved, single-edged blade twenty-four to thirty-six inches long. The katana was worn with its scabbard thrust through the wearer's belt. It was worn with the cutting edge up.

KATA-OSHI (ka'ta oh'shee) *Jp.* "shoulder push" The second judo technique of ju-no-kata, the forms of gentleness.

KATA-SEOI (ka'ta say-oy) *Jp.* The single shoulder throw in judo.

KATA-SEOI-NAGE: See GO-NO-SEN-NO-KATA.

KATATE-AGE (ka-ta'tay a'gay) *Jp.* "one hand raising" The tenth judo technique of ju-no-kata, the forms of gentleness.

KATATE-DORI (ka-ta'tay do'ree) *Jp.* "one-hand seizure from side" 1. The ninth judo technique of ju-no-kata, the forms of gentleness. 2. The single-hand hold of judo, a technique of kote-hodoki, the wrist-releasing techniques.

KATATE-JIME (ka-ta'tay jee-meh) *Jp.* "one-hand wringing" The judo single-handed necklock in which an opponent's lapel is used to choke her or him.

KATSU (kat'soo) *Jp.* "resuscitation," "living," or "being helped" 1. A system of resuscitation used to revive a semiconscious person. Its basis is to stimulate the heart and lungs by sharply tapping their spinal nerve centers.

KATSUGI-JIME (ka-tsoo-gee jee-meh) *Jp.* The shoulder necklock used in judo.

KAUNDE (ka-un'day) *Kr.* "middle" A tae kwon do term representing the middle region of the body. It is specifically used to designate target areas.

KAY-MEN-BO: See HOP-GAR.

KEAGE (kay-a'gay) *Jp.* "kick up" 1. A karate kick directed to the abdomen. 2. The fifteenth judo technique of kime-no-kata, the forms of self-defense.

KEIBO (kay'bo) *Jp.* A wooden club used by the Japanese police.

KEIBO SOHO: See JOJUTSU.

KEIBU (kay-boo) *Jp.* Neck area. In sport karate one of the primary target areas.

KEIKO (kay'koh) *Jp.* "chicken-beak hand" 1. See: CHICKEN BEAK. 2. "training" or "practice" In kendo, there are three main types: gakari-geiko (attack practice) in which a kenshi practices continuous attacks; gokaku-geiko (equal practice) in which two kendoka of equal ability practice in the atmosphere of a real match; and hikitate-geiko (assistant practice) in which a senior works with a junior while fighting.

Kendo

KEIKOGI (kay'koh-gee) *Jp.* "practice uniform" A name often used by martial arts practitioners when referring to their practice outfits.

KEITO: See CHICKEN-HEAD WRIST.

KEKOMI (kay'koh-mee) *Jp.* "kicking" 1. A karate kick usually directed to the center level as opposed to a high or low kick. 2. (to) "thrust."

KEMPO: See CH'UAN FA.

KENDO (kehn'doh) *Jp.* "way of the sword" The modern art and sport of Japanese fencing. Kendoka wear a hakama (divided skirt) with a tare (apron; groin protector). On the upper body they wear a keikogi (jacket) similar to that worn in judo. The hands and forearms are protected by a kote (wrist glove) and the chest is covered by a do (breastplate). The head is protected by a men (headguard) consisting of a nickel-steel grill and heavily padded cloth that covers the head, throat, and shoulders.

The kendoka uses a shinai (practice sword) which consists of four pieces of bamboo held together by cords.

The object of a kendo contest is to deliver scoring cuts to an opponent's predetermined target areas: the center of the head; the left side of the head, right side of the head; left wrist; right wrist; left side of the ribcage; right side of ribcage. The throat and chest are targets for thrusting techniques. Most blows are delivered with two hands on the sword in a cutting action, with the arms fully extended. Many target areas, particularly those on the left side of the body are valid only under specified circumstances.

Today, kendo is practiced not only in Japan but in most Western countries both as a sport and a means of spiritual discipline. Kendo developed from kenjutsu (art of the sword).

KENDOKA (kehn-doh'ka) *Jp.* "kendoperson" A practitioner of kendo.

KENJUTSU (kehn-jut'soo) *Jp.* "art of the sword" An aggressive method of swordsmanship practiced by Japanese feudal warriors in which the combatants pitted naked blade against blade. Today, kenjutsu is practiced chiefly in the form of kata and actual combat is staged only with the bokken (wooden sword). Kenjutsu is the art from which kendo developed.

KEN-KEN (kehn kehn) *Jp.* "skipping" or "hopping" A hopping action used in throwing that greatly facilitates the entry to certain judo techniques.

KENKYAKU (kehn-kya'koo) *Jp.* "fencer" One of many words used to describe those who lived by the sword, especially in literary usage.

KENPO (kehn'poh) *Jp.* "fist method" A modern term describing one of the more innovative martial arts practiced in Hawaii and the Americas. It employs linear as well as circular moves, utilizing intermittant power when and where needed, interspersed with minor and major moves that flow with continuity. Kenpo is flexible in thought and action so as to blend with encounters as they occur.

KENSHI (kehn'shee) *Jp.* "fencer."

KENSHUSEI (kehn-shoo'say) *Jp.* A term used to denote special research students who obtain the most advanced training and are usually expected to become teachers.

KENSUI-JIME (kehn-swee jee-meh) *Jp.* The hanging chokelock in judo.

KENTSUI: See HAMMER FIST.

KENTSUI-UCHI (kehn-tswee oo'chee) *Jp.* "hammer-fist strike" A karate hand technique in which the bottom of the fist delivers a blow, usually to the face.

KENYOHO (kehn-yoh'hoh) *Jp.* A judo method of combining a holding technique with a strangulation in order to effect a submission.

KERI (keh-ree) *Jp.* "kick" or "kicking."

KERI-WAZA (keh-ree wa'za) *Jp.* "kicking techniques."

KESA-GATAME (keh'sa ga-ta-meh) *Jp.* "scarf hold" A judo pinning technique in which an opponent is pinned by the first judo technique of katame-no-kata.

KESA-GATAME-JIME (keh-sa ga-ta-meh jee-meh) *Jp.* "cross chest choke" A judo technique of strangulation in which the opponent is choked while in a cross-chest hold position.

KESA-GATAME-KEI (keh-sa ga-ta-meh kay-ee) *Jp.* "scarf-hold system" One of the three systems into which the holding techniques of judo can be subdivided. This particular system is composed of techniques in which one sits with the upper part of the body held erect and the torso held obliquely in close contact with the opponent.

KEUPSO CHIRIGI (kup'soh chee-roo'gee) *Kr.* The Korean art of attacking the vital points of the body. About forty of these points are used as target areas, to which the practitioner is taught to strike with both the hands and feet.

KI (kee) *Jp.* "spirit" Ideally, the mental and spiritual power summoned through concentration and breathing that can be applied to accomplish physical feats. This centralized energy, possessed by every person, can be manifested through the practice of just about any martial discipline, particularly those subscribing to a sophisticated study of physiology. See also CHI.

KIAI (kee'eye) *Jp.* "spirit meeting" A loud shout or yell of self-assertion most common to the Japanese and Okinawan martial disciplines. It is a method in which the shout, in conjunction with the expulsion of air, can reinforce a striking technique by maximizing bodily strength. Known in Korean as kihap (yelling).

KIAI-JUTSU (kee'eye jut'soo) *Jp.* "art of the spirit meeting" A specific method of combat based on the employment of the voice as a weapon. It was a blending of various factors which composed the entire personality of the warrior to produce through the voice an outward manifestation of the inner spirit.

KIBA-DACHI (kee'ba dach) *Jp.* "horse stance" or "straddle stance" A karate stance in which the feet are extended twice the width of the shoulders and chiefly used when facing an opponent from the side.

KICKING Any of numerous methods of striking with the foot. Known in Japanese as keri, in Korean as chagi.

KICK-BOXING Also known as Muay Thai boxing because of its native origin, it was once the single hand-to-hand combat method used to supplement armed warfare in Thailand. Thai kick-boxing, sometimes called the "sport of kings," is the national pastime of Thailand.

The sport takes place in a rope-enclosed ring much like western boxing. There are usually five rounds of three minutes duration. Fighting is conducted with padded gloves and sometimes semipadded feet, with the object being to render the opponent unconscious. Contests can also be determined by a technical knockout or a decision. Fights are often brutal and bloody and contestants are frequently injured. This is mainly because the rules permit blows with the hands, feet, knees, and elbows. Particularly devastating are the full-power kicks permitted to the legs, knees, and thighs.

The term "kick-boxing" is now synonymous with the sport as it is conducted in Japan, while the Thais maintain the name Muay Thai or Thai-boxing.

KIHAP (kee'ap) *Kr.* "yelling." See also KIAI.

KIHON (kee'hohn) *Jp.* "basics" or "basic training" In karate, the repetition of the fundamental techniques.

KIHON KUMITE (kee'hohn koo'mee-tay) *Jp.* "basic sparring" See ONE-STEP SPARRING.

KIMA SOGI (kee'ma soh'gee) *Kr.* "riding stance." See HORSE STANCE.

KIME: See FOCUS.

KIME-NO-KATA (kee'may noh ka'ta) *Jp.* "kata of self-defense" The fourth judo kata composed of twenty techniques divided into two sets of eight and twelve movements respectively. The first series is the idori, or techniques from a kneeling position; second is the tachiai, or techniques performed from a standing position.

First Series: *Idori (Seated Defense)*

1. ryote-dori (both hand seizure)

2. tsukikake (straight punch to stomach)
3. suri-age (blow against forehead with palm)
4. yoko-uchi (blow at the temple)
5. ushiro-dori (shoulder grab from behind)
6. tsuki-komi (dagger thrust at the stomach)
7. kiri-komi (direct downward cut with dagger)
8. yoko-tsuki (side thrust with dagger)

Second Series: *Tachiai (Standing Defense)*

9. ryote-dori (both hand seizure)
10. sode-tori (side sleeve seizure)
11. tsuki-kake (straight punch to face)
12. tsuki-age (uppercut blow)
13. suri-age (blow against forehead with palm)
14. yoko-uchi (blow at the temple)
15. keage (kick to abdomen)
16. ushiro-dori (shoulder grab from behind)
17. tsuki-komi (stomach thrust with dagger)
18. kiri-komi (direct downward cut with dagger)
19. nuki-kake (sword unsheathing)
20. kiri-oroshi (direct downward cut with sword)

KIN-GERI (keen'gay-ree) *Jp.* "front arch kick" A karate kick to the groin using the instep.

KIRIKAESHI (kee-ree-ka-ehsh) *Jp.* "repeated cutting to alternate sides" Kendo warm-up exercises with the shinai.

KIRI-KOMI: See KIME-NO-KATA.

KIRI-OROSHI: See JU-NO-KATA.

KIRITSUKI (kee-ree-tskee) *Jp.* "cut and thrust" The cutting action of the sword; one of the four phases of study in all Japanese iai (sword) techniques.

KITO-RYU (kee'toh-ryoo) *Jp.* One of the early jujutsu schools which especially influenced Jigoro Kano's formulation of Kodokan judo.

KNEE Part of the leg used as a striking point for close-range fighting in many martial disciplines. Known in Japanese as the hiza, in Korean as the mooreup.

KNEE-LOCKING TECHNIQUES Joint-locking techniques used on the knee joints with the object of gaining a submission from an opponent. They are most common in judo and jujutsu. Known in Japanese as hiza-waza.

KNEE SHOULDER THROW A variation of seoi-nage in which the right hand is used to push to the rear of an opponent's knee. Known in Japanese as the hiza-seoi.

KNEE WHEEL: See HIZAGURUMA.

KNIFE HAND An open-hand karate technique delivered with the fleshy edge of the hand. Known in Japanese as the shuto. See also EDGE OF HAND.

KNIFE-HAND BLOCK A karate block performed with the edge of the open hand. Known in Japanese as the shuto-uke.

KOA-SEOGI (ko-ah say-oh-gee) *Kr.* "twisted stance" A tae kwon do stance in which the shin of one leg and the calf of the other are twisted around each other.

KOBAYASHI-RYU (koh-ba-ya'shee ryoo) *Jp.* An Okinawan style of karate stemming from Shuri-te and which is now one of the branches of shorin-ryu. This style, translated as "small forest," should not be confused with the other branches of shorin-ryu karate known as "pine forest" and "young forest," respectively. The English spelling of these Japanese names does not reflect the differences between the arts.

KOBUDO (koh-boo'doh) *Jp.* "weapons way" A generic term coined in the 20th century, which can be used to describe collectively all Okinawan combatives. However, it is more accurate to specify "Okinawan kobudo" in order to distinguish them from "Japanese kobudo."

The use of this term should not be limited, as it popularly is, to describe the ancient weapons systems of Okinawa, for that practice has also been called buki-ho.

When kobudo is used to describe the practice of Okinawan weaponry, it encompasses numerous weapons which were an improvisation of farm implements converted into effective protective devices by ingenious Okinawan farmers. They include the bo (staff), sai (pronged truncheon), kama (sickle), tonfa (handle) and nunchaku (flail). The shuriken (throwing blades) and manriki-gusari (weighted chain), while typically Japanese and not farm tools, are also a part of this classification.

KOBU-JUTSU (koh'boo jut'soo) *Jp.* "art of weapons" The traditional weaponry indigenous to Okinawan karate. The main weapons that form the basis of kobu-jutsu are the bo (staff), sai (short pronged truncheon), nunchaku (flail), tonfa (handle), and kama (sickle). Secondary weapons include the timbei (shield), rochin (short spear), surushin (weighted chain), eku (oar), and the teko (knuckle-duster).

These weapons also came to be classified under kobudo (way of weapons) in the 20th century. See also KOBUDO.

KOCHUNG SOGI (koh'jung soh'gee) *Kr.* "fixed stance."

KODACHI (koh-da'chee) *Jp.* "small sword" A forerunner of the wakizashi (short sword), that boasts a blade between twelve and eighteen inches in length.

KO-DANG (koh'dang) *Kr.* A tae kwon do hyung of thirty-nine movements named after the pseudonym of Cho Man-Sik, a Korean patriot.

KODANSHA (koh-dan'sha) *Jp.* A high-ranking judo black belt of fifth-degree and above.

KODA-ORE (koh-da oh-reh) *Jp.* "log fall" The seventh judo technique of koshiki-no-kata, the forms antique.

KODOKAN (koh'doh-kan) *Jp.* "Hall for teaching the way" The largest single establishment for the practice and promotion of judo, located in Tokyo.

KODOKAN-GOSHIN-JUTSU: See KATA.

KOEIKAN (koh'ay-kan) *Jp.* A system of Japanese karate founded by Eizo Onishi in Kanagawa, Japan, in 1952.

KOGUSOKU (koh-goo-soh'koo) *Jp.* 1. An ancient method of unarmed combat mentioned in connection with kumiuchi and sumo in the oldest records of the Japanese martial arts. 2. A system of unarmed combat similar to jujutsu and a forerunner of modern judo.

KOHAI (koh-heye) *Jp.* A junior in a school or organization.

KOHO-UKEMI (koh-hoh oo-kay-mee) The judo method of falling backward without injury through the use of shock-dispersing action, slapping the mat with the arms.

Kokutsu Dachi

KOJIRI (koh-jee-ree) *Jp.* The chape or end cap of the scabbard of a samurai sword.

KOKEN (coe'ken) *Jp.* "bent-wrist" See: CHICKEN-HEAD WRIST.

KOKO: See TIGER MOUTH.

KOKUTSU-DACHI (koh-kut'soo da'chee) *Jp.* "back stance" A karate stance in which 70 percent of the body weight is supported by the back foot, allowing the front foot greater kicking potential. This stance is often used when blocking a direct frontal attack.

KOKYU (koh'kyoo) *Jp.* "breathing" or "ki."

KOODAN (koo'dan) *Kr.* "ninth rank" Ninth-degree black belt in the Korean martial arts.

KOOGUP (koo'goop) *Kr.* "ninth class" A white belt in tae kwon do and other Korean martial arts.

KOOKUP HWAL BOB: See CHIMGOO SUL PUP.

KOREAN KARATE A name sometimes used for tae kwon do.

KOSHI (koh'shee) *Jp.* "ball of the foot" or "hip(s)".

KOSHIGURUMA (koh'shee-guh-roo'muh) *Jp.* A judo hip throw in which the opponent is grasped around the neck and thrown over the hip.

KOSHIKI-NO-KATA (koh-shee'kee noh ka'ta) *Jp.* "kata of the forms antique" A judo kata composed of techniques in which it is assumed the participants are armor-clad. It is the seventh judo kata and it is composed of twenty-one techniques divided into two sets of fourteen and seven movements respectively.

First Series: *Omote (Frontal Movements)*

1. tai (ready posture)
2. yume-no-uchi (amidst dream)
3. ryo-kuhi (strength dodging)
4. mizu-guruma (water wheel)
5. mizu-nagare (water flowing)
6. hiki-otoshi (drawing drop)
7. koda-ore (log fall)
8. uchi-kudaki (pulverizing)
9. tani-otoshi (the valley drop)

30\. kuruma-daoshi (wheel throw)

11. shikoro-dori (hold on shoulder armor)
12. shikoro-gaeshi (throwing from shoulder armor)
13. yudachi (shower)
14. taki-otoshi (waterfall drop)

Second Series: *Ura (Rear Movements)*

15. mi-kudaki (body smashing)
16. kuruma-gaeshi (wheel throw)
17. mizu-iri (water plunging)
18. ryu-setsu (willow snow)
19. saka-otoshi (headlong drop)
20. yuki-ore (snow break)
21. iwa-name (breaker on the rock)

KOSHI MAWARI (koh'shee ma-wa'ree) *Jp.* "hip turning" An ancient method of unarmed combat similar to jujutsu and a forerunner to judo.

KOSHI-WAZA (koh-shee wa'za) *Jp.* "hip techniques" Throwing techniques employing principally the hips or waist which are used in judo, jujutsu, aikido, and karate.

KOSOTOGAKE (koh-soh-toh-ga-keh) *Jp.* "minor outer sweeping throw" Used in judo, the opponent's foot is swept out from under him or her by a circular sweeping movement coming from the outside.

KOSOTOGARI (koh-soh-toh-ga'ree) *Jp.* "minor outer reaping" A judo throwing technique of the leg or foot, in which the opponent is downed as he steps forward by reaping his heel from the outside.

KOTE (koh-teh) *Jp.* "wrist" 1. Two large heavy gloves worn by kendoka to protect their hands and lower forearms. 2. In kendo, the wrist as a target area.

KOTE-HODOKI (koh-teh hoh-doh-kee) *Jp.* "wrist-releasing techniques" A judo method of freeing the wrists from a hold while leaving the defender in a position for further attack.

KOTE-WAZA (koh-teh wa'za) *Jp.* "wrist-locking techniques" A set of immobilization techniques taught in judo, but prohibited in competition.

KO-TSURI-GOSHI (koh tsu-ree goh-sh) *Jp.* "minor propping hip throw" A judo technique and variation of tsuri-goshi (lifting hip throw).

KO-UCHI-GAKE (koh oo-chee gah-keh) *Jp.* The minor inner hook throw of judo.

KOUCHI GARI (koh-oo-chee-ga-ree) *Jp.* "minor inner reaping" A judo throw in which the opponent is thrown by reaping the back of his heel from the inside.

KO-WAZA (koh wa'za) *Jp.* "minor techniques" In judo, minor techniques requiring a minimum of body movement.

KUBI-JIME (koo'bee jee-may') *Jp.* "necklocks" A collective name for judo necklocks.

KUDAN (koo'dan) *Kr.* "nine;" *Jp.* "ninth rank" Ninth-degree black belt in the Japanese and Okinawan martial arts.

KUEN *Ch.* "fist" The formal exercises of kung-fu. See also KATA.

KUEN HUE HOK PAI *Ch.* "tiger-crane system" A style of kung-fu based on the fighting methods of the tiger and crane. Known as Hu Hao P'ai in Mandarin.

KUEN TAO *Ch.* A method of Chinese boxing practiced in Indonesia, Malaysia, and the Philippines.

KUJI-KIRI (koo'jee kee'ree) *Jp.* "energy channeling" A hypnotic movement of the fingers used by the ninja to confuse their opponents. Known as mudras in Sanskrit. Its origins are in esoteric Buddhism and early Hinduism.

KUKI-NAGE (koo-kee na-geh) *Jp.* "air throw" A judo technique not listed in the Kodokan formal techniques, which is considered a te-waza, a standing throw effected through hand and arm movements.

KUKKIWON (kuk'kee-wan) *Kr.* The largest single facility for the practice and promotion of tae kwon do. It is located in Seoul and was established in 1972.

KUKYU (koo'kyoo) *Jp.* "ninth class" A beginner, or white belt, in many of the Japanese and Okinawan martial arts, particularly karate.

KUMADE (koo-ma'day) *Jp.* "rake" or "fork" See BEAR HAND.

KUMIKATA (koo'me-caw'ta) *Jp.* A judo method of grappling with a standing opponent.

KUMITE (koo'mee-teh) *Jp.* "sparring" A term used in karate for a form of training in which two opponents confront each other in simulated combat. In karate, there are a number of types of kumite, all different: ippon kumite (one-step sparring), sanbon kumite (three-step sparring), and gohon kumite (five-step sparring). In these methods, the attacks are always predetermined.

After predetermined sparring is somewhat mastered, the karate student learns jiyu-kumite (free sparring), in which there is a free exchange of blows, blocks, and counterattacks, none of which is predetermined. However, all blows are pulled just short of contact to prevent injury.

KUMIUCHI (koo-mee-oo'chee) *Jp.* "grappling" Wrestling techniques originally used by the samurai on the battlefield and which give birth to jujutsu.

KUNEH (koo-neh) *Kr.* "bow" or "bowing."

KUNG CHIA *Ch.* "solo exercise" One of the three stages of t'ai-chi ch'uan.

Kung-Fu

KUNG-FU (kung-foo') *Ch.* "skill," "time," "strength," "ability," "task," or "work" A period of time utilized by a person to perform a specific type of task or work and a subsequent generic term used to refer to the Chinese unarmed martial arts. Kung-fu has two main divisions and several subdivisions with respect to the types of blows used, style of practice, and attitude. The southern styles display a clear preference for techniques of strength and power. The contrasting northern styles employ soft, open movements, often emphasizing the lower body. Also known as gwo shu and wushu.

KUO-SHU *Ch.* "national arts" A term replacing wu-shu (war arts) in China in 1928, when a series of nationally organized tournaments were created and continued until the war with Japan.

KUP (kup) *Kr.* The grade levels below black belt in the Korean martial arts.

KUPSO (kup-soh) *Kr.* The vital points of the body.

KURI-GATA (ku-ree ga-ta) *Jp.* "chestnut shape" The cord knob of the scabbard of a samurai sword. The cord (sagea), which helps keep the sword in position in the wearer's belt, passes through a hole in the kuri-gata.

KURO-OBI (koo-row oh-bee) *Jp.* 'black belt" In Japanese martial arts, the black belt is worn by a person who has mastered the basic techniques and beyond.

KURUMA-TAOSHI (koo-roo-ma ta-oh-shee) *Jp.* "wheel throw" The tenth judo technique of koshiki-no-kata.

KURUMA-GAESHI (koo-roo-ma geye-shee) *Jp* "wheel throw" The sixteenth judo technique of koshiki-no-kata.

KURUMA-WAZA (koo-roo-ma wa-za) *Jp.* "wheeling techniques" Judo throws in which an opponent's body travels through a wide arc before landing.

KUSABIDOME (koo-sa-bee-doh-meh) *Jp.* A judo countertechnique to hip throws in which the leg is thrust between the opponent's legs in such a way as to nullify the attempted technique.

KUSANKU (koo-san-koo) A karate kata, named after a famed Chinese martial artist, which was developed in the shorin-ryu school of Okinawa.

KUSARI: See CHAIN.

KUSARIGAMA (koo-sa-ree-ga'ma) *Jp.* "chain and sickle art" A form of armed combat founded in Japan, which centers around a chain-sickle weapon. It is one of a particular group of weapons noted for their efficiency in neutralizing the sword at long range.

KUZURE-KAMI-SHIHO-GATAME: See KATAME-NO-KATA.

KUZUSHI (koo-zoo'shee) *Jp.* "breaking" or "upsetting" In judo, the act of disturbing or breaking an opponent's posture or balance before committing oneself to the actual attack. There are eight basic ways of unbalancing an opponent in judo:

1. mae kuzushi (breaking forward)
2. ushiro kuzushi (breaking backward)
3. hidari kuzushi (breaking to the left)

4. migi kuzushi (breaking to the right)
5. migi-mae sumi kuzushi (breaking to the right front corner)
6. hidari-mae-sumi kuzushi (breaking to the left front corner)
7. migi-ushiro-sumi kuzushi (breaking to the right rear corner)
8. hidari-ushiro-sumi kuzushi (breaking to the left rear corner)

KWANG-GAE (kwang gay) *Kr.* A tae kwon do hyung named after Kwang-Gae-T'o-Wang, the 19th-century king of the Koguro dynasty. The thirty-nine movements are symbolic of the duration of his reign.

KWANKU (kwan'koo) *Jp.* "to contemplate at the sky" The name of a karate kata.

KWAN TAO: See: QUAN DO.

KWONBOP; KWONPUP (kwan-bap; kwan-pup) *Kr.* A Chinese method of unarmed combat that spread to and was popularized in Korea between A.D. 1147–1170.

KWOON *Ch.* "training hall" A facility in which the Chinese martial arts are practiced.

KWUN *Ch.* "staff" or "stave" See BO.

KYOBU (kyoh-boo) *Jp.* "chest area" One of the primary targets in sport karate.

KYOCHA MARKI (kyoh'cha mar'kee) *Kr.* "cross block" See X BLOCK.

KYOKPA (kyohk'pa) *Kr.* "breaking."

KYOKUSHINKAI (kyoh-koo'shin-keye) *Jp.* "extreme truth association" or "school of ultimate truth" A style of Japanese karate founded by Masutatsu Oyama and synthesized from elements of goju-ryu and Shotokan karate combined with certain principles of Chinese boxing. Kyokushinkai emphasizes contact fighting and the development of breaking skills.

KYOSHI (kyoh-shee) *Jp.* "teacher grade," "expert instructor," or "assistant professor" A Japanese martial arts teacher who is of sixth- or seventh-degree black belt rank. While one must have attained at least that level of proficiency, not all instructors of this rank receive the title of kyoshi. See also TASHI; RENSHI; HANSHI.

KYU (kyoo) *Jp.* "grade" A rank designation signifying a level of achievement below black belt or dan rank in the Japanese and Okinawan martial disciplines. In most of these disciplines, the kyu grades progress upward from eighth, the lowest, to first kyu, the highest (some arts such as aikido have only five kyu grades). These grades precede the dan (rank) degrees which designate black belts.

The kyu ranks are:

1. hachikyu (eighth grade)
2. shichikyu (seventh grade)
3. rokkyu (sixth grade)
4. gokyu (fifth grade)
5. yonkyu (fourth grade)
6. sankyu (third grade)
7. nikyu (second grade)
8. ikkyu (first grade)

The color of the belt worn by the kyu grade student becomes darker as one progresses toward black belt. While numerous variations exist today, the most popular belt colors representing the kyu grades are, respectively: white, yellow, orange, blue, green, purple, brown. Some styles designate kyu grades by the use of colored tips or stripes at the end of their belt, instead of changing the color of the whole belt.

KYUDO (kyoo-doh) *Jp.* "way of the bow" The modern Japanese practice of archery as a discipline of coordinated integration. It is based on the use of the longbow against targets of three basic types: a fourteen-inch target, a thirty-two-inch target (hammato), or a sixty-four-inch target (o-mato). The distance may range from eighty-five feet in the close style of shooting (chikamato) to 180 feet or more in the distant style (inagashi).

Kyudo's basis is the clarity of execution, the poise, and the control over the bow. That is, its functional way of achieving the desired coordination. It is the descendent of kyujutsu.

KYUJUTSU (kyoo-jut'soo) *Jp.* "art of the bow" The ancient Japanese discipline of archery that encompassed a complex system of practices and techniques used in time of war. During the Tokugawa era (1600–1867), this art evolved into kyudo (way of the bow).

KYUNG-KI-DO (kyung kee doh) *Kr.* "way of fighting skill" A modern comprehensive system of self-defense simulating actual fighting conditions and integrating the combined skills of judo, karate, and wrestling. Also called the trithlon, it was created and developed by Ken Min, physical education instructor at University of California at Berkeley, whose intention was to simulate the Olympic decathlon with events exclusively devoted to fighting competition.

KYUNGYE (kyung'yay) *Kr.* "bow" A formal command used in Korean martial arts classes to designate when to bow in greeting or respect.

KYUNG-SA-SOGI (kyung sa soh-gee) *Kr.* "diagonal stance."

KYUPKA (kyup'ka) *Kr.* "breaking."

KYU SHIN (kyoo'shin) *Jp.* A concept of judo in which the fundamental principles of motion are obeyed so that stiff postures are avoided and the best of judo is achieved.

KYUSHINDO (kyoo'shin-doh) *Jp.* A precept of judo, its three maxims being: banbutsu ruten—all things in the universe undergo a succession of changes; ritsu do—rhythmic and flowing movement; and cho-wa—all things work and flow in perfect harmony.

KYUSHIN-RYU (kyoo'shin-ryoo) *Jp.* An early school of jujutsu.

LAKAN (la-kan) *Phil.* The male black belt rank in the Filipino art of arnis.

LAMA *Ch.* One of the three schools of white crane kung-fu. See also HOP GAR.

LAPEL Part of the judo uniform commonly used to hold, throw, and choke. Known as eri in Japanese.

LATHI (la-tee) *Ind.* "staff" An Indian fighting art centered around a cane or bamboo staff about five feet in length.

LAW HORN KUEN *Ch.* A style of kung-fu characterized by high leaps and intricate footwork.

LEFT FRONT CORNER: See EIGHT DIRECTIONS OF UNBALANCE.

LEFT REAR CORNER: See EIGHT DIRECTIONS OF UNBALANCE.

LEFT SIDE: See EIGHT DIRECTIONS OF UNBALANCE.

LEG THROWS: See ASHI-WAZA.

LEG WHEEL: See ASHI-GURUMA.

LEVERAGE POINTS (EP) Fixed points at which force, minimum or otherwise, can be used to overthrow an opponent or prevent an action from taking place.

LI-CHIA *Ch.* A southern Chinese style of kung-fu called li-gar in Cantonese.

LIFT-PULL A judo term meaning a fishing action of the hands and arms as a prerequisite to throwing an opponent. This action causes the opponent's weight and balance to be transferred onto the toes.

LI-GAR: See LI-CHIA.

LIGHT CONTACT A term used to designate a type of karate competition in which lightly striking an opponent with controlled force to the body is permitted, but contact to the face is not.

LIMA LAMA (lee-ma la'ma) *Poly.* "hand of wisdom" An American martial art of Polynesian descent, which is composed of a combination of revised movements stemming from thirteen various Polynesian fighting arts.

LINEAR MOVEMENTS (EP) Moves that are direct in nature and follow a straight path. They are primarily offensive, but can be utilized defensively or as follow-ups after meeting resistance.

LIU GAR *Ch.* A basic southern Chinese style of kung-fu centered around close-range fighting. It is characterized by intricate hand movements designed to open up offensive opportunities on an opponent. Also known as liu jya in Mandarin.

LOCK A martial arts term designating a technique that immobilizes the part of the body to which it is applied, usually a joint.

LOCK-OUT (EP) Refers to the delivery of a technique that remains at the target upon contact, instead of being retracted.

LOGISTICS The aspect of positional theory concerned with the use of tactical footwork on a given battlefield to effect the most favorable fighting distances from an opponent.

LONG-HAND BOXING Any system of kung-fu, or Chinese boxing,

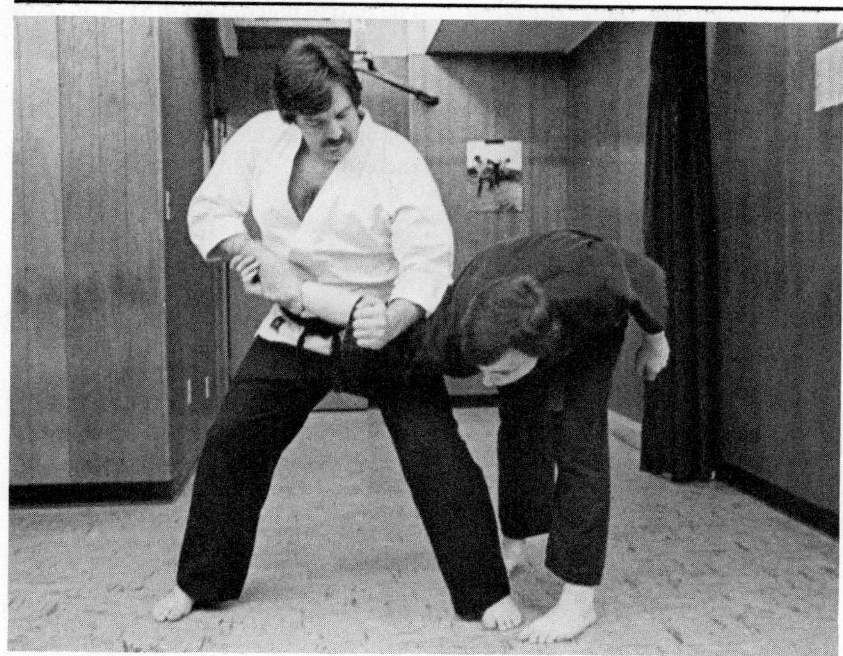

Lock (Elbow Lock)

characterized by the use of the arm's full extension during the execution of a technique.

LONG-RANGE TECHNIQUES Any techniques with which a fighter can reach an opponent at the longest distance, using the full extension of the arms or legs.

LOW FORM Any kung-fu system in which the techniques largely depend on speed and power rather than on timing and positioning.

LOW-LINE GUARD Any guard position where the lead hand is lowered to waist level.

LOW LINES The positional coordinates located below the waist.

L-STANCE A stance in which the feet form an L. The front foot points forward and is perpendicular to the rear foot. Known in Japanese as the renoji-dachi, in Korean as the dwitkoobi or niunja-sogi.

LUA (loo'a) *Poly.* "bone-breaking" The native martial art of Hawaii, now extinct, which was similar to Japanese jujutsu.

LUNGE PUNCH A karate punching technique performed with a step forward. The punch is delivered from the same side of the body as the forward foot. Known in Japanese as the oi-zuki.

MA (maw) *Ch.* "horse" The kung-fu term for the horse stance.

MA-AI (ma'eye) *Jp.* "distancing" The distance between two opponents.

MACHI-DOJO (ma'chee doh'joh) *Jp.* A small training hall for the Japanese martial arts, usually an annex to the main dojo.

MAE (ma'eh) *Jp.* "front" or "forward."

MAE-ASHI-GERI (ma-eh a-shee geh-ree) *Jp.* "front foot kick" A karate technique in which the kick is delivered from the front foot, as opposed to the rear one.

MAE-EMPI-UCHI (ma-eh ehm-pee oo-chee) "front elbow strike" See EMPI-UCHI.

MAE-GERI (ma-eh geh-ree) *Jp.* "front kick."

MAE-GERI-KEAGI: See FRONT KICK.

MAE-GERI-KEKOMI: See FRONT KICK.

MAE-HIJI-ATE: See EMPI-UCHI.

MAE-SANKAKU-JIME (ma-eh san-kah-koo jee-meh) *Jp.* The front triangular choke used in judo.

MAE-SUMI-OTOSHI (ma-eh soo-mee oh-toh-shee) *Jp.* "front corner drop" One of the hand throwing techniques of judo.

MAE-TOBI GERI (ma-eh toh-bee geh-ree) *Jp.* "front flying kick" See also FLYING FRONT KICK.

MAE-UDE-OSAE-UKE: See FOREARM PRESSING BLOCK.

MAE-UKEMI (ma-eh oo-kehm-ee) *Jp.* The front breakfall in judo.

MAIRI (ma-ee-ree) *Jp.* Tapping with the hand on either one's own body or the mat. In judo competition, this signals submission such as to a choke or armbar. In judo or aikido practice, it is used to signal one's partner that the technique being practiced has been applied effectively. One never taps the partner's or opponent's body.

MAJOR MOVES (EP) Strong and positive moves which cause immediate devastation.

MAKERU (ma-keh-roo) *Jp.* "lose" or "to be defeated."

MAKGI: See MARKI.

MAKIAGE-GU (ma-kee-a-geh goo) *Jp.* "lever bar" An Okinawan karate training device used to strengthen the wrist.

MAKI-KOMI (ma'kee koh'mee) *Jp.* "winding" A compound word attached to numerous judo techniques in which the winding of the body represents an important aspect of the throw.

MAKIWARA (ma-kee-wa'ra) *Jp.* "straw-padded striking post" A karate training post designed for toughening various striking points. It is constructed from a piece of wood about sixty inches long and tapered at one end, the thin end of which is mounted on a platform or secured to the ground. Knuckles, elbows, feet, and so on are toughened by repeated strikes to the post. Known in Korean as the dallyon joo (forging post).

MAKURA-KESA-GATAME (mah-koo-rah keh-sah gah-tah-meh) *Jp.* "pillow scarf hold" A judo hold-down technique and variation of kesa-gatame (scarf hold).

Makiwara

MANEUVER (EP) A method one uses to close or extend range.

MAN-MAE (man-ma-eh) *Jp.* "due front" One of the eight directions of unbalance in judo.

MANRIKI-GUSARI (man-ree'kee gu-sar'ee) *Jp.* "ten thousand power chain" A two- or three-foot length of chain with weighted ends used for self-defense. It was devised by a Japanese swordsman in the 18th century and can be applied with devastating effect against both armed and unarmed assailants. In Okinawa, the weapon is known as the surushin (weighted chain).

MARGIN FOR ERROR (EP) The execution of a defensive and/or offensive move that, when delivered, provides greater latitude to work with in the event of error or miscalculation.

MARKI (mar'kee) *Kr.* "block" The defensive motions of tae kwon do. Known also as makgi, it is normally used as part of a compound word.

MARRIAGE TO GRAVITY (EP) The uniting of strength, mind, and breath while dropping with the weight of the body. The merger of all of the above factors at the time the body drops greatly adds to the force of a blow or strike. Known also as gravitational marriage.

MARTIAL Military, warlike, fighting.

MARTIAL ARTS An encompassing term usually reserved for the Asian fighting arts, although it can refer to any fighting discipline with or without weapons.

MASTER A title bestowed on a martial artist who has attained advanced rank after long years of study.

MA-SUTEMI-WAZA (ma soo-tehm'ee wa'za) *Jp.* A collective name for a group of judo throws performed from a prone position. It is a subdivision of sutemi-waza, often referred to as sacrifice throws.

MAT TECHNIQUES: See GRAPPLING TECHNIQUES.

MATE (ma'teh) *Jp.* "wait" A referee's command used in a judo contest or Japanese-style karate match to indicate to the contestants that they must temporarily halt their action.

MATSUBAYASHI-RYU (mat-soo-beye-a'shee-ryoo) *Jp.* "pine forest style" An Okinawan style of karate founded by Sokon Matsumura, later renamed shorin-ryu. See also SHORIN-RYU.

MATWORK Judo techniques employed while both opponents are on the ground, with particular emphasis placed on immobilizing holds and locks. Known in Japanese as ne-waza (ground techniques) or katame-waza (grappling techniques).

MA-USHIRO (ma oo-shee'roh) *Jp.* "due back" One of the eight directions of unbalance in judo.

MAWARU (ma-wa'roo) *Jp.* "to turn around."

MAWASHI-GERI: See ROUNDHOUSE KICK.

MAWASHI-TOBI-GERI: See FLYING ROUNDHOUSE KICK.

MAWASHI-ZUKI (ma-wash'ee zoo'kee) *Jp.* "roundhouse punch" A karate punch whose delivery from the hip is characterized by a three-quarter rotation of the striking fist in a wide circular motion. This technique is applied with a twisting movement of the hip for maximum efficiency.

MECHANICAL (EP) Refers to those whose movements are very staccato in appearance; a sequence of movements that appear as if they are being done by the numbers.

MEIJIN (may'jeen) *Jp.* "expert" One who has mastered an art far beyond the boundaries of physical prowess. One becomes a meijin only after experiencing infinitely painstaking discipline.

MEKUGI (meh-koo'ghee) *Jp.* A bamboo pin used to secure the handle of a samurai sword to the blade.

MEN (men) *Jp.* 1. The head protector used in kendo. It is composed of a nickel steel grill set in cotton headgear heavily padded to absorb the blows received from the shinai (bamboo sword). 2. A scoring point on top of the head. Cuts must be made in an area within 45 degrees of either side of the center line. The area is roughly marked by the cords holding the men in place.

MENKYO-KAIDEN (men'kyoe keye'den) *Jp.* A certificate of full proficiency in a Japanese martial art, usually awarded to an advanced student deemed most suited to carry on the transmission of the art. A master customarily is issued only one menkyo-kaiden in a lifetime.

Men (Kendo Helmet)

MENUKI (mehn-oo-kee) *Jp.* Hilt ornaments of a samurai sword.

METHOD OF EXECUTION (EP) The manner in which a move is executed to produce maximum results. For example, several methods could be used to execute a punch: a direct course, a dipping path, a roundhouse, and so on.

MI (mee) *Jp.* The blade of a knife or sword.

MICARI-OBI (mee-ca-ree o-bee) *Jp.* In karate, a green belt, generally worn after at least nine months of training.

MIDDLE A term often used to refer to the bodily area encompassing the stomach to the neck. Known in Japanese as chudan and in Korean as kaunde.

MIDDLE-FINGER ONE-KNUCKLE FIST A clenched-fist karate technique whereby the second knuckle of the middle finger is extended and used as a striking point. Known in Japanese as ippon nukite.

MIDDLE LINES The positional coordinates located below the shoulders and above the waist.

MIGI (mee'gee) *Jp.* "right" or "right side."

MIGI-ATO-SUMI (mee'gee a'toh soo'mee) *Jp.* "right rear corner" One of the eight directions of unbalance in judo.

MIGI-JIGO-TAI (mee'gee jee'goh teye) *Jp.* "right defensive posture" A judo stance in which the body is lowered with the right foot slightly forward and prepared for an attack.

MIGI-KUZUSHI: See KUZUSHI.

MIGI-MAE-SUMI-KUZUSHI: See KUZUSHI.

MIGI-SHIZENTAI (mee'gee shee'zehn-teye) *Jp.* "right natural position" A judo position in which the body is relaxed and the right foot is placed approximately twelve inches forward.

MIGI-USHIRO-SUMI-KUZUSHI: See KUZUSHI.

MIKAZUKI-GERI: See CRESCENT KICK.

MIKAZUKI-GERI-UKE: See CRESCENT-KICK BLOCK.

MI-KUDAKI (mee koo-dak'ee) *Jp.* "body smashing" The fifteenth judo technique of koshiki-no-kata.

MIKULGI (mee-kul-gee) *Kr.* "sliding" A tae kwon do method of dodging by sliding the feet along the ground. It is effective in covering long distances smoothly.

MINOR MOVES (EP) Subordinate moves that, although not devastating, cause ample damage and delay to allow the execution of a major strike, blow, or kick; moves which are weak but effectively used to set up an opponent.

MIRO MARKI (mee'row mar'key) *Kr.* "pushing block" A tae kwon do block in which the palm or double forearm is used to unbalance an attacker. Known also as miro makgi.

MIT-CHOOMUK (mit choo-muk) *Kr.* "bottom fist" The bottom of the clenched fist used as a striking point in tae kwon do.

MI TSUNG-I *Ch.* "labyrinthine art" A highly deceptive method of kung-fu brought to acclaim by Huo Yuan-Chia, featuring rapid, baffling turns and attacks.

This intricate and seemingly confusing style is also known as Yen Ching Ch'uan, after the figure Yen Ching in a famous Chinese novel, and the Lost Track system of kung-fu. It stems from Chang County, a district noted for producing exquisite kung-fu styles and masters. Huo Yan Chia, the style's foremost practitioner, founded the Ching Wu Athletic Association in Shanghai, which many consider one of the most influential kung-fu organizations in China.

MIZUGUMO (mee-zoo-goo-moh) *Jp.* "water spider" A water-crossing device composed of four carved pieces of wood fastened together to form a circle with a hole in the middle. A rectangular piece of wood, the length of the foot, is secured to the center with a cord attached to the circle. The person using this device strapped her or his feet to the rectangular piece and proceeded to walk across water. The mizugomo was used by the Japanese ninja.

MIZU-GURUMA (mee'zoo gu-roo'ma) *Jp.* "water wheel" The fourth judo technique of koshiki-no-kata.

MIZU-IRI (mee-zoo ee-ree) *Jp.* "water plunging" The seventeenth judo technique of koshiki-no-kata.

MIZUKAKI (mee-zoo-ka'kee) *Jp.* A weblike device placed on the feet during swimming, similar to present-day flippers. It was used by the Japanese ninja.

MIZU-NAGARE (mee-zoo na-ga-reh) *Jp.* "water flowing" The fifth judo technique of koshiki-no-kata.

MIZU NO KOKORO (mee'zoo noh koh'koh-roh) *Jp.* "mind like water" A psychological principle of the martial arts emphasizing the need to calm the mind, much like the surface of undisturbed water, while facing an opponent.

MOA SOGI (moh-a soh-gee) *Kr.* "close stance" A basic tae kwon do stance assumed with the feet together.

MODIFIED HORSE STANCE A karate position similar to the horse stance except the feet are placed at 45-degree angles.

MODOTTE (moh-doh-teh) *Jp.* A command for returning to the original position, used in competition.

MOK-GAR *Ch.* A Cantonese surname representative of a basic southern style of kung-fu. Known as mo-jiya in Mandarin.

MOKPYO (mak'pyoh) *Kr.* "striking point" or "target" In tae kwon do, weak areas of the body that can be effectively struck or kicked.

MOKUJU (moh-koo'joo) *Jp.* The wooden rifle and simulated bayonet used in juken-do (way of the bayonet).

MOKUSOH (mohk-soh') *Jp.* "quiet thought" A quiet form of meditation usually performed before and after a training session in the Japanese martial arts. It is done to achieve mental and physical tranquility.

MOMCHAU MAKGI (ma-choh ma'gee) *Kr.* "checking block" A tae kwon do block in which one forearm is placed inside the other forearm to defend against a strong attack, usually spinning kicks.

MOMDOLLYO-CHAGI: See BANDAE DOLLYO CHAGI.

Mon-Fat-Jong

MOMENTARY CONDITIONING (EP) The ability to condition one's opponent to think one way, only to reverse the conditioned reflex so as to set him or her up for an attack.

MON-FAT-JONG *Ch.* "multi-technique device" A kung-fu training device, resembling a human figure including a spring-mounted head and extensions representing arms. A single improvised "knee" extends from the base of the torso. All of the striking areas are padded and the device allows the student to practice any type of punching, striking, blocking, or kicking technique.

MONKEY One of the five animals whose movements composed the basis of Hua To's exercises.

MONKEY STYLE A form of kung-fu known in Chinese as tai-sing-pek-kwar. In this style, the practitioner imitates the movements of the monkey and practices light, agile, deceptive techniques. There are numerous variations of the style: lost monkey, drunken monkey, tall monkey, stone monkey, and wood monkey.

MOO DUK KWAN (moo'du-kwon) *Kr.* "Institute of Military Virtue" A style of Korean martial arts similar to tae kwon do.

MOON-MOO (moon moo) *Kr.* A tae kwon do hyung.

MOOREUP (moo'rup) *Kr.* "knee" Part of the body used for short-range fighting in tae kwon do.

MOROASHI-DACHI (moh-roh-a-shee da-chee) *Jp.* "one-foot-forward stance" See also FORWARD STANCE.

MOROTE (moh-roh-teh) *Jp.* "double" or "two-handed" A term synonymous with the use of two hands to perform a certain technique, e. g., morote seoi-nage (two-handed shoulder throw).

MOROTE-GARI (moh-roh-teh ga-ree) *Jp.* "two-handed reap" A judo throw to the rear executed by clasping an opponent's legs with both hands; a tackle.

MOROTE-JIME (moh-roh-teh jee-meh) *Jp.* The two-handed necklock in judo.

MOROTE-SEOI-NAGE (moh-roh-teh seh-oy na-geh) *Jp.* "two-handed shoulder throw" See SEOI-NAGE.

MOROTE-SUKUI-UKE (moh-roh-teh soo-koo-ee oo-keh) *Jp.* "two-handed scooping block" A karate blocking technique used against a kick in which the attacker's kick is scooped up.

MOROTE-TSUKAMI-UKE (moh-roh-teh tska-mee oo-keh) *Jp.* "two-handed grasping block" A karate blocking technique used against a punch.

MOROTE-UKE (moh-roh-teh oo-keh) *Jp.* "double forearm block" or "augmented forearm block" A karate block against a hand attack in which the opposite fist is placed close to the elbow of the blocking forearm.

MOROTE-ZUKI (moh-roh-teh zoo-kee) *Jp.* "double fist punch" A karate punching technique in which both hands punch simultaneously.

MO-SEOGI (moh soh-gee) *Kr.* A tae kwon do preparatory stance in which the feet are spread apart and one foot is placed forward.

Morote-Uke

MOTONOICHI (moh-toh-noh-ee-chee) *Jp.* "return to original position" A command used by a referee during a karate match.

MU (moo) *Jp.* "nothing" The Zen nothingness or emptiness. This principle is often used in the Japanese martial arts to make one clear the mind of all thought so the body will respond instantly to any situation.

MUAY THAI See KICK-BOXING.

MUDANSHA (moo-dan'shuh) *Jp.* "one without grade" A martial arts student who has not yet attained the rank of black belt. See KYU.

MUI-FA-JEONG *Ch.* "plum flower stumps" A series of tree stumps driven into the ground on top of which certain styles practice kung-fu, chiefly Hop-Gar and white crane.

MULTIPLE ATTACK (EP) An attack by two or more opponents.

MUNE (moo'neh) *Jp.* "chest" or "abdomen" A target area used in early days of kendo competition. Recently (1978) the International Kendo

Federation reinstated the mune target area if the attacker is using the jodan kamae.

MUNE-ATE (moo-neh a-teh) *Jp.* The early name for the chest protector used in kendo. Today it is called a do.

MUNE-OSHI (moo-neh oh-shee) *Jp.* "chest press" A judo self-defense technique, the twelfth of ju-no-kata.

MUSUBI-DACHI (mu-soo'bee da'chee) *Jp.* "informal attention stance" A preparatory karate stance assumed with the heels held together and the toes open about 45 degrees.

MUTE-UKEMI (moo'teh oo-kehm'ee) *Jp.* The judo breakfall without the use of the hands.

MUTON (mu-tan) *Phil.* The short sticks used in armis, usually about three feet in length.

MYUNG CHI (myoong chee') *Kr.* "solar plexus."

NACHUGI (na-choo-gee) *Kr.* A tae kwon do method of towering the body to evade a flying kick.

NAERYO JIREUGI: See DOWNWARD PUNCH.

NAERYO MARKI: See DOWNWARD BLOCK.

NAFUDAKAKE (na-foo-da-ka-keh) *Jp.* The name board posted in the dojo to show the names and seniority of the members.

NAGASHI-UKE See SWEEPING BLOCK.

NAGASHI-ZUKI: See FLOWING PUNCH.

NAGE-NO-KATA (na-gay noh ka'ta) *Jp.* "forms of throwing" The first judo kata composing fifteen throws divided into five sets of three techniques each. These techniques were selected as the ideal model to aid the study of the theory of throwing methods.

First Series: *Te-Waza (Hand Techniques)*

1. uki-otoshi (floating drop)
2. seoi-nage (shoulder throw)
3. kata-guruma (shoulder wheel)

Second Series: *Koshi-Waza (Hip Techniques)*

4. uki-goshi (floating hip throw)
5. harai-goshi (sweeping hip throw)
6. tsuri-komi-goshi (lifting hip throw)

Third Series: *Ashi-Waza (Leg and Foot Techniques)*

7. okuri-ashi-harai (sweeping ankle throw).
8. sasae-tsuri-komi-ashi (propping drawing ankle throw)
9. uchi-mata (inner thigh throw)

Fourth Series: *Ma-Sutemi-Waza (Sacrifice Techniques)*

10. tomoe-nage (stomach throw)
11. ura-nage (rear throw)
12. sumi-gaeshi (corner throw)

Fifth Series: *Yoko-Sutemi-Waza (Side Sacrifice Techniques)*

13. yoko-gake (side body drop)
14. yoko-guruma (side wheel throw)
15. uki-waza (floating techniques)

NAGE-WAZA (naw'gay wa'za) *Jp.* "throwing techniques" One of the three basic categories into which judo and aikido can be subdivided.

Naginata

NAGINATA (na-ghee-na'ta) *Jp.* "reaping sword" A curved-blade spear, once used by Japanese monks and samurai. It is approximately seven feet long including the blade, which is two to three feet in length. The butt end was used as well. The naginata was used with a circular action to deliver slashes to all portions of the enemy's body, and because of its length was extremely effective against a sword-bearing opponent including those on horseback. Many women of the samurai class became adept at the use of this weapon during the Edo period. (1600–1808).

NAGINATA-DO (na-ghee-na'ta doh) *Jp.* "way of the reaping sword" The art of using a wooden naginata, practiced mostly by women both as a form of physical education and a sport. The sport naginata is a six and one-half-foot pole including a bamboo blade, almost two feet long, attached to one end. Contestants wear protective equipment which is virtually the same as that used in kendo. Points are scored for cuts to the top of the head, the forearms, trunk, or shins. A thrusting attack to the throat can also score a point. Matches between a woman with the naginata and a man with a sword also occur.

NAGINATA-JUTSU (na-ghee-na'ta jut'soo) *Jp.* "art of the long sword" A weapons art practiced almost exclusively by the women of the Japanese samurai class. It has been replaced today by naginata-do, a sport-oriented version of this combat form.

NAGINATAKA (na-ghee-na-ta'ka) *Jp.* A naginata practitioner.

NAHA-TE (na'ha tay) *Okinawan.* "Naha hand" One of the three original Okinawan karate schools whose name derives from the capital city of Okinawa where it was created. It is the forerunner of one branch of shorin-ryu karate.

NAIFANCHIN; NAIHANCHI (neye fan'cheen; neye'han'chee) *Jp.* The Okinawan name for a series of karate kata using lateral footwork only. These kata were designed to protect one strictly from frontal attacks, since they are performed as if the practitioner's back were close to a wall. They are known as tekki (horse riding) in numerous styles of Japanese karate, most notably Shotokan.

NAIWAN (neye-wan') *Jp.* "inner arm" Part of the forearm located on the same side as the thumb; often used in karate blocking techniques.

NAJUNDE (na-joon'da) *Kr.* "low" A tae kwon do term used to refer to the lower area of the body.

NAKADAKA-IPPON-KEN (na-ka-da-ka eep-pohn ken) *Jp.* "middle-finger one-knuckle fist" Also known as nakadaka-ken, a fist formed with the middle joint of the middle finger protruding slightly. It is used in karate to attack the bridge of the nose and the ribcage.

NAKAGO (na-ka'goh) *Jp.* The tang; that portion of a sword blade to which the hilt is attached.

NAMI-ASHI (na'mee a'shee) *Jp.* "inside snapping block" A karate blocking technique in which the foot is used to deflect attacks to the groin or to avoid stamping attacks to the leg.

NAMI-JUJI-JIME (na-mee joo-jee jee-may) *Jp.* "natural cross choke" A judo choke in which the arms are crossed and the opponent's collar is gripped with both hands.

NANAMI-UCHI (na-na'mee-oo'chee) *Jp.* "slanting strike" A judo self-defense technique. The eighth technique of ju-no-kata.

NAOTTE (na-oht-teh) *Jp.* A command to be at ease or to relax.

NARANDE (na-ra-n-deh) *Jp.* A command to line up.

NARANI SOGI (na-ra'nee soh'gee) *Kr.* "parallel stance" A preparatory stance of tae kwon do in which the feet are placed parallel and the heels are approximately a shoulder-width apart.

NATURAL WEAPONS(EP) Parts of the anatomy used as offensive weapons, including parts of the hand, arm, foot, leg, and so on.

NAWANUKE NO JITSU (na-wa-noo-keh noh jee-tsu) *Jp.* A method of escaping from bonds by dislocation of one's own joints. This method was extensively practiced by the Japanese ninja.

NECKLOCK A word usually used in judo for choking techniques.

NEI-CHIA *Ch.* "internal school" An encompassing term for kung-fu styles in which yielding is the most important characteristic. Such styles include t'ai-chi ch'uan, pa-kua, and hsing'yi.

NEIKYA (nay'kya) *Kr.* An advanced system of combat developed from Korean kwonbop.

NEKO-ASHI-DACHI; NEKO-DACHI (nay-koh a-shee da-chee; nay-koh da-chee) *Jp.* "cat stance" A karate position in which most of the body weight is placed on the rear foot and merely the ball of the extended front foot touches the ground.

NEN-RYU: See CHUJO-RYU.

NERVE CENTERS Pressure points of the body that, when attacked, cause a great deal of pain.

NET *Kr.* "four."

NEUTRALIZED HANDS (EP) The positioning of one's hand(s) in a neutral area for maximum availability in nullifying an attack, or for use in rendering a more successful attack.

NEUTRAL RANGE The distance between two opponents at which neither fighter can reach the other with a kick or punch.

NE-WAZA (neh wa'za) *Jp.* "ground techniques," "groundwork," or "grappling techniques" The collective name for judo techniques per-

Neko-Ashi-Dachi

formed while both fighters are on the ground. Often referred to as matwork or holddowns. See also GRAPPLING TECHNIQUES.

NI (nee) *Jp.* "two" or "second."

NIDAN (nee'dan) *Jp.* "second rank" Second-degree black belt in the Japanese martial disciplines.

NIHON NUKITE (nee'hohn noo'kee'tay) *Jp.* "two-finger spear hand" A karate technique in which the tips of the first two fingers are used to attack more vulnerable areas such as the eyes.

NIHON SEOI-NAGE (nee-hohn say-oy na-geh) *Jp.* "two-arm shoulder throw" A judo hand throw often referred to by judoka as the morote-seoi.

NIKYU (nee'kyoo) *Jp.* "second class" Two steps below black belt in the Japanese martial disciplines. Usually represented by a brown belt.

NINJA (nin'ja) *Jp.* "stealer in" or "spy" Japanese warriors hired as spies, assassins, and terrorists in feudal Japan. The ninja sold their clandestine services to the great and small lords of Japan when certain disreputable tasks had to be undertaken. The ninja families worked for the highest bidder and owed allegiance to no one.

Flourishing between the 13th and 17th centuries, the ninja became legends in their time, capable of performing astonishing feats. They developed ninjutsu (art of stealing in) which incorporated all the existing martial skills like swordsmanship, archery, spearmanship, stick fighting, and unarmed combat. They also mastered specialty weapons such as dirks, darts, daggers, star-shaped throwing knives, caltrops, brass knuckles, smoke bombs, and various poisons. They became adept at an unusual degree of muscular control enabling them to perform such feats as scaling walls and remaining under water for several minutes.

Out of necessity, ninja were great escape artists. They could dislocate their joints and slip out of the most complicated knots. They were equally skilled at camouflage and could blend in with their immediate surroundings so well that many regarded them as "invisible." Because of this talent, ninjutsu has commonly been called the "art of invisibility."

Ninja were impeccable actors and masters of disguise. They could appear as priests, carpenters, soldiers, or courtesans and switch roles almost instantly as necessity dictated. Since most missions were carried out at night the ninja outfit was normally black, but occasionally green or white was worn to blend in with foliage or snow.

Ninja

A ninja was an expert survivalist who could cook, prepare medicines, explosives, and any other necessities for survival.

One was born a ninja and died one. Since secrecy was imperative few ninja achieved renown. A ninja on the verge of capture usually committed suicide rather than face torture.

NIPPON-DEN KODOKAN JUDO (nee-pohn dehn koh-doh-kan joo-doh) *Jp.* The full name of Jigoro Kano's judo, which is almost never used today.

NIPPON KEMPO (neep-pohn kehm-po) *Jp.* A combination of several martial practices including judo, karate, and aikido. It consists of strikes, kicks, throws, and body locks. During practice, protective gear is worn since full contact is encouraged.

NISHI KEN (nee-shee ken') *Jp.* "split fingers" See TWO-FINGER SPEAR HAND.

NIUNJA-SOGI: See L-STANCE.

NOGARE (noh-ga'ray) *Jp.* A style of breathing used in karate that advocates proper breath control even in the face of danger.

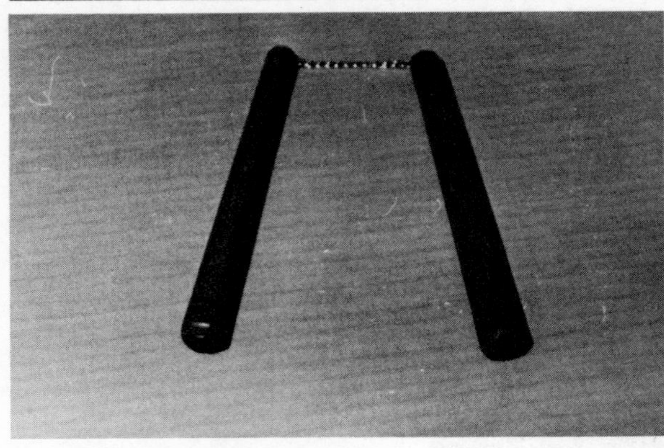

Nunchaku

NON-CONTACT KARATE A type of karate competition in which the players are permitted to make only light contact to the body with the various blows but are forbidden to strike the face. This restriction is most particularly necessary to prevent injuries among beginners. Non-contact is most widely practiced among traditional Japanese karate stylists. See LIGHT CONTACT.

NOOLLO CHAGI (nool-loh cha-gee) *Kr.* "pressing kick" An encompassing term for tae kwon do kicks directed to the knee and calf.

NOOLLO MAKGI (nool-loh ma-gee) *Kr.* "pressing block" A tae kwon do block used against low-line attacks.

NOPUNDE (noh-pun'day) *Kr.* "high" A tae kwon do term used to represent the upper part of the body.

NOPUNDE MAKGI (noh-pun'day ma-gee) *Kr.* "high block" A tae kwon do block in which the blocking hand reaches the defender's eye level. It can be delivered with many different parts of the hand: the palm, fist, forearm, backhand, and so forth.

NORTHERN STYLES A name given to kung-fu systems developed in northern China. These styles usually emphasize kicking techniques and gymnastic-type movements.

NUKI-KAKE: See KIME-NO-KATA.

NUKITE (noo'kee-tay) *Jp.* "spear hand."

NUNCHAKU (nun-cha'koo) *Jp.* "wooden flail" An Okinawan rice thresher made of two unequal lengths of hardwood hinged together by a cord originally made of hair, either human or horse. During the Japanese occupation of the Ryukyu Islands, the nunchaku developed as one of the five systematized weapons of Okinawa that were used in conjunction with empty-hand fighting arts. The modern nunchaku is made with both sticks the same length. Lighter woods and even plastic have replaced the heavy red oak and nylon cords or swivel-mounted chains are used in place of hair.

The nunchaku can be swung with tremendous velocity in a wide variety of patterns and can thus deliver devastating blows. It can also be used to block or parry an attack or as a thrusting weapon, and the cord can be used to choke or catch an opponent's wrist and apply severe pressure to immobilize and bring about a submission.

NUNTE (nun'teh) *Jp.* A weapon similar in shape and size to the sai except that one prong points toward the bearer and the other projects outward. The central shaft extends on both ends beyond the point where the prongs are connected. The nunte, a weapon developed by Okinawan farmers, is usually placed on the end of the bo or long staff.

O (oh) *Jp.* "major," "big," or "great."

OBI (oh'bee) *Jp.* "belt" In many of the Japanese martial arts, the color of the belt worn around a practitioner's waist denotes rank.

OBI-OTOSHI (oh'bee oh-toh'shee) *Jp.* "belt drop" A devastating judo technique in which it is possible to reduce an opponent to unconsciousness with the impact of the head and body against the mat. This technique is seldom used in competition.

OBI-SEOI (oh-bee seh-oi) *Jp.* "belt shoulder throw" A judo throw and variation of seoi-nage in which the loose ends of the opponent's belt is used to lift the opponent onto the shoulders and then throw him.

OBI-TORI (oh-bee toh'ree) *Jp.* "belt seizure" The eleventh judo technique of ju-no-kata.

ODACHI (oh-da'chee) *Jp.* "great sword" or "oversized sword" See TACHI.

OFFENSE Any act of attacking.

OFFENSIVE CHECK (EP) A single move which first acts as a check before becoming a strike or hit.

OGOSHI (oh-goh/vshee) *Jp.* "major hip throw" One of the most basic throws of judo, chiefly used to teach students how to develop full hip movement in their early training. It is done by grasping the opponent around the hip with one hand, then turning while throwing the opponent over one's own hip.

OGURUMA (oh-goo-roo'ma) *Jp.* "major wheel" A judo leg throw in which the opponent is thrown over the extended feet placed across the front of the opponent's body just below the abdomen.

OH (oh) *Kr.* "fifth" or "five."

OHDAN (oh'dan) *Kr.* "fifth rank" The fifth-degree black belt in tae kwon do.

OHGUP (oh'gup) *Kr.* "fifth class" A green belt in tae kwon do.

OI-ZUKI: See LUNGE PUNCH.

OKINAWA GOJU-RYU A form of unarmed combat related to Japanese goju-ryu karate. The present-day masters of both styles studied with Okinawan karate master, Chojun Miyagi, founder of goju-ryu.

OKINAWA KEMPO A spinoff style of Chinese kempo.

Ogoshi

OKINAWA-TE (oh-kee-na-wa teh) *Jp.* "Okinawa hand" The forerunner of modern karate. This style, native to Okinawa, was an early synthesis of several Chinese combatives introduced to the Ryukyu Islands by visiting Chinese monks and government officials.

OKURI-ASHI-HARAI (oh-koo-ree a-shee ha-reye) *Jp.* "sweeping ankle throw" The seventh judo technique of nage-no-kata. In this technique, the opponent is thrown by sweeping his foot out from under him as he steps forward. See also ASHI-WAZA.

OKURI-ERI-JIME (oh-koo-ree eh-ree jee-meh) *Jp.* "sliding collar choke" A popular judo choke in which both hands are clamped on an opponent's lapel to apply a choke by drawing the gi across the windpipe and/or carotid artery. It is the eighth technique of katame-no-kata.

OMGYO DIDIGI (om'gyo di-di-ghee) *Kr.* "stepping" A tae kwon do term for movements covering long distances.

OMGYO MIKULGI (om'gyoh mee-cool'ghee) *Kr.* "step-sliding" A form of tae kwon do footwork.

OMOTE (oh-moh'tay) *Jp.* "front."

ONE-ARM SHOULDER THROW: See IPPON-SEOI-NAGE.

ONE FINGER A purported Chinese training method in which the forefinger is repeatedly struck against an iron bell until, through this practice, one can supposedly cause serious injury or death to anyone at whom one points.

ONE-FINGER SPEAR HAND A karate hand technique employing the tip of the extended forefinger as the striking point. Known in Japanese as ippon-nukite.

ONE HUNDRED EIGHT DUMMIES One hundred and eight wooden dummies erroneously reputed to be constructed in a hallway of the Shaolin Temple for the purpose of testing a graduate's skill in the martial arts. Students who failed the test remained in the temple until they were able to pass the test.

ONE-KNUCKLE FIST A karate hand technique in which the second knuckle of the forefinger is extended and employed as the striking point. Known in Japanese as ippon-ken.

ONE-LEG STANCE A karate position in which the body is supported on one foot while the other is placed behind the knee, usually in conjunction with a low-line block. It is often referred to as the crane stance.

ONE POINT 1. The center of ki believed to be located within the abdomen, approximately two inches below the navel. Known in Japanese as tanden or seika tanden. 2. A score awarded in many different types of martial arts contests when a player has successfully executed a technique against his opponent. Known in Japanese as ippon.

ONE-STEPS A method of practicing martial arts techniques where one step is taken and then a technique is delivered.

ONE-STEP SPARRING In karate, a method of prearranged practice fighting in which the designated attacker takes one step forward to deliver a single technique, and the designated defender blocks and immediately counters. Known in Japanese as ippon kumite and in Korean as ilbo daeryon.

ONI KEN (oh'nee kehn) *Jp.* "extended-knuckle fist."

OPEN-HAND TECHNIQUES Those offensive and defensive martial arts techniques executed with the fingers partially or fully extended. When any of the fingers meet the palm, the fist is in some way clenched and the technique can no longer be categorized as open-hand.

OPEN-LEG STANCE: See HACHIJI-DACHI.

OPPOSING FORCE (EP) Two forces going in opposite directions from each other.

ORANGE BELT The color of a belt worn in the beginning level of karate or tae kwon do study; approximately seventh kyu or seventh gup.

OREI (oh-ray') *Jp.* "respect" or "etiquette" An expression of formal greeting in karate. The honorific prefix "o" assumes the meaning of thanks, appreciation, and remuneration. Rei means to bow or a salutation.

ORUN (oh'run) *Kr.* "right" A directional term used in the Korean martial arts.

OS (oos) *Jp.* "good morning," "request," "entreat," or "push ahead" A common greeting in Japanese karate circles, which holds many connotations, the most common being to push ahead or never give up.

OSAEKOMI (oh-sa-eh-koh-mee) *Jp.* "holding" A term used by a judo referee to denote that a holding technique is being applied. If the opponent is successfully held down for twenty-five seconds, a point is scored.

OSAEKOMI-TOKETA (oh-sa-eh-koh-mee toh-keh-ta) *Jp.* "hold is broken" A term used by a judo referee to denote that a holding technique has been broken.

OSAEKOMI-WAZA (oh-sa-eh-koh-mee wa-za) *Jp.* "holding technique" See OSAE-WAZA.

OSAE-UKE (oh-sa-eh oo-keh) *Jp.* "pressing block" A karate blocking technique in which the attacking arm is pressed downward with the open hand. It is used chiefly against attacks to the groin or solar plexus.

OSAE-WAZA (oh-sa-eh wa-za) *Jp.* "holding techniques" A collective name for immobilizing holds used in judo groundwork. Also called osaekomi-waza.

O-SENSEI (oh'sehn-say) *Jp.* "great teacher" The honorific prefix "o" attached to the word sensei (teacher) indicates respect and acknowledgment of the chief instructor of a system, even though other high-ranked teachers are present. In aikido this title refers only to the founder, Morihei Uyeshiba.

OSOTOGAKE (oh-soh-toh-ga'keh) *Jp.* "major outer dash" A judo leg technique in which the opponent's leg is hooked behind the knee. As the opponent becomes unbalanced, she or he is thrown backward.

OSOTOGARI (oh-soh-toh-ga'ree) *Jp.* "major outer reap" A judo leg technique in which the opponent is unbalanced to the rear while one leg is swept out from under her or him thus throwing the opponent backward.

OSOTOGURUMA (oh-soh-toh-goo-roo-ma) *Jp.* "major outer wheel" A judo throw in which both of the opponent's feet are swept out from behind, landing the opponent flat on her or his back.

OSOTOMAKIKOMI (oh-soh-toh-ma-ke-koh-mee) *Jp.* "major outer winding" A judo sacrifice throw.

Ouchi-Gari

OSOTO-OTOSHI (oh-soh'toh oh-toh'shee) *Jp.* "major outer drop" A judo leg throw in which the opponent is tossed backward.

OTOSHI (oh-toh-shee) *Jp.* "drop."

OTOSHI-EMPI-UCHI: See EMPI-UCHI.

OTOSHI-HIJI-ATE: See EMPI-UCHI.

OTOSHI-UKE: See DROPPING BLOCK.

OTSURI-GOSHI (oh-tsu-ree goh-shee) *Jp.* "major lifting hip throw" A judo throw of the hip category.

OUCHI-GARI (oh-oo-chee ga-ree) *Jp.* "major inner reap" A judo foot throw in which one foot is swept out from under an opponent in a circular sweeping motion.

OUCHI-MATA (oh-oo-chee ma-ta) *Jp.* "major inner thigh throw" See UCHIMATA.

OUTER RIM (EP) That imaginary oval within which defensive and/or offensive moves should be confined so as not to overextend or overcommit. Employing this principle reduces openings and the chances of being hit.

OUTSIDE BLOCK In karate, any block executed from outside the boundary of the body to the inside.

OVEREMPHASIS The act of exaggerating a technique to the point of unnaturalness.

OVEREXTENSION The act of extending a technique to the point where one's balance becomes unstable.

OVERHAND According to some karate styles, any hand technique performed where the hand is raised above the elbow.

OVERHAND FIST A clenched fist employing the back portion of the knuckles as the striking point. A technique common to the long-hand systems of kung-fu.

OVER-REACH (EP) To overextend oneself needlessly with a blow or kick; to reach above or beyond a certain point unnecessarily.

O-WAZA (oh-wa'za) *Jp.* "major technique" A judo technique requiring a large body movement.

OX-JAW HAND A karate blocking technique in which the outside edge of the palm heel is used to parry downward or laterally. It can be used as a striking point when delivered to the collar bone. Known in Japanese as the seiryuto; as a block it is called seiryuto-uke.

P

PACHIGI (pa-chee'gee) *Kr.* A Korean martial art in which the head is used to butt an opponent.

PAI-HAO-CH'UAN *Ch.* A kung-fu system based on the movements of the white crane: long swinging arms, acrobatic high kicks, and graceful mobility. It developed approximately five hundred years ago at a Tibetan monastery. According to legend, a lama priest observed a fight between a crane and an ape in which the crane neutralized its foe through the agility of its long legs, huge wings, pecking, and clawing. Known as pac hoc in Cantonese.

PAI SHIH *Ch.* A ceremony for a kung-fu novice denoting his acceptance as a disciple.

PAK HOC *Ch.* Another name for white crane boxing. See also PAI-HAO-CH'UAN.

PAK SAO *Ch.* A wing chun kung-fu exercise to develop control over reflex actions.

PA-KUA (ba-gwa) *Ch.* "eight trigrams" One of the three internal methods of kung-fu. Pa-kua is composed of various circling and linear postures named after and based on the movements of the snake, stork, dragon, hawk, lion, monkey, and bear, and has many of its roots in the *Book of Changes.*

PAL (pal) *Kr.* "eighth" or "eight."

PALDAN (pal'dan) *Kr.* "eighth rank" Eighth-degree black belt in the Korean marital arts.

PALGUP (pal'goop) *Kr.* "eighth class" Gold belt, a beginner's level in tae kwon do.

PALKOOP: See ELBOW.

PALKUMCHI: See ELBOW.

PALM HEEL The heel or bottom part of the palm used in karate, both for attacking and defending. Known in Japanese as the teisho.

PALM HEEL BLOCK A karate blocking technique using the palm heel to block an opponent's forearm or leg. Known as the teisho-uke in Japanese. A combined palm heel block, also used in karate, has the heel of the palms placed together and thrust forward to block an opponent's kick. Known in Japanese as the teisho-awase-uke.

PALM-HEEL STRIKE A karate technique delivered with the heel of the hand in a thrusting motion, usually to the face or chin. Known in Japanese as the teisho-uchi.

PALMOK (pal'mohk) *Kr.* "forearm" or "wrist" Part of the body used for tae kwon do blocks.

PANKRATION (pan-kray'shun) *Greek* "game of all powers" An early Greek sport developed as a combination of earlier native forms of boxing and wrestling. Any technique except eye-gouging and biting was permitted. Kicking was common, and pankration is the first fighting discipline known to have devised methods of kicking and integrate them with blows of the fist and empty-hand strikes.

Pankration is the most well-documented fighting art of the pre-Christian era. It was introduced into the Olympic Games in 648 B.C., the same year as the horse race.

PARALLEL PUNCH A karate punch delivered with both fists simultaneously. Known in Japanese as the heiko-zuki.

PARRO *Kr.* "return" A tae kwon do command used in formal classes.

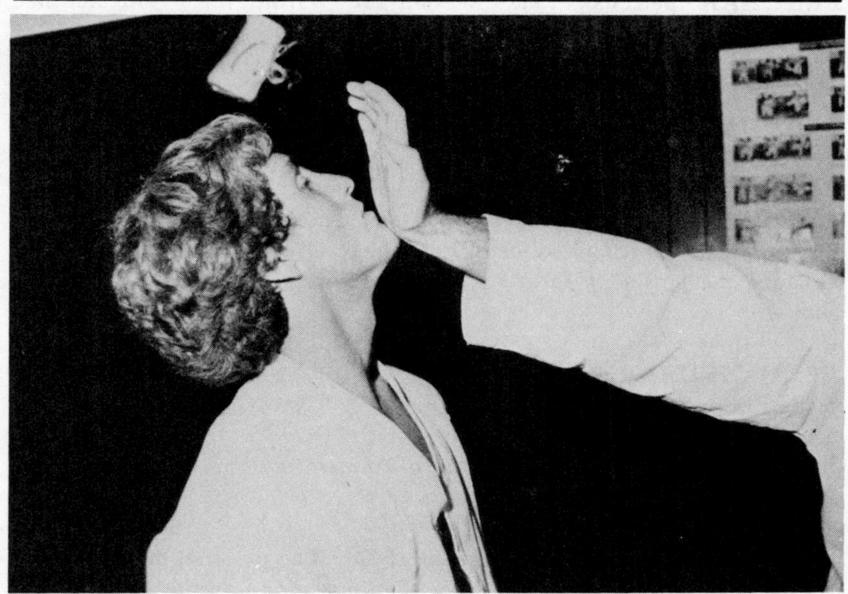

Palm-Heel Strike

PARRY To evade, ward off, or redirect the force of a blow or kick.

PASSAI: See BASSAI.

PAT MEI P'AI *Ch.* The white eyebrow style of kung-fu named after Pat Mei, a monk whose beard, hair, and eyebrows were strikingly white. This style, which is quite popular in southern China, is known as Bok Mei P'ai in Cantonese.

PAT-SAI (pat-seye') *Jp.* "to breach" or "to go through fortifications" Another name for the bassai kata of karate. The full title is Matsumura Patsai. See also BASSAI.

PATTERN A series of prearranged offensive and defensive maneuvers executed against one or more imaginary attacking opponents. The word pattern is the English translation of the Korean word "hyung" and is common to tae kwon do. See also HYUNG; KATA.

PEICHIN (pay'cheen) *Jp.* An Okinawan feudal title bestowed on a samurai by a lord for distinguished services rendered.

PENCHAK (pen'chak) *Indo.* "evasion" or "warding off" An unarmed Indonesian art similar to a two-person dance. Because of its dancelike execution it is not always viewed strictly as a martial art.

PENDULUM/MOTION: See ITSUTSU-NO-KATA.

PENETRATION POINT (EP) That imaginary point beyond the intended target, which compels the attacker not to prematurely tense the punch, kick, strike, and so forth. Fulfillment of this principle will greatly enhance the power of an attack and therefore cause greater damage or shock.

PENG CH'UAN *Ch.* "crushing fist" One of the five basic techniques of hsing-i kung-fu.

PENTJAK (pent-jaak) *Indo.* One of numerous terms used to indicate Indonesian unarmed combat.

PENTJAK-SILAT (pent-jaak se-lat) *Indo.* The national martial arts of Indonesia. It encompasses the study of empty-hand fighting as well as the use of numerous weapons such as the blade, staff, stick, and projectile weapons. Much of pentjak-silat is practiced in the form of solo exercises similar to karate kata, and sometimes background music is used in training. There are many different styles of pentjak-silat, all with their own variations but similar basic concepts.

PERCUSSION A term used in aikido to designate other arts that advocate any form of strong physical contact.

PERIMETER Another name for critical distance, the area between opponents.

PHIHAGI *Kr.* "dodging" A tae kwon do method of evasive footwork.

PI CH'UAN *Ch.* "splitting fist" One of the five basic techniques of hysing-i kung-fu.

PIN (EP) 1. The pressing of joints or other key areas on an opponent's body to one's own body. This momentarily keeps an opponent stationary and prevents him or her from taking action. 2. A term used by judoka when referring to matwork or groundwork.

PINAN (pee'nan) *Jp.* "peaceful mind" A series of karate kata developed by Yasutsune Itosu in 1903 and first taught to Okinawan children when karate was incorporated into the public school system in Okinawa Prefecture. Known also as the ping-an or heian katas. See also HEIAN.

PING-AN: See PINAN.

PINNING CHECK (EP) A restraining vicelike move used to hinder an opponent from taking action.

PIVOT The act of swinging or turning the body while keeping the center of gravity fixed at a central point.

PIVOT POINT (EP) That point, spot, position, level, and so forth that various body parts use as an axis upon which to turn.

PLANNED REACTION (EP) A predetermined scheme for making an opponent respond prematurely, thus creating an opportune opening.

PLANTAR ARCH That part of the underfoot between the heel and the ball of the foot and used in executing many ankle throws, or foot sweeps.

PLUM BLOSSOM: See PRAYING MANTIS.

POINT OF ACTIVITY (EP) The center of action where attention should be focused.

POINT OF FOCUS In karate, any so-called pinpoint location of a striking point to which the entire force of the body is concentrated in conjunction with the execution of a technique.

POISON FINGER A kung-fu technique by which an opponent can reputedly be killed by the mere touch of a finger. No proof of this technique, or any variation, actually exists, but many kung-fu practitioners nevertheless believe it is possible.

POKE (EP) Refers to the thrusting of the tips or joints of the fingers to particular target areas on an opponent's body.

PON-GAI-NOON (pon-guy-noon') *Ch.* The Chinese counterpart of Okinawa's Uechi-ryu karate.

POOMSE: See HYUNG.

POSITION 1. A set or arranged posture. 2. A command used when teaching to have a student assume his original starting position.

POSTURE The position of the body in relation to the technique being executed.

PO-UN (poh-un') *Kr.* A tae kwon do hyung named after the Korean poet Chong Mong-Chu.

PRAYING MANTIS A style of kung-fu characterized by fierce grasping movements, clawing attacks, and punches. There are several variations of this style. Originating in the Shao-lin Temple, praying mantis branched out into several subsystems including the seven stars system, the plum blossom system, t'ai-chi-ch'uan, and so on.

PREARRANGED SPARRING In karate, a method of prearranged practice fighting in which both participants are aware of the intended attacks, blocks, and counters. Known in Japanese as yakusoku kumite and in Korean as yaksok daeryon.

PREMEDITATED COMMITMENT (EP) Purposeful moves pre-planned to be used in setting up an opponent.

PRESSING BLOCK In karate, a downward, pressing motion with the open hand to neutralize an opponent's low-line attack. Known in Japanese as the osae-uke and in Korean as noollo makgi.

PRESSURE POINTS Nerve centers located on various parts of the body and serving as primary target areas for most martial arts. These points include the temple, throat, solar plexus, kidneys, and so on.

PREVENTIVE MOTION (EP) Movements used to ward off attacks or to stabilize a particular body target when delivering a major move. These motions can be parries, light blocks, or even pushing moves. They can be used as the opponent delivers an attack or when the opponent is merely posed in position.

PRIMARY TECHNIQUES: See FIVE PRIMARY TECHNIQUES.

PROFESSIONAL KARATE The dual branch of American karate competition in which participants compete for financial rewards. While it tends to be confusing, pro karate flourishes in two forms: semi-contact and full-contact. The difference is that in the former, contestants restrain their blows and attempt to score points; in the latter, the objective, like boxing, is to render the opponent unconscious.

PROJECTION The act of bringing forth additional energy while performing martial arts kata or forms. Performers having this projection generate intense feeling in a stylish display, as if they are actually involved in a realistic fighting situation.

PROSECUTOR A police weapon which is a combination of the billy club and the Okinawan tonfa (rice grinder). See also TONFA.

PUKULAN (poh-ku-lan) *Indo.* One of numerous terms used to designate an Indonesian form of martial arts.

PUNCHING TECHNIQUES Any clenched-fist technique in which the force is transmitted in a straight line through the forearm to the striking point. Known in Japanese as tsuki and in Korean as jirugi.

PURPLE BELT The color of a belt usually worn in the intermediate level of study in some martial arts; usually it represents sixth kyu.

PUSH-DRAG (EP) Involves slightly raising the forward or rear leg as the opposite leg pushes the body forward or back before catching up to resume the original distance between feet. One of the three methods of shuffling in the martial arts.

PYRAMID THEORY The popular analysis that all martial arts, in early practice, are far removed from one another, but eventually reach a synonymous purpose or point, much like the symbol of the pyramid.

PYRRHIC An early Greek war dance depicting the motions of eluding blows and shots of every kind by various means of swerving, yielding ground, leaping, or crouching. The Pyrrhic was practiced to music in both armed and unarmed fashion, and was similar in content and form to modern karate katas.

PYUGI (pyoo'gee) *Kr.* "stretching."

Q R

QUANDO (kwan'doh) *Ch.* A large, heavy shafted weapon with an axelike cutting blade affixed to one end. Known as kwan tao in Mandarin.

RANDORI (ran-doh'ree) *Jp.* "free exercise" A judo term similar in meaning to free-sparring, in which two contestants practice throwing and grappling under the conditions of actual contest. Randori is also practiced in aikido where one person defends against any number of opponents in a fluid and continuous fashion, and is known as jiyu waza.

RANDORI-NO-KATA (ran-doh'ree noh ka'ta) *Jp.* "forms of free exercise" An overall judo term given to the nage-no-kata and the katame-no-kata.

RANDORI-WAZA (ran-doh'ree wa'za) *Jp.* "free exercise techniques" The free practice of throws and groundwork in judo, jujutsu, and aikido.

RANGE (EP) That distance existing between opponents.

RANK A term used in the martial arts to designate the level of proficiency one has achieved anywhere from white belt to tenth-degree black belt.

REACTIONARY SET-UP (EP) Having an opponent respond to a faked stimulus, thus creating vulnerability to one's attack.

READY STANCE A preparatory karate position assumed at the beginning or conclusion of training from which one waits for another command to continue or to stop.

REAP An action of the leg or foot to sweep away the legs or feet of an opponent in the execution of a throw. Known in Japanese as gari.

REAR CROSSOVER (EP) A type of maneuver involving the back foot crossing over and back of the forward leg, or the forward leg moving over and back of the rear leg. This form of footwork is applicable when moving forward or back.

REAR FOOT STANCE: See DWIT BAL SOGI.

REAR LOCK A judo technique of holding or immobilization used in groundwork.

RECOIL (EP) To spring back after a blow or kick has been delivered; a fast retrieve after delivery.

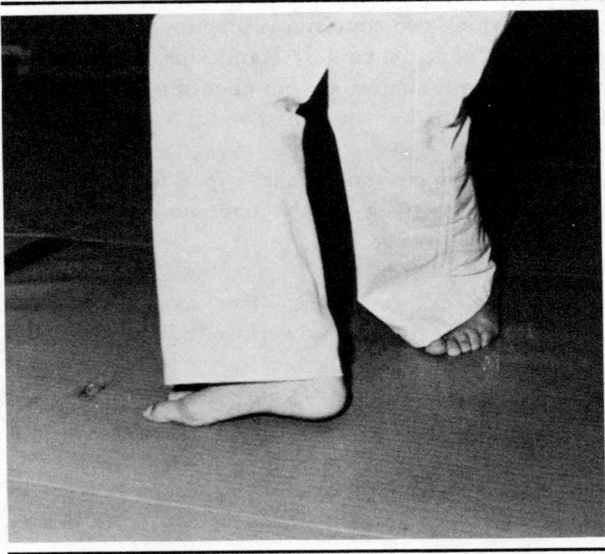

Rear Crossover

RED BELT 1. If maroon, the color of a belt worn by the recognized master of a certain martial arts system. It is usually awarded as an honorary degree after a lifetime of study and denotes tenth-degree black belt. In judo from the sixth dan to the eighth dan, the belt is white with red stripes while the ninth and tenth dan is all red. 2. If bright red, the color of a belt worn in the intermediate level of tae kwon do study directly before black belt. This belt encompasses the ranks of third, second, and first gup.

REFEREE In any martial arts contest, the chief official who oversees the actions of the contestants.

REFERENCE POINT (EP) That point of origin in a sequence that one can refer to before proceeding to the opposite side. The same sequence can then be executed on the opposite side. It also indicates the directing of attention to a particular point in a technique sequence.

REFLEX ACTION Designating an involuntary action to an attack. It is the ultimate aim in all martial arts to attain lightning reflex action against any type of attack so as to eliminate the momentary hesitation that accompanies the thinking process. See also SPONTANEITY.

REI (ray) *Jp.* A command to bow. Other expressions with rei are: Shomen ni rei (bow to the front); Sensei ni rei (bow to the teacher); and Otagai ni rei (bow to each other).

REIGISAHO (ray-gee-sa-hoh) *Jp.* "etiquette" The formal dojo customs and mannerisms indigenous to the Japanese martial arts and ways.

REINFORCED BLOCKS Blocking techniques used in karate in which one arm performs the actual blocking while the other supports it. Known also as augmented blocks.

RELAXED MOVES (EP) Moves that are completely relaxed in nature when used offensively or defensively. Tension, however, does come into play at the conclusion of these moves. Such moves become faster and more flexible, to the point where pain is lessened, and can easily be redirected to another target.

RENMEI (ren'may) *Jp.* A federation, league, or union of Japanese martial arts clubs.

RENOJI-DACHI: See L-STANCE.

RENRAKU-HENKA-WAZA (rehn-rah-koo hehn-ka wa-za) *Jp.* "combination techniques" The successive attacking by different judo methods against an opponent, whereby each preceding technique is a preparatory move to the following technique so that all attacks are connected. Combination techniques are also used by other Japanese martial arts.

RENRAKU-WAZA (rehn-ra'koo wa'za) *Jp.* "continuation techniques" A judo method of offense whereby a diversionary attack in a direction the opponent least expects is followed by a strong attack in another direction, thereby culminating in a victory.

RENSHI (rehn'shee) *Jp.* "polished expert" A Japanese martial arts teacher who is of fifth- to sixth-degree black belt rank, although not all such black belts are awarded this title. Renshi is one of several titles that include tashi (expert), kyoshi (teacher grade), and hanshi (master). One attaining this title is usually an assistant to a kyoshi.

RENSHU (ren'shoo) *Jp.* "practice" or "training period."

RENZOKU-WAZA (ren-zoh'coo waw'za) *Jp.* "continuous techniques."

RENZUKI (ren-zoo'key) *Jp.* "continuous attack."

REPETITION Something repeated such as a technique or combination. It is the key to reaching mechanical proficiency in the martial arts.

RESPONSE-HIT A counterattack coming in immediate response to an opponent's attack.

RETRACTION The act of drawing back a technique following execution, usually as rapidly as it was delivered.

REVERSE GRIP: See GYAKU-NI-TORU-TOKOTO.

REVERSE KNIFE HAND 1. A ridge hand. 2. An open-hand karate thrust executed in a backhand motion with the palm upward.

REVERSE PUNCH A punch executed by the hand opposite the forward leg. It is snapped forward in a torquing motion while the forward fist is retracted to the hip. Known in Japanese as the gyaku-zuki.

REVERSE ROUNDHOUSE KICK A karate kicking technique that

Reverse Punch

moves opposite to that of the roundhouse kick. Known in Japanese as the gyaku-mawashi-geri.

REVERSE SIDE The side of the body furthest from an opponent.

RIDGE HAND An open-hand karate technique delivered laterally with the thumb side of the hand as the striking point. It is sometimes referred to as a reverse knife hand. Known in Japanese as the haito.

RIGHT FRONT CORNER: See EIGHT DIRECTIONS OF UNBALANCE.

RIGHT REAR CORNER: See EIGHT DIRECTIONS OF UNBALANCE.

RIGHT SIDE: See EIGHT DIRECTIONS OF UNBALANCE.

RIKEN (ree'ken) *Jp.* "backfist."

RISING BLOCK: See UPWARD BLOCK.

RITSU DO: See KYUSHINDO.

RITSUREI (reet-suh-ray) *Jp.* "standing bow."

ROCHIN: See KOBU-JUTSU.

RO-HAI (roh'heye) *Jp.* "crane on a rock" An Okinawan shorin-ryu karate kata characterized by one-leg stances, symbolic of a crane standing on a rock. Also known as lohai or gankaku.

ROKKYU (roh'kyoo) *Jp.* "sixth class" A beginner's rank in the Japanese and Okinawan martial arts.

ROKU (roh'kuh) *Jp.* "six."

ROKUDAN (roh'koo-dan) *Jp.* "sixth rank" Sixth-degree black belt in the Japanese and Okinawan martial arts.

ROKUSHAKUBO (roh-koo-sha-koo'boh) *Jp.* "six-foot staff" A hardwood polelike weapon whose use is closely related to the movements of the Okinawa-te karate system.

ROLLING FALL A method of falling to the mat in which the person falling is thrown head over heels and then rolls smoothly up onto the feet again. It is used in judo and aikido. Known in Japanese as the zempo-ukemi. This is often also known as a rollout.

ROLLOUT: See ROLLING FALL.

ROOTED STANCE: See FUDO-DACHI.

ROUNDHOUSE KICK A karate kick in which the kicking foot is snapped outward in a motion from the knee, thereby acting as a pivot like that of a gate, to strike the intended target. In this motion the hip rotates forward to add power to the technique. Known in Japanese as the mawashi-geri and in Korean as the tolyo chagi.

ROUNDHOUSE PUNCH A karate punch that follows a circular path to its target.

ROUNDING THE CORNERS (EP) An expression when teaching to emphasize the importance of continuing a move so that a student does not abruptly stop one action in order to start another but makes a smooth transition. It is another method used to conserve time.

RYOGAN-TSUKI (ree-oh-gan tsu-kee) *Jp.* "both eyes poke" The fifteenth technique of ju-no-kata.

RYO-KATA-OSHI (ryoh ka'ta oh'shee) *Jp.* "both shoulders press down" The seventh technique of ju-no-kata.

RYO-KUHI (ryoh koo'heye) *Jp.* "strength dodging" The third judo technique of koshiki-no-kata.

RYOTE-DORI (ryoh'tay doh'ree) *Jp.* "both hands seizure" The third judo technique of ju-no-kata. When sitting, it is the first technique of kime-no-kata; when standing, the ninth of kime-no-kata.

RYU (ryoo) *Jp.* "way," "school," "style," or "method" A term used as a suffix after almost all styles of Japanese and Okinawan martial arts, e.g., Shito-ryu, goju-ryu, wado-ryu, Uechi-ryu, and so on. Ryu basically means a formalized martial tradition under an established teacher and school.

RYU-SETSU (ryoo seht'sue) *Jp.* "willow snow" The eighteenth judo technique of koshiki-no-kata.

RYUTOKEN: See DRAGON'S HEAD FIST.

Roundhouse Kick

S

SA (sa) *Kr.* "four."

SABOM (sa'bam) *Kr.* "teacher" or "instructor" A tae kwon do instructor. Known also as sabum, sah bom, sabumnim.

SABUM: See SABOM.

SABUMNIM: See SABOM.

SACRIFICE THROWS A system of judo throws in which one sacrifices the upright posture to bring down an opponent. These are performed with either the back or the side flat on the ground. Known in Japanese as the sutemi-waza.

SADAN (sa'dan) *Kr.* "fourth rank" Fourth-degree black belt in tae kwon do and the Korean martial arts.

SAFE-T-EQUIPMENT The trade name for foam rubber hand and foot pads used in karate and related martial arts. Invented by Jhoon Rhee of Washington, D.C., in 1972. Rhee's innovative equipment, introduced at the Top 10 National Karate Championships in 1973, brought about the creation of semi-contact karate competition and for the first time allowed fighters to make contact without fear of injury. Today, Safe-T-Equipment, of all types (rubber, leather, foam, etc.), is almost universally used throughout the United States both for semi-contact competition and as a training aid in martial arts studios.

SAGUP (sa'gup) *Kr.* "fourth class" An intermediate rank in tae kwon do.

SAH BOM : See SABOM.

SAI (seye) *Jp.* A pronged truncheon about fifteen to twenty inches long used as a defensive instrument against various weapons, specifically the sword and staff, as well as empty-hand attacks. It is believed to have originated from the pitchfork, and is one of the five systemized weapons developed by the early karate practitioners of Okinawa. It is practiced today as an extension of a black belt's training.

SAKA-OTOSHI (sa'ka oh-toh'shee) *Jp.* "headlong drop" The nineteenth judo technique of koshiki-no-kata.

SAKASU-JUJI-JIME (sa'ka-su joo'jee jee-may) *Jp.* "inverse cross necklock" A judo choking technique.

Salutation

SALUTATION A traditional greeting or paying of respects indigenous to the Chinese martial arts. It is generally performed by placing one clenched fist against the open palm of the opposite hand.

SAM (sam) 1. *Ch.* The traditional uniform of kung-fu. 2. *Kr.* "three" or "third."

SAMBO (sam'boh) *Russian* A compound word for samo-aborona bez oruzhia, or "self-defense without a weapon." It is the name of a Soviet martial art that bears a similarity to Japanese judo, in that it consists of throws, grips, and hold-downs. Trunks, sneakers, and a belted jacket are worn in sambo competition. Matches are won by the contestant who gains the most points in a given time period.

SAMBO DAERYON (sam'bo da'ryohn) *Kr.* "three-step sparring."

SAMDAN (sam'dan) *Kr.* "third rank" Third-degree black belt in tae kwon do.

SAMGUP (sam'gup) *Kr.* "third class" An intermediate rank in tae kwon do, three levels below chodan.

SAM-IL (sam'eel) *Kr.* A tae kwon do hyung consisting of thirty-three movements.

SAMPO-WAZA (sam'poh wa'za) *Jp.* "walking techniques" Okinawan karate techniques executed while simultaneously taking three steps forward.

SAMURAI (sam'uh-reye) *Jp.* "warrior" or "one who serves" The swordsmen of feudal Japan who were impeccably adept at a wide variety of martial practices, particularly the sword, and served a lord and fief. Strict rules and regulations were established for feudal lords and their samurai after A.D. 1600 under the Tokugawa shogunate. They regulated even the length of sword, type of dress, and manner of speech.

SAN (san) *Jp.* "three" or "friend" A formal Japanese title equivalent to the English titles Mr. and Ms. which is used as a suffix to a person's last name, i.e., Tanaka-san.

SANBON KUMITE (san'bohn koo'mee-tay) *Jp.* "three-step sparring" A method of prearranged karate practice fighting in which one partner attacks with three consecutive techniques while the opponent retreats and blocks each attack.

SAN CHIEH PANG: See THREE-SECTIONAL STAFF.

SANCHIN (san'cheen) *Jp.* A karate kata created by Okinawan karate master Chojun Miyagi, the founder of goju-ryu, which promulgates the hardness of his style by emphasizing forceful breathing and graduated dynamic tension. This concept postulates the ability to absorb shock and the so-called impenetrable guard.

SANCHIN-DACHI (san'cheen da'chee) *Jp.* "hour-glass stance" A basic karate stance in which the front foot is pointed inward at 45 degrees with the rear foot pointing forward. It is the primary stance used in the sanchin kata.

SANDAN (san'dan) *Jp.* "third rank" A third-degree black belt in the Japanese and Okinawan martial arts.

SANDAN MARKI: See UPWARD BLOCK.

SAND PALM A purported Chinese technique in which the hand is thrust repeatedly into sand until, through this practice, a mere gesture will upend an opponent.

SANDWICHING (EP) The striking of a target from both ends, greatly increasing the pressure and effect. This causes a vice-like effect since the target is not able to ride with any of the two striking forces. Here the principle of preventive motion is employed.

SANGDAN (sang'dan) *Kr.* "upper" or "upper level" A directional term used in tae kwon do.

SANGDAN MARKI: See UPWARD BLOCK.

SANGDAN KYOCHA MARKI: See UPWARD X BLOCK.

SANKAKU (san-ka'koo) *Jp.* A triangular leg position used when holding an opponent in judo groundwork. It is similar to a figure four.

SANKAKU-JIME (san'ka-koo jee'meh) *Jp.* "triangular necklock" A judo stranglehold in which the opponent's neck and one of his arms are squeezed together with the legs.

SANKAKUTAI (san-ka-koo-tai) *Jp.* "triangle shape" or "triangular formation" The geometric figure of stability and potential motion with the feet in a triangular position, practiced in aikido and other martial arts.

SANKUKAI (san'koo-keye) *Jp.* A style of karate based on a combination of many other systems. It was founded by Yoshinao Nanbu, and places great emphasis on escaping techniques and aikido-like defenses.

SANKYU (san'kyoo) *Jp.* "third class" First-degree brown belt in many Japanese and Okinawan martial arts; three steps below shodan.

SANREN-ZUKI (san'rehn zoo'kee) *Jp.* A karate practice method in which three consecutive punches are delivered straight forward from a stationary position.

SAN-SHOU (san su) *Ch.* "free fighting" One of the three stages of tai chi ch'uan.

SAPPO (sap-poh) *Jp.* A method of attacking vital points of the body in order to cause a coma or death.

SASAE-TSURI-KOMI-ASHI (sa-sa-eh tsu-ree koh-mee a-shee) *Jp.* "propping drawing ankle throw" A judo leg throw in which the opponent is thrown by a lifting, sweeping motion. It is the eighth technique of nage-no-kata.

SASAE-TSURI-KOMI-ASHI-HARAI (sa-sa-eh tsu-ree koh-mee a-shee har-eeye) *Jp.* "propping drawing ankle sweeping throw" A judo leg technique.

SASH A silk band worn around the waist to denote a level of skill or achievement in some styles of the Chinese martial arts.

SASUN SOGI See DIAGONAL STANCE.

SAVATE (sa-vat') *French* French hand and foot fighting. A method of fighting to the knockout once popular with the aristocracy of France. It is noted for its flamboyant kicking techniques, but is practiced by relatively few people today.

SAYA (sa′ya) *Jp.* The scabbard of a samurai sword.

SCARF That part of the judo jacket that encircles the neck and is used for chokes.

SCISSORS PUNCH: See HASAMI-ZUKI.

SCISSORS TECHNIQUE A method of attack in judo in which the legs are employed like scissors to squeeze the abdomen or chest of an opponent during groundwork.

SCOOPING BLOCK In karate, a scooping, circular motion with the open hand or fist to neutralize an opponent's attack.

SCOOPING THROW: See SUKUI-NAGE.

SECOND PUNCHING A term used in non- and semi-contact karate matches when a fighter strikes an opponent immediately after the opponent has already scored and the referee has intervened.

SEIKA TANDEN (say′ka tan′dehn) *Jp.* "lower abdomen."

SEIKEN (say′kehn) *Jp.* "forefist" The first knuckles of the index and middle fingers when clenched into a fist.

SEIKEN-ZUKI (say′kehn zoo′kee) *Jp.* "forefist punch" A straight punch using the forefist as the striking point, a technique common to many martial arts.

SEIKOTSU (say-koh′tsoo) *Jp.* The art of bone setting.

SEIPEI (say′pay) *Jp.* An advanced kata practiced in goju-ryu karate.

SEIRYOKU-ZEN-YO KOKUMIN-TAIIKU-NO-KATA (say-ryoh-koo zehn yoh koh-koo-meen teye-eekoo noh ka-ta) *Jp.* "The all-applied power building people's physical education form" Forms of natural physical education based on the principle of maximum efficiency. One of the katas of judo, it consists of various movements aiming at the harmonious development of the body while also practicing attack and defense maneuvers.

SEIRYUTO: See OX-JAW HAND.

Seiken

SEISAN (say'san) *Jp.* An Okinawan karate kata bearing the name of its founder. Seisan was the first kata taught by Okinawan karate masters prior to 1903 when Yasutsune Itosu taught in the public school system. Since then most karate schools have taught the pinan kata before moving into the classical ones. Some masters, however, still cling to tradition and teach this form first. See also HANGETSU.

SEISHIN (say'sheen) *Jp.* "mind," "soul," or "spirit."

SEITO (say'toh) *Jp.* "pupil" or "student."

SEIZA (say'za) *Jp.* "correct sitting" A full kneeling position used in many martial arts when performing the ceremonial bow or receiving formal instruction.

SE-JONG (say'johng) *Kr.* A tae kwon do hyung consisting of twenty-four movements and named after King Se-Jong.

SEKIZUI-WAZA (seh-kee-tsu-ee wa-za) *Jp.* "spine-locking techniques" An encompassing term for various immobilization techniques used in judo, strictly taught for self-defense and are forbidden in competition.

SEMI-CLASSICAL STYLE A term used in the United States and Europe when referring to karate styles that find their roots in the Orient, but which have deviated either philosophically or technically from the original system. Many American karate instructors fall into this category by having synthesized two or more styles to suit their needs and those of their students.

SEMI-CONTACT KARATE A term used to describe karate competition in which the contestants wear protective equipment on both hands and feet and are permitted to deliver controlled techniques with moderate contact. Overaggressive contact or a knockout blow leads to disqualification. This form of competition is the mid-step between non-contact and full-contact karate.

SEMI-FREE ONE-BLOW SPARRING A method of prearranged karate practice fighting in which both participants move freely about while the attacker delivers only a single technique and the defender blocks and immediately counters. Known in Japanese as jiyu-ippon-kumite.

SEMPAI (sehm'peye) *Jp.* "senior" A title usually given to senior level kyu (grade) holders, normally of brown belt rank, if no black belts are present. In many traditional karate schools, first-degree black belts are also called sempai or senior. Usually it denotes any senior by age, rank, position, or social standing. Used as a name in informal speech only.

SEN (sehn) *Jp.* Initiative in using mental faculties, technical skill, and physical power to defeat an opponent. It connotes a judo situation in which an opponent has attempted a technique unsuccessfully, and one executes successfully a countertechnique to either check or counterattack.

SEN-I (sehn-ee') *Jp.* "fighting will" or "fighting spirit."

SENSEI (sehn'say) *Jp.* "teacher" or "instructor" A term used in all Japanese and Okinawan martial arts.

SENSEI NI REI: See REI.

SENSEN-NO-SEN (sehn-sehn noh sehn) *Jp.* A judo term denoting correct anticipation of an opponent's intended move. In the split second between intention and action, one can take advantage of the opponent's preoccupation with the intended technique and execute one's own attack first. Known in kendo as debana waza.

SEOI-HANE-GOSHI (seh-oy ha-neh goh-shee) *Jp.* "shoulder spring hip throw" A judo hip technique.

SEOI-MAKIKOMI (seh-oy mah-kee-koh-mee) *Jp.* "winding shoulder throw" A judo hand technique.

SEOI-NAGE (seh-oy na-geh) *Jp.* "shoulder throw" A judo hand technique in which the opponent is tossed over the shoulder. There are two types of shoulder throws: ippon-seoi-nage (one-arm shoulder throw) and morote-seoi-nage (two-arm shoulder throw). Most judoka use the term seoi-nage when referring to the latter technique. Seoi-nage is the second technique of nage-no-kata.

SEPPA (seh-pah) *Jp.* The washers above and below the guard of a samurai sword.

SEPPUKU: See HARA-KIRI.

SET 1. *Kr.* "three." 2. (EP) Another term used to describe kata or form, a dancelike routine of offensive and defensive maneuvers.

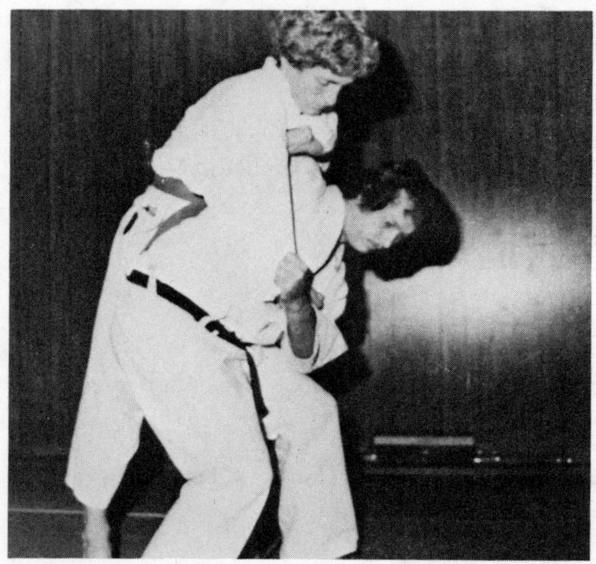

Seoi-Nage

SETTING The act of lowering the center of gravity while striking in order to enhance power.

SEVEN STARS: See PRAYING MANTIS.

SEWAO-JIREUGI: See VERTICAL PUNCH.

SEWO CHIRUGI (say'woe chee-rue'ghee) *Kr.* "vertical punch."

SHAO-LIN (shau-lin') *Ch.* "young forest" or "small forest" A method of kung-fu based on eight postures and five animal forms: the dragon, snake, tiger, crane, and leopard. It is the name of the famed Shao-lin Temple in the Hunan province of China.

SHEER (sheer) *Kr.* "at ease" A Korean command used in tae kwon do.

SHEJAK (shee'jak) *Kr.* "begin" A Korean command used in tae kwon do.

SHI (shee) *Jp.* "four."

SHIAI (shee'eye) *Jp.* "match" or "contest" A competitive match between Japanese martial artists.

SHIAIJO (shee-eye'joh) *Jp.* "contest area" The area where martial arts contests are conducted.

SHIB (shib) *Kr.* "tenth."

SHIBORI-WAZA (shee-boh'ree wa'za) *Jp.* "strangulation techniques" Another name for judo choking techniques.

SHIBUM (shee'bum) *Kr.* "demonstration."

SHICHI (shee'chee) *Jp.* "seven."

SHICHIDAN (shee'chee-dan) *Jp.* "seventh rank" Seventh-degree black belt in the Japanese and Okinawan martial arts.

SHICHIKYU (shee'chee-cue) *Jp.* "seventh class" A beginner's rank in some Japanese and Okinawan martial arts.

SHIDOGEIKO (shee-doh-gay-koh) *Jp.* "learning practice" A form of judo practice in which student and instructor train together, but often stop for discussion and to correct flaws in the student's technique.

SHIHAN (shee'han) *Jp.* "doctor," "master teacher," or "model teacher" A title representing a master in Japanese martial arts. Usually, these instructors are of very high rank, sixth-degree black belt and above, and some head their own styles or schools.

SHIHAP (shee'hap) *Kr.* "bout" or "match" A tae kwon do contest.

SHIHO-GATAME-KEI (shee-hoh ga-ta-mee kay) *Jp.* "four quarters locking system" One of the three systems into which the holding techniques of judo can be subdivided. In this system are classified all techniques in which the user is either on all fours or lying on the stomach in such a way as to maintain contact between the user's body and the opponent's chest and abdomen.

SHIKKO (shee'koh) *Jp.* "knee walking" A method of moving forward while keeping one knee constantly on the ground. Knee walking was originally a polite way of moving in a house, especially before a lord. It is commonly used in aikido training.

SHIKO-DACHI (shee'koh da'chee) *Jp.* A modified horse stance used in goju-ryu karate and in sumo wrestling. The principal difference between this and the conventional horse stance is that the feet are turned outward at a 45-degree angle.

SHIKORO-DORI See KOSHIKI-NO-KATA.

SHIKORO-GAESHI: See KOSHIKI-NO-KATA.

SHIME (shee'may) *Jp.* "strangling" or "choke."

SHIME-WAZA (shee'may wa'za) *Jp.* "strangulation technique" A collective name for judo techniques in which an opponent is subdued by choking or strangulation.

SHIMOSEKI (shee-moh-sek'ee) *Jp.* "lower seat" In a traditional Japanese dojo, the area where students line up and face their instructor(s). It is located to the right of the kamiza (upper seat).

SHIMOZA (shee-moh'za) *Jp.* "lower seat" In a traditional Japanese dojo, the meeting place for all students. It is located directly opposite the kamiza (upper seat).

SHIMPAN (shim'pan) *Jp.* The referee in a Japanese martial arts contest. Known also as the shinpan.

SHINAI (shuh-neye') *Jp.* A fencing practice sword, made of bamboo strips, and used in the practice of kendo.

SHINPAN: See SHIMPAN.

SHINKEN (sheen'kehn) *Jp.* "real sword" An actual life or death encounter. The term originated in feudal Japan where such encounters took place regularly.

SHINKYU-SHIAI (sheen'kyoo shee'eye) *Jp.* An examination event to determine the rank advancement of kyu-grade in the Japanese martial arts.

SHINOBI SHOZOKU (shee-noh-bee shoh-zoh-koo) *Jp.* The uniform worn by the ninja. It consisted of a jacket, hood, and tight pants, which were tied at the knee and ankle for maximum mobility. The shoes were split at the toe, designed for silence and easy gripping. The ninja's clothing was reversible, usually black on one side and dark blue, green, or white on the other.

SHINOBI-JUTSU (sheen-noh'bee jut'soo) *Jp.* The original form for ninjutsu.

SHINSHIN (shin'shin) *Jp.* "stopped mind" A condition in which one remains exclusively defensive, giving an opponent opportunities for victory.

SHINTAI (shin-teye') *Jp.* "movement" or "linear motion" A method of advancing or retreating, or of moving to the left or right of an original position.

SHIRO OBI (shee-roh oh-bee) *Jp.* In karate, a white belt or novice.

SHISEI (shee'say) *Jp.* "posture" or "stance" A term used in Japanese martial arts.

SHITAHARA (shee-ta-har'a) *Jp.* "lower abdomen."

SHITA-UKE: See DOWNWARD BLOCK.

SHITO-RYU (shee'toh ryoo) *Jp.* A style of karate founded by Kenwa Mabuni and influenced directly by both Naha-te and Shuri-te, two early Okinawan karate systems. The name Shito was contractively derived when Mabuni combined the Japanese characters of his teachers' names, Ankoh Itosu and Kanryo Higashionna. Shito-ryu is one of the four major Japanese karate systems.

SHIZEN-HONTAI (shee-zehn hon-teye) *Jp.* "basic natural posture" A relaxed judo position in which the feet are placed approximately twelve inches apart and the arms are held loosely at the sides.

SHIZENTAI (shee'zehn-teye) *Jp.* "natural position" An encompassing term for numerous karate stances in which the body remains relaxed but alert. From these postures, any position of attack or defense can be quickly assumed.

SHOBU-HO (shoh-boo-hoh') *Jp.* "contest tactics" Regulations and rules employed in a tournament contest.

SHOCHUGEIKO (shoh-choo-gay'koh) *Jp.* A traditional event in Japan in which vigorous training is practiced for up to thirty days during the hottest time of the year.

SHODAN (shoh-dan) *Jp.* "first rank" First-degree black belt in the Japanese and Okinawan martial arts.

SHOMEN (shoh'mehn) *Jp.* "front" or "forward" Often refers to the front wall of a dojo, which is the direction students bow to show respect to the dojo.

SHOMEN NI REI: See REI.

SHOREI-RYU (shoh'ray ryoo) *Jp.* "Shorei way" An Okinawan karate system developed from Naha-te. It is one of the three chief Okinawan styles from which numerous karate kata have been derived. Shorei-ryu is characterized by slow, powerful movements.

SHORINJI KEMPO (shoh-reen'jee kehm'poh) *Jp.* "Shorinji fist way" A modern Japanese martial art with religious direction, tracing its roots back to the kung-fu of the Shao-lin Temple.

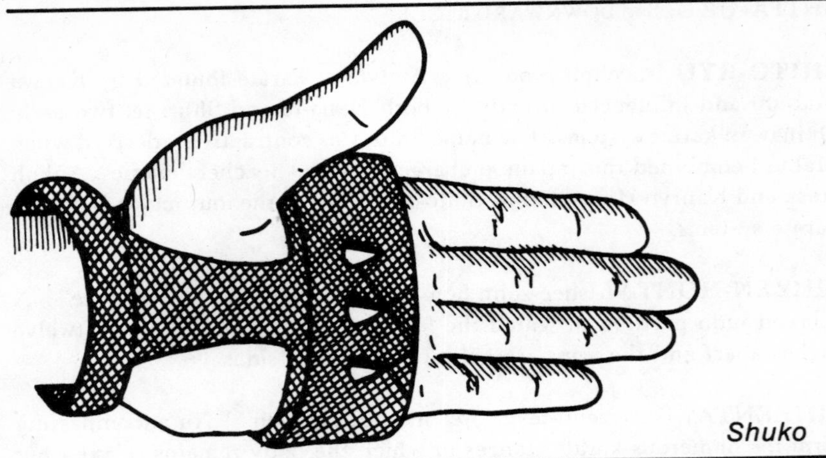

SHORINJI-RYU (shoh-reen'jee ryoo) *Jp.* "Shorinji way" A style of karate which is a synthesis of Okinawan and Japanese karate. It emphasizes rapid footwork and mobility.

SHORIN-RYU (shoh'reen ryoo) *Jp.* Any one of three Okinawan karate systems that go by the same name. The three, according to the various translations of their Japanese characters, are: pine forest way, also called Matsubayashi-ryu; young forest way, which was originally called Naha-te after the city where it was spawned and which was founded by Sokon Matsumura; and small forest way, founded by Choshin Chibana, a Matsumura disciple.

Shorin-ryu represents major branches of Okinawan karate. From these styles numerous karate kata have been derived.

SHORT-HAND BOXING A southern Chinese system of fighting characterized by close-range techniques.

SHORT SWORD: See WAKIZASHI; KOTACHI.

SHOSHINSHA (shoh-sheen'sha) *Jp.* "novice" or "beginner" Any unranked Japanese martial artist.

SHOTEI (shoh'tay) *Jp.* "palm heel."

SHOTOKAN (shoh'toh-kan) *Jp.* "Shoto's house" A popular Japanese karate system founded by Gichin Funakoshi and influenced directly by the

Okinawan style of Shuri-te. It is characterized by powerful linear techniques and deep, strong stances.

Funakoshi practiced calligraphy and signed his work with his penname, Shoto. Hence, the school where he taught came to be known as Shoto's school. Today, his style is one of the four major Japanese karate systems and is practiced throughout the world.

SHOULDER That part of the body which can be used for an immobilization hold, or over which an opponent can be thrown in judo. Known in Japanese as the seoi.

SHOULDER NECKLOCK A judo strangulation technique whereby an opponent's collar is held with both hands and the opponent's neck is then brought into close contact with the attacker's shoulder, thereby effecting a submission as pressure is increased.

SHOULDER THROW: See SEOI-NAGE.

SHUAI CHIAO *Ch.* Along with chin-na, this form of Chinese wrestling possibly influenced the formation of Japanese jujutsu.

SHUBAKU (shoo-ba'koo) *Jp.* A system of empty-hand combat similar to jujutsu which is considered a forerunner of judo.

SHUCHU-SURU (shoo-choo soo-roo) *Jp.* To concentrate or devote undivided attention; integration.

SHUDOKAN (shoo-doh'kan) *Jp.* A minor style of Japanese karate founded by Kanken Toyama.

SHUFFLE (EP) The shifting of the body forward or back to close or increase the distance between oneself and an opponent. In kenpo, there are three methods that accomplish this: push-drag, drag-step, and step-drag.

SHUGYOSHA (shoo-gyoh-sha) *Jp.* One who is in intense training. It usually refers to those who devote their entire lives to discipline. It originally referred to those who practiced magical rites or esoteric Buddhism deep in the mountains of Japan.

SHUGYO (shoo'gyoh) *Jp.* "training" or "practice."

SHUKO (shoo'koh) *Jp.* A type of feudal age brass knuckle used by the Japanese ninja. Besides the small metal plate that slipped over the knuckles, the shuko had spikes extending from the palm so an enemy's face could be raked. It was also useful for gripping when climbing walls.

SHUKOKAI (shoo'koh-keye) *Jp.* "way for all" A style of karate founded by Chojiro Tani which advocates higher stances for smooth mobility.

SHUMATSU UNDO (shoo-ma-tsoo un-doh) *Jp.* "ending exercise" Cooling-off exercises performed at the end of a training session.

SHURIKEN (shoo-ree'kehn) *Jp.* Bladed instruments commonly used as throwing weapons by the ninja.

SHURI-TE (shoo'ree tay) *Jp.* "Shuri hand" One of the three original Okinawan karate schools, which derived its name from the city where it originated. It is the forerunner of shorin-ryu.

SHUSHIN (shoo'sheen) *Jp.* The chief referee in a judo contest or a Japanese-style karate match.

SHUSOKU GARAMI: See SUIEI-JUTSU.

SHUTO (shoo-toh) *Jp.* "knife hand," "sword hand," or "edge of hand" The edge of the hand used for karate chopping techniques.

SHUTO-UKE: See KNIFE-HAND BLOCK.

SI BOK *Ch.* "older uncle" A title given to a senior ranking instructor in some styles of kung-fu.

SICKLE A common farming implement developed in Okinawa and Japan as a significant weapons art. Known in Japanese as the kama.

SIDE BREAKFALL A method of breakfalling to the side while striking the mat with the hand and arm to avoid injury. Used in Japanese martial arts such as judo and aikido.

SIDE ELBOW STRIKE: See EMPI-UCHI.

SIDE KICK A linear karate kick executed laterally. Known in Japanese as the yoko-geri.

SIDE ROLLING FALL A judo falling method in which the body rolls sideward to avoid injury.

Side Kick

SIDE ROUND ELBOW STRIKE: See EMPI-UCHI.

SIDE THRUST KICK A karate kick delivered to the side, in which the foot is thrust toward the opponent and the knee is locked momentarily.

SIFU (see′foo) *Ch.* "teacher" or "instructor" A master or instructor of kung-fu.

SILAT (see-lat′) *Indo.* "quickness of action" A martial art similar to a two-person dance where the practitioners stare hypnotically at each other and then, at a given moment, begin a series of slow movements resembling combat. As the dance progresses, the moves become faster and the fighting spirit of the participants rises. Because of this intensity the dance is usually halted after only a few minutes.

It is believed silat originated in China and was transmitted to Indonesia between A.D. 900 and 1200.

SILAT BUAH: See BERSILAT.

SILAT PULOT: See BERSILAT.

SIL-LUM *Ch.* The Cantonese name for Shao-lin kung-fu.

SIMSA (sim'sa) *Kr.* "test" The tae kwon do test for rank advancement.

SIMPLE TECHNIQUES Those techniques executed in one movement, either direct or indirect.

SINGLE-HANDED NECKLOCK A judo strangulation hold using one hand to apply pressure to the carotid arteries.

SIPDAN (sip'dan) *Kr.* "tenth rank" Tenth-degree black belt in tae kwon do; the master rank.

SIPGUP (sip'gup) *Kr.* "tenth class" A beginner in tae kwon do.

SIXTEEN WAYS (OF THE SWORD) The traditional sixteen methods of using the Chinese sword. They are:

piercing (thrusting upward)
hacking (swinging down)
splitting (moving right to left, then downward)
jabbing upward
thrusting upward
chiseling (cutting with the back edge)
groping (holding the sword parallel to the body)
throwing (wielding the sword flatly right to left)
thrusting (with the point held upward)
deflecting (by horizontal crosscutting)
hooking (with the point dangling down)
upholding (parrying with the sword crosswise)
spinning (to and fro maneuvering)
scraping (with the edge half-cutting)
stretching (poking the point upward)
whirling (with the point moving circularly)

SKIRT SHOULDER THROW A judo variation of the shoulder throw in which the skirt or loose end of the jacket is held instead of the more conventional hold on the lapel.

SLICE (EP) A method of attack that, when executed, skims the surface of the target. Though not penetrating, it is effective. It is a minor move used to set up an opponent for a major move.

SLIDING KICK A method of kicking in which the rear foot is slid beside the forward kicking foot before execution in order to keep the center of gravity low and diminish the distance to the target area by using the forward side.

SMASHING TECHNIQUES Karate hand techniques other than punches or strikes, such as elbow blows.

SNAP (EP) A particular method of execution that involves the use of a whipping-type attack or blow, but with greater magnitude than a whip.

SNAP KICK A method in which the kicking foot is snapped quickly outward and sharply retracted without extending the hip into the kick as in a thrusting motion.

SOATARI-SHIAI (soh-ta-ree shee'eye) *Jp.* "round-robin contest" A judo contest in which opponent is pitted against opponent until, through process of elimination, all contestants have fought one another.

SOCHIN-DACHI (soh'cheen da'chee) *Jp.* "diagonal straddle-leg stance" See FUDO-DACHI.

SODEUGURUMA (soh-deh-goo-roo-ma) *Jp.* "sleeve wheel" A judo grappling technique.

SODE-GURUMA-JIME (soh-deh goo-roo-ma jee-meh) *Jp.* "lapel wheel choke" A judo grappling technique.

SODE-TORI (soh-deh toh-ree) *Jp.* "hold on sleeve" The tenth judo technique of kime-no-kata.

SODE-TSURI-KOMI-GOSHI (soh-deh tsoo-ree koh-mee goh-shee) *Jp.* "sleeve-lifting hip throw" A judo throw in which both the opponent's sleeves are grasped and she or he is pulled up and thrown over the hip.

SOFT STYLE A term designating a martial art that advocates fluid, circular techniques coupled with an emphasis on chi, such as in many kung-fu systems.

SOGI (soh-gee) *Kr.* "stance" or "position."

SOJUTSU (soh-jut'soo) *Jp.* "art of the spear" An armed combative practiced by Japanese feudal warriors who used many types and styles of spears.

SOKDO (sak'doh) *Kr.* "speed."

SOKIM (soh-keem') *Kr.* "fake" or "feint."

SOKUTEI-ASAE-UKE (soh-koo'tay oh-sa'eh oo'kay) *Jp.* "pressing block with sole" A karate block using the sole of the foot to check an opponent's kick before it is fully extended.

SOKUTO (soh-koo'toh) *Jp.* "foot edge" or "knife foot" See EDGE OF FOOT.

SOLAR PLEXUS A network of nerves in the abdomen behind the stomach commonly used as a critical target area. Known in Korean as the myung chi.

SOLE OF THE FOOT In karate and tae kwon do, a striking point for the crescent kick and the crescent-kick block.

SONBADAK (san-ba'dak) *Kr.* "palm."

SONDUNG (san-doong') *Kr.* "backhand."

SONDUNG MOK MARKI (son-doong' mak mar'kee) *Kr.* "bent-wrist block."

SONKAL (san'kal) *Kr.* "knife hand."

SONO-MAMA (soh-noh ma-ma) *Jp.* "don't move" A judo referee's term calling for contestants to remain still. This usually occurs during matwork when one contestant's body is out of bounds.

SOOPYUNG CHIRUGI (soop-yung' chee-ru'gee) *Kr.* "horizontal punch" A tae kwon do double punch to the side in which one arm is extended, the other sharply bent.

SOORYON (soo-ryan) *Kr.* "training."

SOREMADE (soh-ray-ma'deh) *Jp.* "that is all" A term used by a referee to denote the end of a contest.

SO-RIM YU (soh'reem yoo) *Kr.* The Korean term for Okinawan shorin-ryu karate.

SO-RYONG YU (soh-ryoong yoo) *Kr.* The Korean term for Okinawan shorei-ryu karate.

SOSOKU-GERI (soh-soh'koo ga'ray) *Jp.* A double karate kick in which both feet extend simultaneously, either to the front or side.

SOTO (soh'toh) *Jp.* "outside," "outer," or "exterior."

SOTO MAKIKOMI (soh'toh ma-kee-koh'mee) *Jp.* "outer winding throw" A judo sacrifice technique in which the opponent is thrown by winding the opponent's arm and body around oneself, then rolling forward to the mat.

SOTO-MOROTE (soh'toh moh-roh'tay) *Jp.* "outer two-handed throw" A judo technique similar to the sukui-nage (scooping throw).

SOTO-UKE (soh'toh oo'kay) *Jp.* "outside block" A karate block in which the opponent's arm is deflected to the side with a circular motion of one's forearm.

SOUTHERN STYLES Those kung-fu systems developed in southern China.

SPARRING A form of martial arts training in which two opponents face one another and simulate actual combat. There are numerous types, depending on the practitioners' ability. Usually, the first type of sparring is a basic form in which all offensive and defensive movements are prearranged. One-step sparring, as it is called in karate, has the opponents face each other and practice alternately attacking and blocking with only one technique. Later, as the practitioners' skill increases, so do the number of steps, i.e., three-step sparring and five-step sparring.

The next plateau is semifree sparring where the mode of attack and the target area(s) are still predetermined. Both practitioners are mobile and the attacker must now find an opening and create proper distance for the attack. A more advanced form predetermines the attacker and defender but not the target area.

Free-style sparring is the most advanced version. Here both practitioners attack and defend at will with nothing prearranged. See also KUMITE; SPORT KARATE.

SPEAR FINGER A karate hand technique in which one finger is held rigid and thrust forward.

SPEAR HAND An open-hand karate technique in which the four fingers are extended so the tips form a blunt edge and are used as a striking point. Known in Japanese as nukite.

SPINE-LOCKING TECHNIQUES Bone-locking techniques of judo used specifically to attack the spine. Although they are an integral part of judo, the inherent danger prohibits their use in competition. Known in Japanese as seikuzi-waza.

SPINNING BACK KICK A karate thrust kick executed to the rear in which the delivery is characterized by the turning of the body 180 degrees.

SPONTANEITY The ability to react naturally to an impromptu attack or situation without conscious effort or restraint.

SPORT KARATE Competitive karate in which two contestants engage in simulated and real combat, depending on the type of fighting. There are three types of karate competition practiced today. In non-contact, contes-

Spear Hand

tants engage in freestyle sparring with the object of scoring points. Here combat is simulated and contact is limited to certain specified areas of the body. Face contact is usually grounds for disqualification. Techniques are pulled short of contact in most cases and points are awarded for blows that, had they made contact, would have resulted in the disabling of the opponent.

In semi-contact, contestants wear hand and foot pads and are permitted to make controlled contact to the face and body with the object of scoring points. The contestant who accumulates the most points in a given time period, usually two minutes in the eliminations and three minutes in the finals, wins the match. Contestants are divided by both weight and rank.

In full-contact karate, also called professional karate, contestants fight in a ring, similar to boxing, with the object of rendering one another unconscious. Monetary purses are awarded to the winner. Fighters wear hand and foot pads and use punching and kicking techniques. Knee and elbow techniques are prohibited.

SPRINGING HIP THROW: See HANE-GOSHI.

STABILITY A state of firm balance imperative for good martial arts performance.

STAFF A wooden stave generally about six feet long. One of the five systemized weapons used by early Okinawan karate practitioners. Known in Japanese as the bo.

STAGES OF DISTANCE (EP) Those varying distances that exist between oneself and an opponent which can be closed or increased by selecting any one of the foot maneuvering sequences.

STAMPING KICK A thrust kick executed downward, usually with the heel.

STANCE A position of the feet allowing maximum balance, stability or mobility for a compatible technique. The hundreds of martial arts movements understandably require different stances compatible to each movement. Known in Japanese as dachi and in Korean as sogi.

STANDING ARMLOCKS Armlocks applied to an opponent's arm when it is extended.

STANDING DEFENSE The second series of judo defense techniques in kime-no-kata.

STANDING THROWS Those judo techniques carried out from a standing position. Known in Japanese as tachi-waza.

STAVE: See STAFF.

STEP-DRAG (EP) The stepping forward or backward with one foot as the other drags to meet it. One of the three methods of shuffling.

STICKING HANDS The practice of certain complicated hand and arm maneuvers that render an opponent immobile and allow the user to dominate and attack the opponent's vulnerable areas. Known as chi sao in Cantonese.

Its operation requires two practitioners, whose hands touch constantly, to engage in specific patterns of well-learned movements. The basic position of both practitioners is a fixed body stance where they are facing one another, with their hands, arms and elbows in a seemingly rolling motion. An awareness and comprehension of the opponent's next movement is sensed by the practitioner through this touch-and-response exercise. Calculating the opponent's next response is a distinct nature of vigorous and dedicated chi sao, and serves as a basis for effective close-range fighting.

STOMACH ARMLOCK An armlock applied when an opponent is face down on the ground and pressure is applied to the elbow joint.

STOMACH THROW: See TOMOE-NAGE.

STONE DROP A very antiquated throwing technique no longer used, but which resembles the judo shoulder throw.

STONE MONKEY Part of the monkey style of kung-fu characterized by somersaults and rolling and falling maneuvers.

STOP-HIT A counterattack that stops the opponent's attacking limb before it reaches full extension.

STORK: See HAKUTSURU.

STRADDLE-LEG STANCE; STRADDLE STANCE: See HORSE STANCE.

STRAIGHT PUNCH Any number of martial arts punching techniques characterized by the straightforward thrusting of the fist. Known in Japanese as choku-zuki.

STRATEGICS The aspect of positional theory concerned with the use of planned attacks to secure the position of advantage on a moment-to-moment basis.

STRATEGY The development of a battle plan through which the utilization of a fighter's advantages are timed to exert maximum offensive and defensive strength, with the minimum of risk to the fighter's personal safety.

STRIKING AREA Another name for target area; any part of the body that one strikes.

STRIKING POINT Any part of the body with which one strikes.

STRIKING TECHNIQUES In karate, any technique where the force is transmitted laterally, usually with a snapping motion of the arm. This method includes punches. Known in Japanese as uchi-waza.

STRIPES A strip of cloth worn horizontally across the tips of a belt denoting progress toward the next belt level. A green stripe or stripes, for example, may appear on a white belt. Some styles sanction the wearing of a red strip for each dan rank on the black belt: one stripe indicating first-degree black belt, and so on. In the United States, this method has been almost completely replaced by solid belt colors.

In judo, until quite recently, women were required to wear belts with a white stripe running lengthwise down the center. This is now optional. In some karate styles, the same white stripe is worn by all youngsters under eighteen.

STYLE A word indicating a type of martial art. There are hundreds of styles throughout the world, some seventy-two in karate alone. Each of these differ in technical, strategic, and/or philosophical approach, yet there are common characteristics that can be found in all of them. Some advocate linear techniques, some circular, some power, and others speed. Many of the modern martial styles, particularly those practiced in the Orient, have a religious or spiritual connotation.

STYLIST Any practitioner of a particular martial art.

SUBAK (soo'bak) *Kr.* A native Korean fighting system that enjoyed its widest popularity during the reign of King Uijong (A.D. 1147–1170).

SUDO (soo'doh) *Kr.* "knife hand" A tae kwon do strike with the edge of the hand. Known also as suto.

SUICIDE THROWS An expression used by judoka when referring to techniques in which one falls on the back or side to perform a throw. Known in Japanese as sutemi-waza.

SUIEI-JUTSU (soo-ee-ay joo-tsoo) *Jp.* "swimming art" A form of combative swimming that was part of the Japanese feudal warrior's training. It included methods of silent swimming, staying afloat for prolonged periods, swimming in full armor, and methods of grappling while in the water. Other skills included inatobi (jumping like a mullet), which taught the warrior to leap from water to land; and shusoku garami, a manner of swimming while the arms and legs were bound.

SUKASHI (soo-ka'shee) *Jp.* An evasive judo action applied against an opponent's attack.

SUKI (soo'kee) *Jp.* "opening" A gap in an opponent's defense or technique.

SUKIMA (soo-kee'ma) *Jp.* "gap," "crevice," or "space" A term used to describe a space or opening in Japanese martial arts.

SUKUI (soo-koo'ee) *Jp.* To scoop up.

SUKUI-NAGE (soo-koo'ee na'gee) *Jp.* "scooping throw" A judo hand throw in which one leg is placed behind the opponent's legs and the hands encircle the opponent's hips. The opponent is then scooped up and dropped on her or his back by a twisting motion of the thrower's body.

SUKUI-UKE (soo-koo'ee oo'kay) *Jp.* "scooping block" A karate blocking technique against a kick.

SUKUSHI-OTOSHI (soo-koo'shee oh-toh'shee) *Jp.* "cajoling drop" A judo technique very similar to the kuki-nage, the air throw.

SUMI-GAESHI (soo'mee ga-eh'shee) *Jp.* "corner turn" A judo sacrifice technique performed from a prone position. The twelfth technique of nage-no-kata.

SUMI-OTOSHI (soo'mee oh-toh'shee) *Jp.* "corner drop" A judo hand technique popularly called kuki-nage. Also used in aikido as a timing throw in which the opponent is caused to trip on his own attack.

SUMO (soo'moh) *Jp.* A basic Japanese form of grappling in which the participants are of gigantic proportions. It was originally known as sumai. Today sumo wrestling is conducted in an elevated circular area about fifteen feet in diameter. Victory is achieved by either forcing the opponent out of the ring, or by forcing him to touch the floor within the ring with any part of his body above the knee. This is accomplished by pushing with the hands, the entire body, or by clinching.

SUMOTORI (soo-moh-toh'ree) *Jp.* Sumo wrestlers.

SUNEATE (suh-nay-a-tay) *Jp.* The shin guards used in naginata-do as a protection against strong sweeping cuts below the knee.

SUN SONKUP CHIRUGI: See SPEAR HAND.

SURI-AGE (su-ree a'gay) *Jp.* "glancing blow against face" Performed from a sitting position, it is the third judo technique of kime-no-kata; standing, the thirteenth technique of kime-no-kata.

SURI-ASHI (sue-ree aw'shee) *Jp.* A judo form of walking when performing shintai in which ones feet lightly graze the mat. The body is held erect and movement is made from the hips.

SURPRISE ATTACK Any planned attack predicated on an understanding of distraction to exploit weaknesses in the opponent's focus of attention.

SURUSHIN: See KOBU-JUTSU.

SUTEGEIKO (soo-tay-gay-koh) *Jp.* A method of judo freestyle in which the more skillful partner accepts the techniques of a junior opponent with little resistance and intermittently offers corrective advice.

SUTEMI (soo-teh'mee) *Jp.* "sacrifice."

SUTEMI-WAZA (soo-teh'mee wa'za) *Jp.* "abandonment techniques" In judo, a method of throwing an opponent by falling to the ground with him or her.

SUTO: See SUDO.

SWEEP A method of throwing or unbalancing an opponent by upsetting one or both feet from under him or her. In judo, a sweep is always accompanied by a push or pull with the hands in order to throw the opponent to the ground. In karate, sweeps are often performed only with the foot and followed up with a punch, strike, or kick once the opponent has been unbalanced. Known in Japanese as harai.

SWEEPING ANKLE THROW: See OKURI-ASHI-HARAI.

SWEEPING BLOCK In karate, the use of a lateral sweeping motion with the open hand to neutralize an opponent's attack. Known in Japanese as nagashi-uke.

SWEEPING DRAWING ANKLE THROW: See HARAI-TSURI-KOMI-ASHI.

SWEEPING HIP THROW: See HARAI-GOSHI.

SWITCH (EP) The changing from one stance or position to another while in place. This is performed while moving the feet from one spot to another and involves a lead leg where one of three actions can take place: moving the back leg forward, moving the forward leg back, or jumping in place.

SWORD HAND: See SHUTO.

SYNCHRONIZATION (EP) Refers to an opponent coordinating moves, timing, and direction with one's own in order to take advantage of opportunities for attacking.

SYNCHRONIZED KATA Two or more performers executing the same form simultaneously or a two-person team simulating an actual fight. This event was introduced to karate tournament competition in the early 1970's, but is more commonly seen in martial arts demonstrations.

SYSTEM: See STYLE.

TA-CHENG CH'UAN *Ch.* "great achievement boxing" An internal system of kung-fu developed from hsing-i by Wang Hsiang-chai.

TACHI (ta'chee) *Jp.* A Japanese long sword worn slung from a sword-belt. Like the katana, the tachi had a single-edged curved blade. It was slung with the cutting edge down. This was the style when wearing armor and was not common after A.D. 1600.

TACHI-AI (ta-chee eye') *Jp* 1. The second series of judo techniques in kime-no-kata. 2. The attack in sumo wrestling.

TACHI-REI (ta-chee ray') *Jp.* "standing bow" A salutation common to numerous Japanese martial arts.

TACHI-WAZA (ta'chee wa'za) *Jp.* "standing techniques" A collective name for judo techniques carried out from a standing position.

TACTICAL FOOTWORK The use of the feet as they pertain to the execution of techniques.

TACTICS The aspect of positional theory concerned with the selection of the most efficient techniques to be used against a given opponent.

TAE KYON (teye kyun) *Kr.* An ancient Korean fighting art from which tae kwon do developed.

TAE KWON DO (teye-kwan-doh) *Kr.* "kick-punch way" or "way of hands and feet" The primary form of Korean unarmed combat named during a conference of chung do kwan masters in 1955. The name tae kwon do had been submitted for consideration by General Choi Hong Hi and was chosen because it closely resembled the old name of "tae kyon" in meaning and pronunciation. The new term is now widely used to represent Korean karate.

Tae kwon do is a combination of techniques derived from earlier Korean combatives and the kata, or forms, of the Okinawan Shuri-te and Naha-te schools of karate. These techniques include punching, kicking, striking, blocking, and dodging. Indigenous to tae kwon do are a large number of spectacular kicks, particularly of the jumping and spinning variety.

Form as well as free-sparring is practiced. More recently, tae kwon do has become a worldwide sport with contests frequently conducted that culminate in a world championship. While the rules are somewhat similar to those used in karate competition, tae kwon do players wear protective body gear and make moderate contact to the head and body.

TA HSING CH'UAN *Ch.* "monkey boxing."

TAI (teye) *Jp.* "ready posture" 1. The first judo technique of koshiki-no-kata. 2. The "body."

T'AI-CHI: See T'AI CHI CH'UAN.

T'AI-CHI CH'UAN (teye-chee chwan') *Ch.* "grand ultimate fist" An internal system of kung-fu, also called soft boxing, characterized by its deliberately slow, continuous, circular, well-balanced, and rhythmic movements. T'ai-chi ch'uan is the most widely practiced form of martial art in the world today, primarily because of its healthful benefits. Modern t'ai-chi ch'uan has evolved from a form of pugilism and is today considered more a calisthenic type of exercise.

The term "ch'uan" affixed to t'ai-chi literally refers to the "fist," or "boxing," whereas t'ai-chi chien would be "grand ultimate sword," and so on.

TAIDO (teye'doh) *Jp.* A relatively new Japanese fighting art whose techniques are based on the principle of changing the body's axis. It is a synthesis of numerous martial arts and modern gymnastics.

TAIHO-JUTSU (teye'hoh jut'soo) *Jp.* "arrest techniques" A self-defense system used by the Japanese police consisting of techniques taken from numerous Japanese martial arts.

TAIJUTSU (teye-jut'soo) *Jp.* "body art" 1. A system of unarmed combat similar to jujutsu and a forerunner of modern judo. 2. The branch of modern judo in which it is necessary only to throw an opponent to secure a contest victory. Strangulations and armlocks are excluded.

TAIKO (teye'koh) *Jp.* The drum used in large Japanese dojo to call all sessions to order and to conclude them.

TAIKYOKU (teye-kyoh'koo) *Jp.* "first cause" A set of three basic karate kata formulated by Gichin Funakoshi in conjunction with his belief that in karate, there is no advantage in the first attack. The term taikyoku can also be translated as "great ultimate."

TAI-OTOSHI (teye oh-toh'shee) *Jp.* "body drop" A judo hand throwing technique in which the opponent is thrown over an extended leg. To execute this throw, the thrower turns his or her back to the opponent.

Tai Otoshi

Tameshiwari

TAI SABAKI (teye sa-ba'kee) *Jp.* "body movement" The turning action of the body. In judo, the circular motion required to perform certain throws. An important principle in aikido relating to one's position in relation to the opponent.

TAISHO (teye'shoh) *Jp.* "leader" The captain of a team.

TAISO (tie'sew) *Jp.* "calisthenics" The preliminary exercises performed in all Japanese martial arts. In some dojo, these are also performed immediately after the training session.

TAIYOKU (teye-yoh'koo) *Jp.* A spherical symbol of Chinese derivation representing completeness and integrative balance.

TAKEDOWN A term used in judo when referring to matwork or hold-down techniques.

TAKE-UCHI-RYU (ta-keh oo-chee ryoo) *Jp.* The name for one of the oldest forms of jujutsu.

TAKI-OTOSHI (ta'kee oh-toh'shee) *Jp.* "waterfall drop" or "cascade drop" The fourteenth judo technique of koshiki-no-kata.

TA LEI TAI *Ch.* Chinese boxing contests in which participants constructed public stages and took on all challengers.

TALL MONKEY A part of the monkey style of kung-fu characterized by long-range sweeping techniques, swinging arm motions, and low stances.

TAMBO (tam'boh) *Jp.* "short stick" The art of using the short stick. Known also as tanbo.

TAMESHIWARI (ta-mehsh-ee-war'ee) *Jp.* "to test and to break" In karate, the practice of breaking a variety of materials barehanded in order to test a karateka's power. See also BREAKING.

TANBO: See TAMBO.

TANDEN (tan'dehn) *Jp.* "abdomen" The center of balance, located about two inches below the navel.

TANDOKO-RENSHU (tan-doh'koh rehn'shoo) *Jp.* The practice of judo techniques without a partner; solitary practice.

TANGIBLE WEAPONS The four limbs of the body for striking, the eyes for increasing peripheral vision, the waist for additional power, and footwork to maneuver the body in or out of combat range. All are believed to be the primary body weapons in many systems of unarmed combat.

TANG SOO DO (tang soo doh') *Kr.* "art of the Chinese hand" A Korean combative differing only slightly from tae kwon do.

T'ANG-SU (tang-soo') *Kr.* "T'ang hand" An original Korean empty-hand fighting method borrowed from the T'ang dynasty of China, and developed and systemized during the Three Kingdoms (after the mid-7th century).

TANI-OTOSHI (taw'nee oh-toh'shee) *Jp.* "valley drop" or "dale drop" A judo sacrifice technique; the ninth technique of koshiki-no-kata.

TAN-TIEN *Ch.* "sea of chi" The psychic center located just below the naval, which protects the center of gravity and produces a reservoir of force upon which to draw. In Japanese, it is pronounced tan-den.

TANTO (tan'toh) *Jp.* A Japanese dagger with a blade eight to sixteen inches long and carried by the samurai in addition to the katana (long sword).

TANTO-JUTSU (tan'toh jut'soo) *Jp.* The art of using or throwing a dagger, practiced by both men and women during Japan's feudal period.

TAO *Ch.* A single-edged Chinese broadsword.

TAO YIN *Ch.* Breathing exercises that are allegedly the forerunner of t'ai-chi ch'uan.

TARE (ta'ray) *Jp.* "hanging" The apron worn in kendo to protect the stomach and hips.

TARGET AREA Any specific part of the body to which an attack or a technique is directed.

TASHI (ta'shee) *Jp.* "expert" An expert of the Japanese martial arts who is of third- to fourth-degree black belt rank. All black belts within this category, however, do not receive this title. See also KYOSHI; HANSHI; RENSHI; SHOGO.

TASUT (ta'soot) *Kr.* "five."

TATAMI (ta-ta'mee) *Jp.* "straw mat" A mat usually measuring three by six feet and three inches thick (with bound straw inside). Nowadays, it is

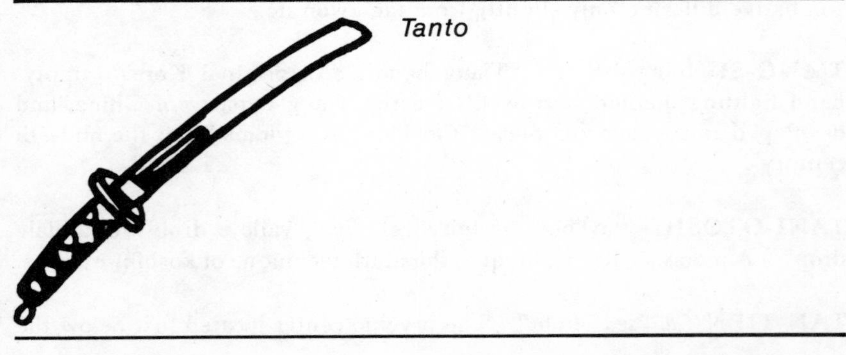
Tanto

covered by vinyl. The tatami is most commonly used for judo and aikido where much falling is required.

TATE (ta'tay) *Jp.* "vertical fist" A karate punch delivered with the fist held vertically.

TATE-EMPI-UCHI: See EMPI-UCHI.

TATE-SHIHO-GATAME (ta-tay shee-hoh ga-ta-meh) *Jp.* "vertical four-corner holding" A judo hold-down technique in which an opponent is straddled and both arms are wrapped about the opponent's neck. Often referred to as the tate-shiho.

TATE-SHUTO-UKE (ta'tay shoo'toh oo'keh) *Jp.* "vertical knife-hand block" A karate blocking technique.

TATTE (tat-teh) *Jp.* A command to stand up from a kneeling position.

TATE-ZUKI (ta'tay zoo'kee) *Jp.* "vertical punch" A karate punch delivered with the fist held vertical upon impact.

TAWARA-GAESHI (ta-wa-ra ga'eh-shee) *Jp.* "bale throw" A judo sacrifice throw.

TE (tay) *Jp.* "hand" A term used in Okinawa as early as A.D. 1629 to describe a fighting art very similar to modern karate. Te was used until the mid-1800's when it was replaced by karate-jutsu.

TEAR (EP) A ripping motion that actually involves grabbing while pulling.

TECHNIQUE CONSCIOUS Term describing a fighter who is more conscious of the form than of the effectiveness of techniques.

TEDORI (tay-doh'ree) *Jp.* "hand movement" An ancient, obscure method of Japanese combat.

TEGURUMA (tay-gu-roo'ma) *Jp.* "hand wheel" A judo countertechnique useful against a poorly attempted sweeping hip throw or similar move.

TEIJI-DACHI (tay'jee da'chee) *Jp.* "T-stance" A basic karate stance in which the feet roughly form an inverted T.

TEISHO: See PALM HEEL.

TEISHO-AWASE-UKE: See PALM HEEL BLOCK.

TEISHO-UCHI: See PALM HEEL STRIKE.

TEISHO-UKE: See PALM HEEL BLOCK.

TEISOKU (tay-soh'koo) *Jp.* Sole of the foot, a striking point.

TEKKI (tehk'kee) *Jp.* "horse riding" A set of three katas formulated in the shorei-ryu school of Okinawan karate.

TEKO: See: KOBU-JUTSU.

TEKUKI-KAKE-UKE (tehk-oo-kee kah-kee oo-kee) *Jp.* "wrist-hooking block" A karate block in which the wrist is hooked over an opponent's wrist as a punch is delivered.

TENBIN-WAZA (tehn-been wa-za) *Jp.* "scales techniques" A judo technique in which the passive opponent's body is kept rigid and is tipped or propped as a scale. This is primarily performed in the practice of hip throws.

TENGUI: See HACHIMAKI.

TEN-NO-KATA (tehn'noh-ka'ta) *Jp.* "kata of the heaven" A Japanese karate formal exercise designed by Gichin Funakoshi consisting of two complementary parts meant to be used as a two-person sparring form.

TENSHIN-SHIN YO RYU (tehn-sheen sheen yoh ryoo) *Jp.* One of the early jujutsu styles studied by Jigoro Kano before the formulation of judo.

TENSHO (tehn'shoh) *Jp.* A goju-ryu karate kata formulated by Chojun Miyagi to transmit the soft aspect of his style and to offset the accentuated hardness indigenous to his sanchin kata. Tensho is characterized by deep breathing and circular hand movements.

TE-OSAE-UKE (tay oh-sa-eh oo-keh) *Jp.* "hand-pressing block" A karate blocking technique applied against an attacker's forearm.

TESSEN-JUTSU (tehs-sehn joo-tsoo) *Jp.* A Japanese method of unarmed combat centered around the tessen (iron fan) and used by the samurai.

TET-KI (teht' kee) *Jp.* "iron horse" An Okinawan karate kata formulated in the shorei-ryu school. The majority of movements throughout this form are executed from a horse stance.

TETSU BISHI (teh-tsoo bee-shee) *Jp.* A four-pointed caltrop used by the ninja to slow down a pursuer. No matter which way a tetsu bishi landed one sharp point always protruded upward.

TETSUBO (teht-soo'boh) *Jp.* "iron staff" A weapon used by the samurai from either a horse-mounted or ground position.

TETSUBO-JUTSU (teht-soo-boh joo-tsoo) "iron staff art" The technique of using the tetsubo.

TE-WAZA (tay wa'za) *Jp.* "hand techniques" Standing judo throws effected through hand and arm movements.

THAI-BOXING: See KICK-BOXING; MUAY-THAI.

THREE-SECTIONAL STAFF A Chinese weapon consisting of three

Three-Sectional Staff

rods connected by chain or rope. It can be used to strike, block, or choke; and in the hands of an expert, is one of the most devastating weapons in the martial arts arsenal. Known as san chieh pang in Mandarin.

THREE-STEP SPARRING A method of prearranged practice fighting in karate in which the attacker takes three steps forward to deliver a series of techniques, and the defender blocks throughout the sequence and counters the final blow. Known in Japanese as sanbon kumite.

THRUST (EP) A particular method of execution involving the use of a propelling, push-type attack or blow.

THRUST KICK In karate, a method of execution in which the kicking foot is thrust outward with driving force and strengthened momentarily before contact by locking out the hip.

TI (tee) *Kr.* "belt" The belt worn around the waist to designate rank in tae kwon do.

TIEH DA JYOU *Ch.* An ointment used by kung-fu practitioners to enhance circulation and to help prevent bruises and similar injuries. This ointment is also supposed to help strengthen the skin, bones, and muscles. It is massaged into the skin after being heated.

TIEN HSUEH *Ch.* The art of striking the vital points, similar to Japanese atemi. See also DIM MOK.

TIGER One of the five animals whose movements composed the basis for Hua To's exercises and which are still used in various contemporary kung-fu schools.

TIGER CLAW An open-hand martial arts technique employing the fingers in a thrusting or claw-like motion.

TIGER MOUTH An open-hand karate technique employing the area between the thumb and forefinger in a thrusting motion. Known in Japanese as the koko.

TIGER TAIL A Chinese foot technique similar to tae kwon do's spinning back kick.

TIMBEI: See KOBU JUTSU.

Thrust Kick

TIME-HIT A counterattack that hits the opponent at about the same time the attacking limb reaches full extension.

TIMING A fighter's ability to impose his or her cadence on the opponent's so attacks are able to penetrate the opponent's defense, and his or her defense stops the opponent's attack. Efficient timing is the essence of skill in unarmed combat.

TI-SHA SHOU *Ch.* "devil's hand" One of the original names for Chinese wrestling, or chin-na.

T'I-T'ANG *Ch.* "ground roof" or "ground shelter" A northern Chinese kung-fu system containing forms characterized by techniques for fighting when falling to or lying on the ground.

TJABANG (t-ja-bang) *Indo.* An iron truncheon similar to the Okinawan sai. See also SAI.

TOBI-GERI (toh'bee gay'ree) *Jp.* "jump kick" Any one of numerous karate kicks executed in midair.

TOBI-GOSHI (toh'bee goh'shee) *Jp.* "jumping hip throw" A judo countertechnique to most hip throws.

TOBU (toh-boo) *Jp.* An expression referring to the head area except the face. It is used in karate competition when referring to a target area.

TO-DE (toh'day) *Jp.* "T'ang hand" Chinese kempo reportedly introduced to Okinawa about A.D . 1372 and, together with ch'uan-fa, considered the combination of arts that subsequently developed into karate.

TOI-GYE (toy'gyay) *Kr.* A tae kwon do hyung named after a 16th-century scholar.

TOKETA (toh-keh-ta) *Jp.* "hold broken" A term used by a judo referee to denote that a holding technique has been broken.

TOKUI-WAZA (toh-ku-ee wa-za) *Jp.* "pet technique" A generic term representing a judoka's personally favorite throw.

TOKUSHU-KEIBO (to-koo-shoo kay-boh) *Jp.* A collapsible tubular truncheon made of metal. When collapsed, it is easy to carry concealed; when fully extended, it measures about fifteen inches.

TOKUSHU-KEIBO-SOHO (to-koo-shoo kay-boh soh-hoh) *Jp.* A combat system used by the Japanese police centering around the tokushu keibo.

TOLYO CHAGI: See ROUNDHOUSE KICK.

TOMARI-TE (toh-ma-ree tay) *Jp.* "Tomari hand" One of the three original Okinawan karate schools. It derived its name from the city where it was founded.

TOMOE (toh-moh'ay) *Jp.* "circular" or "stomach."

TOMOE-NAGE (toh-moh-ay na-gay) *Jp.* "circle or comma throw" A judo sacrifice technique in which the thrower falls flat on his or her back and, placing one foot into the opponent's stomach, throws the opponent over his or her head. It is the tenth technique of nage-no-kata.

TONFA (tohn'fa) *Jp.* "handle" An old Okinawan farming implement developed as a weapon by the early karate developers of Okinawa. The tonfa consists of a hardwood billet between fifteen and twenty inches long with a short projecting stub set about six inches from one end. It can be used to block or parry, thrust, or be spun circularly to strike. Known also as the tuifa.

TONG-CIREUM: See CIREUM.

TONG IL (tong ill′) *Kr.* A tae kwon do hyung.

TORI (toh′ree) *Jp.* "taker" In judo, the partner who performs the technique on the other partner.

TORI-NIKUI (toh-ree nee-koo-ee) *Jp.* "difficult to take" A term used to describe the defensive attitude of a judoka to avoid being thrown.

TORITE (toh-ree′tay) *Jp.* "taking hands" A Japanese system of unarmed combat similar to jujutsu and a forerunner of modern judo.

TO-SAN (toh′ san) *Kr.* A tae kwon do hyung named after a Korean patriot.

TOSHU KAKUTO (toh′shoo ka-koo′toh) *Jp.* A system of unarmed combat used by the Japanese defense forces. Founded in 1952, it combines techniques from many of the Japanese martial arts.

TO TE (toe′ te) *Ch.* "Chinese hand" Another early name given to the Okinawan arts of unarmed combat. See also TO-DE.

TOUCH MASTERS Kung-fu masters who taught the art of tien-hsueh, the art of attacking the vital points. See also DIM MOK.

TRADITIONALIST Any practitioner who conforms to the customs, beliefs, and philosophies handed down through tradition.

TRANSITORY MOVE (EP) The intermediate move that often takes place when moving from one position to another. In most cases, it has definite meaning and can be used effectively.

TRAPPING HANDS The name for various defensive tactics whereby one or both hands trap both of the opponent's hands, sometimes using one of the opponent's arms to block his other arm.

TRIANGULAR NECKLOCK A judo strangulation hold in which both legs encircle an opponent's neck and constrict it from either side.

TSO-KU SHU *Ch.* "twisting skill" One of the original names for Chinese wrestling, or chin-na.

T-STANCE A karate position in which the front foot is placed perpendicular to the rear foot to form a T.

TSUBA (tstsoo-ba) *Jp.* The guard of a samurai sword.

TSUBAME-GAESHI (tsoo-bh-meh ga-ay-shee) *Jp.* "swallow counter" A judo defense method against a hip throw in which the hips are thrust forward and the arms backward, thereby simulating the flight of a swallow. Also the name of the special technique used by Sasaki Koviri, who was a famous swordsman defeated by Miyamoto Musashi.

TSUGI-ASHI (tsoo-gee a-shee) *Jp.* "following foot" A method of walking or maneuvering in which one foot follows the other but never passes it.

TSUKA (tska) *Jp.* The grip or handle of a samurai sword.

TSUKA ITO (tska ee-to) *Jp.* "handle cord" A strong binding usually of silk or leather for the handle of the samurai sword.

TSUKAMI-UKE: See GRASPING BLOCK.

TSU KEN SHITA HAKU SAI KATA (tsoo kehn shta ha-koo seye ka-ta) *Jp.* A kata for the Okinawan sai carrying the name of the district where it was created.

TSUKI (tskee) *Jp.* "thrust" An encompassing term for various types of punching techniques. In kendo and other weapons arts, it refers to thrusting techniques using the point of the sword, butt of the naginata, and so forth.

TSUKI-AGE (tskee a-gay) *Jp.* "uppercut" The thirteenth judo technique of ju-no-kata and the twelfth of kime-no-kata.

TSUKI-DASHI (tskee da-shee) *Jp.* "hand thrust" The first judo technique of ju-no-kata.

TSUKI-KOMI (tskee koh-mee) *Jp.* A judo self-defense technique against a dagger thrust to the stomach. Standing, it is the seventeenth technique of kime-no-kata, sitting, the sixth.

TSUKI NO KOKORO (tskee-noh koh-koh-roh) *Jp.* "mind like the moon" A psychological principle of combat emphasizing the need to be totally aware of an opponent and his movements, much like moonlight shining equally on everything within its range.

TSUKI-TE (tsoo-kee teh) *Jp.* Hand attacks used in karate.

TSUKI-UKE (tskee oo-keh) *Jp.* "punching block" A karate block that simultaneously becomes a punch to an opponent's face.

TSUKI-WAZA (tskee wa-za) *Jp.* Punching techniques used in karate.

TSUKURI (tsoo-koo-ree) *Jp.* The combined actions of arms and body when breaking an opponent's balance in judo. It is the preparatory action for attack in a judo throwing technique.

TSUMASAKI (tsoo-ma-sa-kee) *Jp.* "tips of the toes" Sometimes used as a striking point for karate kicks by compressing the toes. It is usually aimed at the groin.

TSUMAZUKASE-WAZA (tsoo-ma-zoo-ka-seh wa-za) *Jp.* "tripping techniques" In judo, the art of throwing a person by tripping the foot or leg.

TSURI (tsoo-ree) *Jp.* To pull and lift in a circular motion, often used in judo.

TSURIGOSHI (tsoo-ree-goh-shee) *Jp.* "lifting hip throw" A judo hip technique in which an opponent's hips are circled with one hand and he is then thrown over the hips by a twisting motion of the body.

TSURIKOMI (tsoo-ree-koh-mee) *Jp.* "lift-pull" Hand and arm action leading to the breaking of an opponent's balance in judo.

TSURIKOMI-ASHI (tsoo-ree-koh-mee a-shee) *Jp.* "drawing ankle throw" A judo ankle trip in which uke's rear leg is tripped as uke is about to step forward to regain balance.

TSURIKOMI-GOSHI (tsoo-ree-koh-mee goh-shee) *Jp.* "propping drawing hip throw" The sixth judo technique of nage-no-kata. It is often called tsuri-komi.

TSURUASHI-DACHI (tsoo-roo-a-shee da-chee) *Jp.* "crane stance" A karate stance in which one foot is placed on the opposite knee and all balance maintained on one foot.

TSUZUKETE (tsoo-zoo-keh-teh) *Jp.* "continue" A term used by the referee in a karate match, most frequently after a scoreless exchange, to keep the match moving smoothly.

TUIFA: See TONFA.

TWICHIBO CHIRUGI (twee-chee'boh chee-roo'gee) *Kr.* "overturn punch" A tae kwon do punch with the palm of the striking fist inverted, as in an uppercut.

TWISTED STANCE: See KOA SEOGI.

TWISTING KICK A variation of the karate front kick whereby the kicking foot travels straight forward, then, before making contact, is redirected to the side. It is chiefly used when an opponent is facing at an angle.

TWO-FINGER SPEAR HAND An open-hand karate strike employing the tips of the index and middle fingers as striking points. Known in Japanese as nihon nukite.

TWO-KNUCKLE FIST: See FOREFIST.

TWO-STEP SPARRING A method of prearranged practice fighting in karate in which the attacker steps forward twice to deliver a series of blows, and the defender blocks the initial technique and counters the other.

UCHI (oo'chee) *Jp.* 1. "strike" A collective term for karate striking techniques usually performed with the snapping motion of the elbow. Uchi is also a compound term for these various striking techniques. 2. "inner" or "interior" A term used in reference to the execution of certain judo techniques.

UCHI DESHI (oo'chee deh'shee) *Jp.* "apprentice" An old Japanese practice where a student was apprenticed to a martial arts master in order to become an instructor in turn. The master, under this arrangement, is expected to instill moral and character-building virtues in the student as well as overseeing his or her martial arts training.

UCHIHACHIJI-DACHI (oo-chee-ha-chee-jee da-chee) *Jp.* "inverted open-leg stance" A basic karate position in which the feet are spread shoulder width and the toes point inward at a 45-degree angle.

UCHIKOMI (oo-chee-koh-mee) *Jp.* The nonthrowing attack drills practiced in judo. Uke stands erect while tori begins the throw. The throw, however, is never actually completed. Usually, the same technique is repeated many times.

UCHI-MAKIKOMI (oo'chee ma-kee-koh'mee) *Jp.* "inner winding throw" A judo sacrifice technique.

UCHIMATA (oo-chee-mata) *Jp.* "inner thigh throw" A judo leg technique performed by sweeping up with one leg in between the opponent's legs, thus raising the opponent's body off the mat and throwing her or him in a circular motion. The ninth technique of nage-no-kata.

UCHIMATA-SUKASHI (oo-chee-ma'ta soo-ka'shee) *Jp.* "inner thigh slip" A defensive judo move in which the defender slips from the attacker's hip.

UCHI-OROSHI (oo'chee oh-roh'shee) *Jp.* "direct head strike" The fourteenth judo technique of ju-no-kata.

UCHI-UKE: See FOREARM BLOCK.

UCHI-WAZA: See STRIKING TECHNIQUES.

UDE (oo'day) *Jp.* "forearm" or "arm."

UDE-ATE (oo'day a'tay) *Jp.* Judo hand and arm striking techniques. These techniques are prohibited in competition and are taught to advanced students for purposes of self-defense.

UDE-GARAMI (oo'day ga-ra'mee) *Jp.* "entangled armlock" A judo armlock in which the opponent's arm is bent and pressure is applied against the elbow. It is the eleventh technique of katame-no-kata.

UDE-GATAMI (oo'day ga-ta'mee) *Jp.* A judo armlock in which the opponent's arm is locked at the elbow joint. It is the thirteenth technique of katame-no-kata.

UDE-HISHIGI (oo'deh hee-shee'gee) *Jp.* A collective name for the straight-arm locks used in judo.

UDE-HISHIGI-HIZA-GATAME: See HIZA-GATAME.

UDE-HISHIGI-JUJI-GATAME: See JUJI-GATAME.

UDE-HISHIGI-WAKI-GATAME (oo-deh hee-shee-gee wa-kee ga-ta-mee) *Jp.* "side armlock" A judo armlock in which pressure is applied to the opponent's elbow joint.

UDE-UKE (oo'deh oo'keh) *Jp.* "forearm block" A karate block chiefly used to stop attacks to the solar plexus and sometimes the face.

UDE-WAZA (oo'day wa'za) *Jp.* Judo techniques in which pressure is applied against the elbow to force a submission from an opponent.

UECHI-RYU (oo-eh-chee ryoo) *Jp.* "Uechi way" An Okinawan style of karate founded by Kanbum Uechi. It is characterized by linear patterns and forceful sanchin breathing. Uechi-ryu is the counterpart of an earlier Chinese martial art called Pon-gai-noon.

UKE (oo'kay) *Jp.* "receiver" 1. The partner upon whom the technique is executed in judo and aikido practice. 2. To block.

UKE-GATAME-KEI (oo-kay gah-ta-mee kay-ee) *Jp.* "floating hold system" One of the three systems into which judo holding techniques can be subdivided.

UKEMI (oo-kay'mee) *Jp.* "art of falling" or "breakfalling" The art of using shock-dispersing actions to avoid injury when falling. Ukemi is an instrumental practice to both judo and aikido.

UKE-TE (oo'kay tay) *Jp.* "hand blocks."

UKE-GOSHI (oo-kee goh'shee) *Jp.* "floating hip throw" A judo hip technique; the fourth technique of naga-no-kata.

UKI-OTOSHI (oo-kee oh-toh'shee) *Jp.* "floating drop" A judo hand throwing technique; the first technique of nage-no-kata.

UKI-WAZA (oo'kee wa'za) *Jp.* "floating technique" A side sacrifice technique in judo; the fifteenth technique of nage-no-kata.

UL-JI (ul'jee) *Kr.* A tae kwon do hyung named after a 7th-century Korean general.

UMJI CHOOMUK (um'jee choo'muk) *Kr.* "thumb-knuckle fist" A tae kwon do striking technique directed to the chin, temple, or solar plexus.

UNCOMMITTED ACTION (EP) The realization that one is not to move in such a way as to be bound to a certain line of action.

UNDOO (un-doh-oh) The calisthenics usually done before a karate or judo class.

UNDONG (oon'dong) *Kr.* "exercise."

UNIFORM Any one of various types of outfits traditionally worn by practitioners of the martial arts. See also DOBOK; GI; HAKAMA; JUDOGI; SAM.

UNINTENTIONAL MOVES (EP) Accidental and unplanned moves by an opponent that, when unchecked or unanticipated, can defeat you.

UPPERCUT A close-range karate punch directed to the chin or abdomen. In this punch, the wrist is not twisted.

U PUNCH A simultaneous double punch whereby one fist aims for the face, the other for the body when the opponent is positioned to the side. Known in Japanese as yama-zuki and in Korean as digutja chirugi.

UPWARD BLOCK Any one of numerous blocks used to neutralize an opponent's high line attack. Known in Japanese as jodan-uke and in Korean as sandan marki.

UPWARD ELBOW STRIKE: See EMPI-UCHI.

UPWARD X BLOCK A high karate block augmented by crossing one arm over the other.

URA (oo'rah) *Jp.* "reverse," "rear," or "reverse side."

URAKEN (oo'rah-ken) *Jp.* "reverse fist."

URA-NAGE (oo-ra na'geh) *Jp.* "rear throw" A judo sacrifice technique; the eleventh technique of nage-no-kata.

URA-WAZA (oo-ra wa'za) *Jp.* "reverse technique" The judo action in which one nullifies an opponent's intended technique by anticipation coupled with the application of an effective countertechnique.

URA-ZUKI (oo'ra zoo'kee) *Jp.* "close punch" or "reverse punch" A karate technique similar to the uppercut.

USHIRO (oo-shee'roh) *Jp.* "back," "rear," or "behind."

USHIRO-ASHI-GERI (oo-shee-roh a-shee gay-ree) *Jp.* "rear leg kick" A karate kick in which the rear foot kicks forward. It is the same as the mae-geri (front kick). See also FRONT KICK.

USHIRO-DORI (oo-shee'roh doh'ree) *Jp.* "hold on the shoulders from behind" Sitting, the fifth technique of kime-no-kata; and standing, the sixteenth.

USHIRO-EMPI-UCHI: See EMPI-UCHI.

USHIRO-GERI (oo-shee-roh gay-ree) *Jp.* "back kick" A karate kick directed to an opponent behind oneself. The heel is the striking point. Closely related kicks include the ushiro-geri-keage (back snap kick), in which the snapping motion of the knee is used; and the ushiro-geri-kekomi (back thrust kick), in which the leg is thrust backward in a straight line.

USHIRO-GERI-KEAGE: See USHIRO-GERI.

USHIRO-GERI-KEKOMI: See USHIRO-GERI.

USHIRO-GOSHI (oo-shee-roh goh'shee) *Jp.* "rear hip throw" A judo hip technique chiefly used as a counter.

Ushiro-Geri

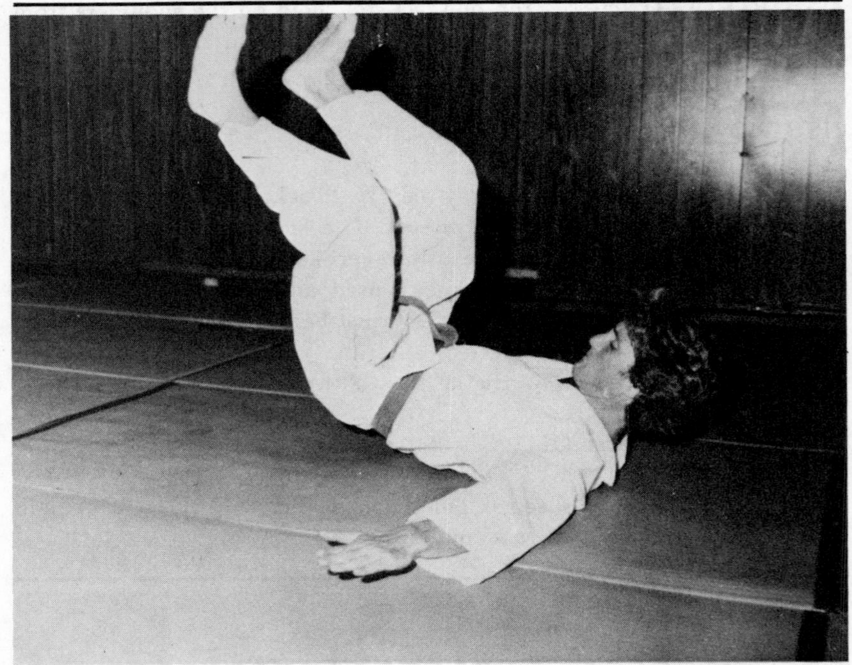

Ushiro-Ukemi

USHIRO-HIJI-ATE: See EMPI-UCHI.

USHIRO-KUZUSHI: See KUZUSHI.

USHIRO-NAGE (oo-shee-roh na-geh) *Jp.* "rear throw."

USHIRO-UKEMI (oo-shee′roh oo-kay′mee) *Jp.* "backward fall" A judo and aikido technique for falling without injury.

UTSU (ut′soo) *Jp.* "to strike" or "to hit" The act of striking with the sword or staff.

UTSURI-GOSHI (oo-tsoo-ree goh-shee) *Jp.* "changing hip throw" A judo technique chiefly used as a counterthrow against hip techniques.

UYE (oo′eh) *Jp.* "up" or "upward."

V

VAJRAMUSHTI (vah-ra-moos'ti) *Ind.* A system of unarmed combat that allegedly existed in India prior to 1000 B.C. While little is known to substantiate its existence, the Kshatriya, or warrior class of that period, were said to have practiced vajramushti, a fighting technique that used the closed fist as a weapon. There are also numerous statues dating back to the first century B.C. that depict temple guardians in poses similar to those used in latter day fighting arts.

VERTICAL PUNCH A clenched-fist karate blow executed straight forward and terminated with the fist held in a vertical position. Known in Japanese as the tate-zuki and in Korean as the sewao-jireugi.

VERTICAL ZONES (EP) One of the three categorical zones of protection encompassing four vertical, or width, segments requiring protection: left outside shoulder to middle of left chest; middle of left chest to sternum; sternum to middle of right chest; and the middle of right chest to the outside of the right shoulder.

VIBRATING PALM: See IRON PALM.

VITAL AREAS (EP) Essential body parts that, when struck, can be injurious or fatal.

WA (wa) *Jp.* "accord" An ancient Japanese term for harmony, accord, and coordination; a principle inherent to many martial systems, when it denotes nonresistance to one's opponent.

WADO-RYU (wa'doh ryoo) *Jp.* "way of peace" or "peace-way system" A Japanese system of karate developed from jujutsu and earlier karate styles by Hironori Ohtsuka. It is one of the four major Japanese karate systems practiced in the world today.

WAI-CHIA *Ch.* "outside group" or "eternal system" A classification of those Chinese martial arts that rely on external power and are characterized by hard, vigorous muscular exertion.

WAKI (waw'kee) *Jp.* "side" or "flank."

WAKIZASHI (waw-ke-zaw'she) *Jp.* "short sword" The shorter of the samurai's two swords. The wakizashi was the same as the katana except that its blade was only sixteen to twenty-three inches long. It was carried in the belt with the katana.

WALKING TECHNIQUES A series of karate exercises involving five steps forward then back, during which various basic techniques are executed.

WANSU (wan'sue) *Jp.* An Okinawan karate kata named after its founder. It was later renamed empi. See also EMPI.

WASHIN-RYU (wa-sheen ryoo) *Jp.* "harmony-truth way" A form of Japanese karate characterized by strong linear techniques and ibuki breathing.

WASTED MOTION (EP) A move that lacks economy, or is delivered needlessly, or does not produce the intended effect.

WAY: See DO.

WAZA (wa-za) *Jp.* "technique(s)."

WAZA-ARI (wa'za a'ree) *Jp.* "technique" 1. In a Japanese-style karate match, a half point, given when a technique is delivered but not cleanly enough to earn a full point. 2. A judo referee's term for an attempted technique that is almost successful, or, for a holding technique broken after twenty-five seconds but before thirty seconds. In both cases, a score of one-half point is awarded.

WAZA-ARI-AWASETE-IPPON (wa-za a-ree ah-wa-seh-teh eep-pohn) *Jp.* A verbal command used by a judo referee to indicate completion of scoring one point by adding an incomplete technique.

WAZARI: See WAZA-ARI.

WEAPON (EP) A term used to describe any particular striking point, *e.g.*, elbow, knee, palm, heel, fist.

WEDGE BLOCK: See KAKIWAKE-UKE.

WEIGHT DISTRIBUTION (EP) The apportionment of weight to each leg related to a particular stance and/or movement. It may vary from 50/50, 60/40, 90/10, and so on.

WEIKYA (way'kya) *Kr.* One of the two advanced systems developed from kwonpup.

WELL FIST A trick from Chinese folklore in which one stands in a horse stance at midnight and gestures with the fist at the water in a well. After ten years of this exercise, one will supposedly be able to cause a "distance death" to an opponent.

WHEEL KICK In karate or tae kwon do, a circular kick whose delivery is characterized by the turning of the body 180 degrees.

WHIP (EP) A particular method of execution involving the use of a snapping type of attack or blow, but with less magnitude than a snap.

WHITE BELT The color of the belt worn by martial arts novices when they begin their training.

WIDE HOUR-GLASS STANCE A defensive karate position in which the knees are tensed inward, the feet are spread approximately twice shoulder width, and the body weight is evenly distributed.

WING CHUN *Ch.* "Beautiful Springtime" A form of Chinese kung-fu that chiefly centers around strong linear punches. Known also as wing tsun and ving tsun in Cantonese. Named after a nun of the Shao-Lin Temple who developed it.

WON-HYO (wan-hyoh') *Kr.* A tae kwon do hyung named after a Buddhist monk.

WOOD MONKEY Part of the monkey style of kung-fu, which relies chiefly on deceptive techniques to lure an opponent into a trap.

WORKING SEQUENCE (EP) Any technique sequence that is highly practical.

WRISTLOCK A hold whereby one is controlled by a painful twisting grip on the wrist. These techniques are commonly used in judo and aikido.

WUSHU; WU SHU (woo'shoo) *Ch.* "war arts" Although wushu can properly be said to encompass all martial arts, today it is used primarily to denote that strain of martial art being developed by the People's Republic of China. Wushu is a highly gymnastic, traditional sportlike artform characterized by several styles. See also CHANG CH'UAN.

WUTANG *Ch.* An ancient school of kung-fu.

WU-TANG-SHAN *Ch.* Another name for wutang kung-fu.

XY

X BLOCK Any block where one arm overlaps the other, usually at the wrist or forearm. Known in Japanese as the juji-uke. See also AUGMENTED BLOCK.

YAKSOK DAERYON (yok'sohk da'ryohn) *Kr.* "prearranged sparring" See also SPARRING.

YAKUSOKU KUMITE (ya-koo-soh'koo koo'mee-teh) *Jp.* "prearranged sparring" See also KUMITE; SPARRING.

YAKUSOKU-GEIKO (ya-koo-soh'koo gay'koh) *Jp.* "prearranged practice" A method of judo practice similar to karate kata in which neither opponent offers any real resistance to the other.

YAMA-ARASHI (ya'ma a-ra'shee) *Jp.* "mountain storm" A judo hip technique similar to the harai-goshi.

YAMA-ZUKI: See U-PUNCH.

YAME (ya-meh') *Jp.* "halt" or "stop" A Japanese command chiefly used in competition.

YAME SOREMADE (ya-meh soh-ray-ma-deh) *Jp.* A Japanese command signaling the end of a match.

YANG *Ch.* "active"; "positive" In yin-yang theory, the positive aspect associated with what is described as centrifugal, expansive, and extroversive. Its dynamic equilibrium with yin, its opposite yet complementary counterpart, permeates the universe.

YARI (yar'ee) *Jp.* "spear."

YASURI-ME (yaw-sore'ee may) *Jp.* "file marks" The file marks on the tang of a samurai sword; since these varied with the maker, they can be used to confirm or deny the validity of a signature.

YAUDAL (ya'dul) *Kr.* "eight."

YAUL (yal) *Kr.* "ten."

YAUP CHOOMUK (yohp choo'muk) *Kr.* "hammer fist."

YAUSUT (ya'soot) *Kr.* "six."

YAWARA (ya-war'a) *Jp.* "gentle" or "soft" An ancient method of unarmed combat believed by many authorities to be the oldest form of unarmed combat practiced in Japan. In some forms of yawara, a short rod is used, called the yawara stick.

YEEBO DAERYON (ee'boh da'ryohn) *Kr.* "two-step sparring."

YELLOW BELT The color of a belt worn by some martial arts novices.

YELLOW CRANE: See CRANE.

YICHOONG CHAGI (ee'choong cha'gee) *Kr.* "double kick."

YICHOONG MARKI (ee'choong mar'kee) *Kr.* "double block."

YIDAN (ee'dan) *Kr.* "second rank" Second-degree black belt in tae kwon do.

YIGUP (ee'gup) *Kr.* "second class" A second-degree brown belt in tae kwon do.

YIKWON (ee'kwan) *Kr.* "backfist" or "back knuckle."

YIN *Ch.* "passive" or "negative" One of the fundamental metaphysical elements of yin and yang whose balance is believed to be the center of existence.

YING CHIAO FAN TZU: See DRUNKEN STYLE.

YIN-YANG SYMBOL A symbol representative of two opposing forces flowing into one another in a continuous state of change.

YOI (yo-ee) *Jp.* "prepare" or "get ready" A Japanese command used in formal classes for the students to prepare for training or competition.

YOJIMBO (yoh-jim'boh) *Jp.* "bodyguard" The name given to masterless samurai (ronin) who hired themselves out as professional bodyguards.

YOKO (yoh'koh) *Jp.* "side" or "lateral" A directional term used in the Japanese martial arts.

YOKO ARUKI (yoh'koh a-roo'key) *Jp.* "sideways walking" One of the unique ninja walking techniques to move stealthily through woods or narrow areas.

YOKO-EMPI-UCHI: See EMPI-UCHI.

YOKO-GAKE (yoh'koh ga-keh) *Jp.* "side body drop" A judo side sacrifice technique and the thirteenth technique of nage-no-kata.

YOKO-GERI (yoh'koh geh'ree) *Jp.* "side kick" A karate kick delivered to the side with the edge of the foot. There are two types: the side snap kick

Yoko-Geri-Keage

Yoko-Ukemi

(yoko-geri-keage), in which the snapping action of the knee is used; and the side thrust kick (yoko-geri-kekomi), in which the kick is thrust to the side with the knee locked upon extension.

YOKO-GERI-KEAGE: See YOKO-GERI.

YOKO-GERI-KEKOMI: See YOKO-GERI.

YOKO-GURUMA (yoh'koh gu-roo'ma) *Jp.* "side wheel" A judo countertechnique against a hip throw and the fourteenth technique of nage-no-kata.

YOKO-HANTEI (yoh-koh han-teh-ee) *Jp.* "side turnover" A judo stranglehold in which an opponent's neck is encircled in a scissor lock.

YOKO-HIJI-ATE: See EMPI-UCHI.

YOKO-JIME (yoh'koh jee-may') *Jp.* "cross side choke" A judo stranglehold applied when the opponent attempts to rise.

YOKO-MAKIKOMI (yoh'koh ma-kee-koh-mee) *Jp.* "side winding throw" A judo throwing technique.

YOKO-MAWASHI-EMPI-UCHI: See EMPI-UCHI.

YOKO-MAWASHI-HIJI-ATE: See EMPI-UCHI.

YOKO-MIGI (yoh'koh mee'gee) *Jp.* "right side" One of the eight directions of unbalance in judo.

YOKO-OTOSHI (yoh'koh oh-toh'shee) *Jp.* "side drop" A judo sacrifice technique.

YOKO-SHIHO-GATAME (yoh-koh shee-hoh ga-ta-meh) *Jp.* "locking of the side four quarters" A judo holding technique in which the opponent's collar and belt is grasped for applying pressure to the chest. It is the fourth technique of katame-no-kata.

YOKO-SUTEMI-WAZA (yoh'koh soo-teh-mee wa'za) *Jp.* "side sacrifice techniques" A collective name for judo sacrifice throws executed with the side of the body touching the ground.

YOKO-TOBI-GERI (yoh'koh toh'bee geh'ree) *Jp.* "flying side kick."

YOKO-TSUKI (yoh'koh tsoo-key) *Jp.* A judo self-defense technique against a side thrust with a dagger. It is the eighth technique of kime-no-kata.

YOKO-UCHI (yoh'koh oo'chee) *Jp.* A judo self-defense technique against a blow to the temple. It is the fourth and the fourteenth technique of kime-no-kata.

YOKO-UKEMI (yoh'koh oo-keh-mee) *Jp.* The side breakfall of judo and aikido.

YOKO-USHIRO (yoh'koh oo-shee'roh) *Jp.* "side rear throw" A judo throwing technique.

YOKO-WAKARE (yoh-koh wa-ka-reh) *Jp.* "side body separation" A judo sacrifice technique.

YOK SUDO (yohk soo'doh) *Kr.* "reverse knife hand" or "ridge hand."

YONDAN (yohn'dan) *Jp.* "fourth rank" Fourth-degree black belt in the Japanese and Okinawan martial arts.

YONHON NUKITE (yohn-hohn noo-kee-tay) *Jp.* "four-finger spear hand" See also SPEAR HAND.

YONSOK (yohn-sohk') *Kr.* "combination."

YONKYU (yan'kyoo) *Jp.* "fourth class" In the Japanese and Okinawan martial arts, an intermediate rank; in judo, a white belt, four grades below shodan.

YOOKDAN (yook'dan) *Kr.* "sixth rank" A sixth-degree black belt in tae kwon do.

YOOKGUP (yook'gup) *Kr.* "sixth class" A green belt in tae kwon do; six grades below chodan.

YOP CHAGI (yohp cha'gee) *Kr.* "side kick."

YOP MARKI (yohp mar'kee) *Kr.* "side block."

YOSEIKAN (yoh-say-kan) *Jp.* A Japanese style of karate.

YOSHI (yoh'shee) *Jp.* "carry on" or "go ahead" A referee's term used in a judo contest or a Japanese-style karate match.

YUBI (yoo'bee) *Jp.* "finger."

YUBIJUTSU (you-bee-jut'soo) *Jp.* A method of using the thumb and fingers against vital points of the body to incapacitate an opponent.

YUBI-WAZA (you'bee wa'za) *Jp.* "finger techniques" Immobilizing techniques that are an integral part of judo, although forbidden in competition. These techniques are also used by jujutsu and aikido practitioners.

YUDACHI (you-da'chee) *Jp.* "shower" The thirteenth judo technique of koshiki-no-kata.

YUDANSHA (yoo-dan'sha) *Jp.* "black belt holder" A title designating a black belt holder.

YUDANSHAKAI (you-dan'sha-keye) *Jp.* "black belt holders group" 1. An association of judo black belts chartered by the Kodokan. 2. Any association of black belts or their equivalent in the martial arts.

YUDO (yoo'doh) *Kr.* The Korean form of judo.

YUKI-ORE (yoo'key oh-reh') *Jp.* "snow break" The twentieth judo technique of koshiki-no-kata.

YUL-KOK (yool′ kohk) *Kr.* A tae kwon do hyung consisting of thirty-eight movements.

YUME-NO-UCHI (you′may noh oo′chee) *Jp.* "amidst dream" The second judo technique of koshiki-no-kata.

YUSEI-GACHI (yoo′say ga′chee) *Jp.* "win by superiority" A judo referee's term denoting a decision in a very close contest.

YU-SIN (yoo′sin) *Kr.* A tae kwon do hyung consisting of sixty-eight movements.

ZANSHIN (zan'sheen) *Jp.* "perfect posture" 1. A term designating mental alertness in Japanese martial arts. 2. To remain in perfect posture; correct mental alertness and posture after executing an attack or a block.

ZAZEN (za'zehn) *Jp.* "sitting meditation" The meditative posture and exercise of the Zen school.

ZEMPO-UKEMI (zehm-poh oo-keh-mee) *Jp.* "rolling fall."

ZEN (zehn) *Jp.* The discipline of enlightenment related to the Buddhist doctrine that emphasizes meditation, discipline, and the direct transmission of teachings from master to student. Known as Dhyana in India and Ch'an in China.

ZENKUTSU-DACHI (zehn-kut'soo da'chee) *Jp.* "forward stance."

ZENSHIN (zehn'sheen) *Jp.* The entire human body.

ZONES OF DEFENSE; ZONES OF PROTECTION (EP) The shielding of the body, with consideration given to three protective zones: horizontal, depth, and vertical.